MATTHEW SARDON

The God Who Bears Our Sorrows
A Biblical Theology of Suffering

First published by Theosis House Press 2025

Copyright © 2025 by Matthew Sardon

All rights reserved. No part of this publication may be reproduced, stored or transmitted in any form or by any means, electronic, mechanical, photocopying, recording, scanning, or otherwise without written permission from the publisher. It is illegal to copy this book, post it to a website, or distribute it by any other means without permission.

Matthew Sardon asserts the moral right to be identified as the author of this work.

First edition

This book was professionally typeset on Reedsy. Find out more at reedsy.com

"Surely He has borne our griefs and carried our sorrows."

- Isaiah 53:4

Contents

Introduction — 1

I The Human Cry

1. The Question That Won't Die: "What kind of God allows this?" — 7
2. The Culture of Pain-avoidance — 26
3. The Human Heart Under Trial — 44
4. At the Threshold of Mystery — 60

II The Story God Tells

5. Genesis And The Wound Of The World — 65
6. Israel And The School Of Affliction — 79
7. Christ The Man Of Sorrows — 94
8. The Resurrection And The Rewriting Of Pain — 108
9. When the Victory Becomes a Vocation — 122

III The Church, the Saints, and the Fire

10. Why The Saints Embrace The Cross — 129
11. Redemptive Suffering And Participation In Christ — 143
12. Suffering, Love, And The Human Vocation — 158
13. When Love Meets A Wounded Age — 170

IV　The Modern Crisis

14　The World That Cannot Suffer　177
15　The Rise Of Assisted Dying And The Culture Of Escape　197
16　Mental Suffering And The Age Of Fragile Souls　212
17　The Problem Of Innocent Suffering　227
18　When Revelation Becomes the Road　241

V　Living the Mystery

19　How To Face Suffering Without Losing Faith　247
20　How to Accompany Someone Who Suffers　271
21　Hope: The Last Word　287

Epilogue　306
About the Author　314

Introduction

Suffering has a way of interrupting the script we thought our life would follow. It breaks into the ordinary rhythms — the school drop-offs, the steady job, the quiet evenings — and asks questions we were not prepared to answer. A phone call in the middle of the night, a diagnosis, a broken relationship, a sudden loss... these are not moments that ask politely for room in our schedule. They arrive like unwelcome prophets, tearing open what we had tried to keep neat and manageable.

Yet the strange thing is that the whole story of Scripture seems to expect this. The Bible never treats suffering as an accident or a cosmic glitch. From the moment Adam and Eve step east of Eden, the people of God walk through a world that groans. Every covenant is forged in the furnace of affliction; every promise God makes seems to pass through the narrow door of trial before it flowers into blessing. Abraham hears God's voice only after leaving everything familiar. Jacob becomes Israel after a night of painful wrestling. Joseph saves the world through years of betrayal and imprisonment. Israel becomes God's chosen people in the crucible of slavery, not the comfort of ease. Even the Psalms — the very prayers God teaches us to pray — ring with lament, questions, and cries from the depths. Scripture's expectation is simple: sooner or later, suffering knocks at every door. The question is not whether we will suffer, but what suffering will make of us.

Our age, however, has forgotten this central truth. We have come to believe that suffering is not simply a burden but a failure — a sign that something has gone wrong in the design of the world or the competence of God. The modern world is built on the assumption that pain should be eliminated, not endured; avoided, not examined. Pharmaceutical miracles promise escape. Entertainment offers distraction. Technology offers the illusion that everything fragile can be controlled. Even death itself is now presented as a problem that medicine can "manage," and in some countries, even schedule. We live in a world that wants Easter without Good Friday, glory without Golgotha, and salvation without sacrifice. Yet the more we try to outrun suffering, the more anxious and fragile we become.

This book begins from a simple confession: suffering is not an obstacle to faith but a doorway into its depths. It is the point where human weakness meets divine fidelity. It is the place where the covenant God reveals not His absence but His nearness. The Christian tradition does not treat suffering as a riddle to be solved but as a mystery to be lived — a mystery that only Christ can illuminate. When we look to the Cross, we do not find an explanation of evil so much as a revelation of love. We discover a God who does not stand above our pain but steps directly into it, carrying it, transforming it, and transfiguring it.

The thesis of this book is not complicated, yet it is demanding. Suffering, when united to Christ, becomes the very means by which the human heart is shaped into love. It is the chisel in the Carpenter's hands, the fire that refines gold, the pruning that bears fruit. This does not mean God delights in our affliction. Quite the opposite. God hates suffering more than we do — so much so that He entered history to bear it Himself. But until the day He wipes every tear from every eye, He permits suffering to become the narrow gate through which grace enters. He allows what He does not love to accomplish what He does.

This is why the saints speak with such paradoxical clarity about the

INTRODUCTION

Cross. They are not romantic about pain; they are realistic about love. Their lives reveal a truth the world has forgotten: the heart learns its deepest wisdom not in comfort but in surrender. The saints show us that suffering does not have the last word — love does. Yet love, to be real, must pass through the test of the Cross. This is the wisdom that runs through every page of Scripture, echoed in every generation of the Church: suffering is not the enemy of the spiritual life; it is the path through which the spiritual life becomes authentic.

Still, there is a kind of suffering that resists explanation: the suffering of the innocent, the suffering that strikes without warning, the suffering that seems wildly disproportionate or brutally senseless. The Bible never ignores this. Job's cry still echoes through every hospital corridor and every graveyard. The prophets wept over the ruins of Jerusalem. The Blessed Mother stood beneath the Cross while the world's Redeemer hung dying above her. Christianity never pretends that every sorrow can be neatly explained. What it offers instead is a Person — a God with wounded hands and a pierced side who meets us in the very place where our questions are sharpest.

If we listen carefully, we begin to hear the heartbeat of Scripture: God does not abandon His people in suffering; He accompanies them. He is the Lord who walks through fire with the three young men in Babylon, who wrestles with Jacob in the night, who strengthens Elijah under the broom tree, who touches the leper with His own hands. From Genesis to Revelation, God is Emmanuel — God with us — even and especially in affliction. Suffering does not reveal a God who is unjust, but a God who is nearer than breath. The Cross is not the failure of divine justice; it is the unveiling of divine mercy.

Modernity's revolt against suffering has left us unprepared for the very thing life inevitably brings. Our culture has mastered comfort but forgotten meaning. Yet the human heart cannot live without meaning. A life without suffering is not promised to us, but a life without meaning is unbearable. The great gift of the Christian faith is not the removal of pain but the transformation of pain into participation — participation in Christ's own redemptive love. When united with Him, suffering becomes seed. It becomes offering. It becomes intercession. It becomes the way a soul learns to love with God's own heart.

That is the vision this book hopes to restore. Not a stoic acceptance of suffering, nor a romantic glossing-over of pain, but a return to the biblical imagination where suffering becomes the place of encounter. Each chapter will trace the story of suffering from Genesis to Christ, from Calvary to the saints, from the ancient world to our own age of assisted dying and spiritual fragility. We will explore why God permits suffering, how He uses it, how the saints understood it, and how we can live it without losing faith or hope. Above all, we will discover that the wounds we carry — physical, emotional, spiritual — can become the very places where God writes His mercy most clearly.

Suffering is not the final word of the Christian story. Glory is. Yet no one reaches glory without first walking the path marked by the Cross. This book begins at that crossroads, where human sorrow meets divine love. It begins with the conviction that every heart, sooner or later, must learn to say with Christ: "Into Your hands." It is there, in that surrender, that suffering stops being an argument against God and becomes the doorway into His heart.

By the end, my hope is that you will see not only why suffering exists, but why God never wastes it. The very wounds that burden you now may become — through grace, through trust, through union with the Crucified — the places where God makes you whole.

I

The Human Cry

1

The Question That Won't Die: "What kind of God allows this?"

Suffering presses upon the human heart with a weight that cannot be ignored. It does not ask whether we are ready for it, nor does it wait until life feels stable. It enters without ceremony and often without warning, disrupting what we assumed would continue undisturbed. A diagnosis, an accident, a loss, a moment of irreversible news—these events mark turning points in life, and they frequently awaken questions that lie dormant until something painful forces them to the surface. Among these questions, one rises more persistently than any other: *What kind of God allows this?* No matter how much theological training a person receives, no matter how devout or disciplined their prayer, this question has a way of returning whenever life has been shaken.

It is important to recognize that this question is not a modern invention. It is not the mark of a fragile age, nor the sign of a shallow faith suddenly confronted with reality. It is one of the oldest questions voiced in Scripture, woven into the experience of the people of God from the earliest pages of the Bible to the final chapters of Revelation. The cry of the suffering is not dismissed as irreverent or immature. It is preserved as part of divine revelation because God understands the human heart far better than we do. He knows that the most honest questions are often born from the places where life has wounded us, and He does not require His children to offer polished phrases when their hearts are breaking.

The book of Job introduces this question with a clarity that is almost startling. Job is described as a righteous man, faithful to God and upright in all his ways. Yet he becomes the figure through whom Scripture gives voice to the anguish of innocent suffering. His losses come in rapid succession: his livelihood is destroyed, his children die, his health collapses. The man who once stood as a model of blessing becomes a symbol of bewilderment. Sitting in the dust, covered in sores, Job asks the one question that rises almost instinctively from every wounded heart: *Why?* He does not ask it with defiance but with desperation, and Scripture allows his words to stand without apology.

This pattern continues throughout the Psalms, where cries of lament occupy a significant portion of Israel's prayerbook. These prayers reveal the inner landscape of believers facing abandonment, injustice, fear, and despair. They show us that the people who trusted God most deeply were not ashamed to ask hard questions: "How long, O Lord?" "Why do You hide Your face?" "Why have You forgotten me?" These prayers are not the polished expressions of spiritual calm. They are the honest cries of covenantal relationship. The psalmist speaks *to* God even when he does not understand what God is doing, and in this very act we see that lament is not a departure from faith but an expression of it.

The prophets echo the same struggle. Jeremiah, often called the weeping prophet, speaks with a candor that leaves no room for sentimentality. He accuses, he questions, he pleads, and he confesses. His ministry unfolds in the midst of national collapse, moral confusion, and personal isolation. Yet all his pain is carried into conversation with God. Habakkuk argues with God over the problem of injustice. Isaiah speaks to a people who walk in darkness and long for light. These are not voices of unbelief. They are voices of believers who know that God can bear the weight of their confusion.

The question reaches its most profound expression in the New Testament, when Jesus Himself takes up the words of the psalms and cries from the Cross, "My God, my God, why have You forsaken Me?" These words are not merely a quotation; they are the entrance of God into the full depth of human suffering. In Christ's cry we see the mystery of divine compassion unveiled: God does not remain above human agony; He enters it. He does not dismiss the human question; He speaks it from within the human condition. This moment reveals that the question "What kind of God allows this?" is not an obstacle to faith. It is part of the path of faith, a question sanctified by the One who carried the Cross.

At the same time, we live in an age that experiences this question with a particular intensity. Modern people often feel the weight of suffering more sharply than previous generations, not because our suffering is greater, but because our expectations of life have shifted dramatically. The world our ancestors inhabited—marked by fragility, limitation, and a constant nearness to death—is vastly different from the world we now take for granted. Advances in medicine, technology, and social stability have given rise to a conviction that suffering is something exceptional rather than something woven into the fabric of human life. When suffering does break through the surface of our comfort, it feels like an intrusion, a violation of what we assumed life should be.

A culture accustomed to comfort naturally finds suffering scandalous. We have been trained to expect convenience, immediate solutions, and control over the circumstances of our lives. When these expectations fail, the resulting confusion leads many to believe that something has gone fundamentally wrong with the world or with God. This expectation of uninterrupted ease is historically unusual and spiritually dangerous. Scripture never portrays life this way. Instead, it portrays a world that is good, yet wounded; created by God, yet distorted by sin; filled with beauty, yet marked by struggle. When we forget this biblical realism, any encounter with suffering feels like a direct contradiction of God's goodness.

In addition to this comfort culture, the medicalisation of suffering has reshaped our perception of what is normal. Modern medicine is an extraordinary gift, one that has alleviated enormous amounts of human pain. But its success has also led to the assumption that all suffering should be treatable, preventable, or curable. When medicine reaches its limits—as it inevitably must—we are left with a sense of failure rather than acceptance. Ancient Israel knew the limitations of the earthly condition. Modern society often refuses to accept those limitations, and in that refusal, suffering becomes all the more bewildering.

Another factor intensifying the contemporary struggle is the rise of radical individualism. In past centuries, suffering was experienced within families, tribes, or communities. People rarely faced hardship alone. Today, loneliness has become one of the defining conditions of modern life, and suffering experienced in isolation becomes heavier and more emotionally destabilising. Without a community to interpret suffering through a shared faith or a shared story, the burden falls entirely on the individual, who often lacks the spiritual or relational resources needed to carry it.

Still another layer is added by the secular worldview that has taken root in modern culture. When transcendence is removed from the horizon of life—when heaven, eternity, and divine providence are no longer part of one's understanding of reality—suffering loses any framework of meaning. It becomes a brute fact, presented without context or purpose. The human heart was not designed to carry suffering in a universe stripped of God. Without transcendence, suffering appears not only painful but absurd. In such a world, the question "What kind of God allows this?" becomes even more anguished, because people no longer believe that there is a story large enough to hold their pain.

These modern dynamics—comfort culture, medicalisation, individualism, secularism—do not create suffering, but they do create a climate in which suffering feels more traumatic and disorienting. They shape the expectations we bring to life and to God, and when those expectations collapse, the result is often a crisis of faith. The difficulty is not simply that we suffer, but that we suffer without understanding how suffering fits within the larger drama of existence. When Scripture is removed from the frame of reference, suffering becomes an unanswerable riddle. When Scripture is restored to its proper place, the question does not disappear, but it is drawn into the wider context of God's covenantal love.

When Scripture becomes the lens through which suffering is viewed, the question itself begins to take on a different shape. We no longer ask it as isolated individuals attempting to interpret our own circumstances in the absence of a larger story. Instead, we find ourselves standing within the same question that generations before us have brought before the Lord. It becomes clear that the people of God have never been shielded from the sorrows of life, nor have they ever been expected to carry those sorrows in silence. What distinguishes biblical faith from modern assumptions is not the elimination of the question, but the context in which the question is asked.

It is striking that the Bible does not rush to defend God against the charge that suffering seems to contradict His goodness. The sacred writers never appear embarrassed by the existence of pain, nor do they attempt to disguise the difficulties that accompany human life. The story of salvation unfolds in the midst of a world marked by struggle from the moment the first sin disrupts the harmony of Eden. Yet the biblical account never portrays suffering as evidence of divine neglect. Instead, it consistently reveals a God who remains faithful to His covenant even when His people suffer deeply. This covenantal framework is the key difference between a merely philosophical reflection on suffering and a theological understanding grounded in revelation.

The Psalms, perhaps more than any other part of Scripture, show how suffering becomes a place of encounter rather than alienation. The psalmists do not deny their pain; they articulate it with stunning clarity. They speak of enemies who pursue them, illnesses that weaken them, fears that haunt them, and injustices that discourage them. Yet every lament is addressed to God. The psalmist does not interpret his suffering apart from the Lord; he places it squarely within the relationship that defines Israel's existence. This is why lament is not a rejection of faith. It is an act of faith, because it assumes that God hears, cares, and responds even when His ways are not yet understood.

We see this same covenantal instinct in the lives of the patriarchs. Abraham is called by God yet experiences trials that would unsettle any believer. His journey includes famine, danger, and prolonged uncertainty, culminating in the agonising test of being asked to offer his son Isaac. The narrative does not present these events as divine cruelty. Rather, it reveals the deepening of Abraham's trust in a God whose promises extend beyond immediate circumstances. Similarly, Jacob's life is marked by conflict, deception, and fear, yet it is through a night of wrestling—a moment of both struggle and intimacy—that he receives a new name and a new identity within the covenant.

Joseph's story introduces another essential dimension of biblical suffering: that God can bring forth good even from the most unjust circumstances. Sold into slavery by his brothers, wrongfully imprisoned, and forgotten by those he aided, Joseph endures hardships that would embitter most hearts. Yet the narrative repeatedly affirms that "the Lord was with Joseph." The presence of God does not spare Joseph from trial, but it sustains him through it, guiding him toward a future in which his suffering becomes the means of salvation for many. The message is not that all suffering has an immediately visible purpose, but that no suffering lies outside the reach of God's providence.

Israel's national story reinforces this pattern on a larger scale. Their years in Egypt, marked by forced labour and oppression, evoke one of the most powerful lines in the Old Testament: "God saw the people of Israel—and God knew" (Ex 2:25). The suffering of the people does not indicate divine abandonment. It becomes the occasion for God's decisive act of redemption in the Exodus. This theme continues through the wilderness, the period of the judges, the monarchy, the exile, and the restoration. At every turn, Israel discovers that suffering is never allowed to sever the covenant. Even when suffering arises from their own unfaithfulness, God remains steadfast, continually drawing His people back to Himself.

Yet despite this rich biblical heritage, many Christians today still find themselves unprepared when suffering enters their lives. This is not because Scripture has failed to speak clearly, but because our culture has taught us to think about suffering in ways that are far removed from the biblical worldview. When suffering arrives unexpectedly, people often assume that something has gone wrong in their relationship with God. They imagine that a life of faith should insulate them from hardship, or that obedience should be rewarded with uninterrupted peace. But Scripture never presents the covenant in these terms. God promises His presence, not a pain-free existence; His fidelity, not the absence of trials.

The modern reader must therefore recover a truth that ancient

Israel understood instinctively: suffering does not fall outside the providence of God. It is not proof that God has grown distant or indifferent. Rather, it is part of the larger drama of salvation through which God reveals His mercy, strengthens faith, and shapes His people for the destiny prepared for them. To say this is not to trivialise human pain or to reduce suffering to a simple formula. It is to recognise that without the biblical story, suffering becomes a riddle with no answer. With the biblical story, suffering becomes an experience through which God draws His people deeper into the mystery of His love.

At this point, the question arises again with renewed force: if God is present, if He is faithful, and if suffering can be understood within the divine economy, then why does the question "What kind of God allows this?" still feel so urgent? The answer lies in the fact that suffering touches not only the body but the soul. It exposes our vulnerabilities, confronts our illusions of control, and forces us to acknowledge the limits of our understanding. This emotional and spiritual weight is intensified by the cultural forces shaping modern life. When people lack a theological framework for suffering, they interpret it through the lens of fear or resentment rather than faith and trust.

A culture that honours personal autonomy above all else finds suffering particularly destabilising because it exposes the fragility of human power. The modern emphasis on self-determination clashes with the reality that suffering comes unbidden and resists our attempts to manage or eliminate it. Medical progress has reduced many forms of suffering, but it has also reinforced the expectation that all suffering should be fixable. When illness or tragedy defies even the most advanced treatments, the result is not only grief but disorientation. People feel betrayed by a world that taught them to expect control.

The absence of transcendence further complicates this experience. When suffering is viewed within the horizon of eternity, it becomes possible to endure it with patience and hope, trusting that God's justice and mercy extend beyond this life. But when life is understood only in temporal terms, suffering becomes an intolerable burden. It appears as a disruption to personal plans rather than as a moment within a larger divine narrative. Without transcendence, the soul becomes too small a container for the weight of suffering.

These cultural dynamics help explain why the ancient question "What kind of God allows this?" has become sharper in our time. The question is the same, but the context has changed. Modern people bring different assumptions to the problem of suffering, assumptions that often obscure the biblical understanding of God, humanity, and the world. This does not make the modern question illegitimate; it simply reveals the need for a return to the scriptural worldview in which suffering has meaning because it has a place within God's saving work.

To understand suffering in a way that is faithful to Scripture, we must acknowledge that the Bible approaches the question along a very specific path. It begins not with philosophical speculation but with the story of God's relationship with His people. This is essential because suffering cannot be understood apart from that story. When suffering is lifted out of the biblical narrative and examined in isolation, it appears arbitrary and cruel. When it is placed back within salvation history, it becomes part of a larger pattern in which God continually brings life out of situations that appear hopeless.

This requires us to adopt the biblical habit of reading our lives in continuity with the people who came before us. The experiences of Abraham, Joseph, Israel, the prophets, the apostles, and most of all Christ, form the interpretive lens for the Christian. Their encounters with suffering were not detached from God's promise but deeply intertwined with it. The same must be true for us. The covenant that shaped their lives is the covenant into which we have been drawn through Christ. If we lose sight of this continuity, we will inevitably misinterpret the role suffering plays in our own lives.

At the heart of this misinterpretation lies a common assumption: that God's goodness is equivalent to our comfort. This assumption is not drawn from Scripture. It arises from cultural expectations that have gradually replaced biblical ones. In the biblical worldview, God's goodness is expressed through His steadfast love, His mercy, His presence, and His faithfulness to His covenant promises. It is not measured by the absence of hardship. In fact, many of the greatest moments of grace in Scripture unfold precisely in situations where suffering is most acute. God led Israel out of Egypt through trials that tested their trust. He formed David through adversity and exile. He deepened the faith of the prophets through experiences that demanded complete reliance upon His word. And He redeemed the world through the suffering, death, and Resurrection of His Son.

When we equate God's goodness with the removal of suffering, we set ourselves up for confusion and disappointment. This does not mean that God wills suffering or that it is, in itself, something desirable. The Christian tradition has always maintained that suffering is a consequence of a fallen world, not a direct expression of God's will. Yet within this fallen world, God brings forth good from circumstances that appear entirely contrary to His purposes. Joseph could say to his brothers, "You meant evil against me; but God meant it for good." This does not excuse the evil, but it reveals the mystery of providence at work within it.

Understanding this distinction protects us from simplistic answers to the problem of evil. Some people, in their desire to defend God, rush to provide explanations that Scripture itself does not offer. They claim confidently to know why a particular tragedy occurred, or they insist that suffering always produces a visible spiritual benefit. But Scripture does not reduce suffering to a single purpose. The reasons for suffering are as varied as the circumstances of human life. Some suffering arises from human sin; some from the consequences of living in a world wounded by the Fall; some from the mystery of God's permissive will; some from the spiritual growth that emerges only through trial. The Bible avoids universalising any one explanation.

For this reason, the problem of evil must be approached with humility. It is not a puzzle to be solved with a few logical steps, nor is it a riddle whose answer will satisfy every emotional wound. The problem of evil forces us to acknowledge the limits of our understanding and to rely on the revelation that God has given us. Scripture's response to suffering takes the form of a story rather than a syllogism. It shows us who God is and how He acts. It unveils His faithfulness across generations and His unbreakable commitment to the covenant He established. It reveals that He enters human suffering rather than observing it from afar, and that He transforms the meaning of suffering through His redemptive work.

Yet even this does not eliminate the emotional struggle. The heart still cries out for clarity. The question still rises: *Why does God allow this?* And here Scripture offers a surprising insight. The Bible does not treat this question as a threat to faith. It treats it as part of the journey of faith. Job asks it. The psalmists ask it. Jeremiah asks it. Jesus Himself gives voice to it. The question is not a sign of disbelief. It is the cry of a heart seeking to reconcile what it knows of God's goodness with what it experiences in the world. This tension does not indicate the absence of grace; it is often the place where grace begins to deepen.

By preserving these cries within the inspired text, Scripture teaches us that God welcomes the honesty of His people. He does not demand silence in the face of suffering. He invites us to bring our confusion and sorrow to Him as part of our relationship with Him. This becomes clear when we observe how God responds to the suffering of His people. He never chastises Job for asking his questions. Instead, He engages Job directly, not by offering a detailed explanation, but by revealing His majesty, His wisdom, and His intimate involvement in creation. The answer God gives is personal rather than theoretical. Job's suffering is not explained, but it is embraced within a vision of God's sovereignty and care that leads Job into deeper trust.

This same pattern appears throughout Scripture. When the psalmist cries out, God does not always remove the suffering, but He meets the psalmist with the assurance of His presence. When the prophets lament the brokenness of Israel, God responds with promises of restoration. When the apostles face persecution, God strengthens them through the Holy Spirit. These responses do not explain suffering in a way that satisfies curiosity, but they reveal a truth that satisfies the heart: God is with His people, even—and especially—in the moments that cause them to question His nearness.

Bearing all this in mind, we begin to see why the biblical approach to suffering differs so markedly from the modern one. The biblical view is grounded in covenant: a relationship initiated by God, sustained by His fidelity, and fulfilled in Christ. Within this relationship, suffering becomes a place where the covenant is tested but not broken. Modern culture, by contrast, approaches suffering through the lens of autonomy, efficiency, and emotional fulfilment. Without the covenant framework, suffering appears meaningless. Within the covenant, suffering becomes something through which God reveals His love, deepens trust, and prepares His people for the fullness of redemption.

This does not mean that suffering becomes easy or that believers are expected to welcome it without struggle. Scripture is entirely realistic about the pain of suffering. It acknowledges grief, fear, and the desire for relief. But it also insists that suffering is not the final word. God's promise extends beyond suffering. His purpose encompasses more than we can perceive in the present moment. And His covenant remains firm even when circumstances appear to contradict His goodness.

If we are to make any progress toward understanding suffering in the light of faith, we must begin by framing the question the way Scripture frames it. The Bible never presents suffering as an abstract difficulty detached from the identity of God or the nature of the covenant. It presents suffering as something that must be read within the story of creation and the subsequent drama of redemption. When this larger narrative is forgotten, suffering appears to stand alone as a challenge to God's goodness; when this narrative is recovered, suffering is understood as a consequence of the world's wounded condition and as a place where God's fidelity is revealed rather than contradicted.

To appreciate this, we must return to the beginning. Genesis introduces us to a world that is ordered, harmonious, and good. Human beings are created in the image and likeness of God and placed within a creation that reflects His generosity. There is no hint of suffering in God's original design. Pain, fear, and disorder enter the biblical story only after humanity turns away from God. This turning is not merely a moral failure; it is a rupture that distorts the entire fabric of creation. The world remains good because it remains God's creation, but it becomes wounded because the communion between God and His children has been fractured.

This initial rupture provides the biblical explanation for the origin of suffering. It does not attribute suffering to divine will; it attributes suffering to a world no longer in perfect harmony with its Creator. But the Bible does not end the story there. Immediately after announcing the consequences of sin, God speaks a promise: the seed of the woman will one day crush the serpent's head. This promise, traditionally called the protoevangelium—the first gospel—becomes the foundation for all that follows. Even in the moment of humanity's greatest failure, God reveals His intention to heal and restore what has been broken. From this point onward, the story of salvation unfolds as God's response to a wounded world.

It is essential to recognize that this response is not merely corrective; it is relational. God does not simply intervene to remove suffering. He establishes a covenant with His people. This covenant shapes Israel's understanding of their trials. When they suffer, they call upon the God who bound Himself to them. Their lament is not a rejection of the covenant but a reaffirmation of it. When they question God, they do so from within a relationship that He Himself initiated. The covenant gives them the language to bring their pain before Him and the confidence to believe that He hears.

Yet even within this covenantal frame, suffering remains complex. The Old Testament does not attempt to provide a single explanation for all suffering. Some suffering arises from human sin—both personal and communal. Some suffering results from the reality of living in a world wounded by the Fall. Some suffering is allowed by God to test, purify, or strengthen His people. And some suffering remains mysterious, defying any attempt to assign a specific cause. Scripture's honesty about this complexity protects us from reducing suffering to a simplistic principle or formula. The biblical writers refuse to pretend that every sorrow fits neatly into our categories. Instead, they continually draw the reader's attention back to God's character and His covenant fidelity.

It is here that the problem of evil must be framed with theological clarity. The question "Why does God allow suffering?" cannot be answered adequately if it is separated from the biblical account of creation, fall, covenant, and redemption. If suffering is viewed apart from this narrative, it becomes an accusation against God. If it is viewed within this narrative, it becomes part of a larger story in which God reveals His love, His justice, and His mercy. This does not eliminate the emotional difficulty of suffering, but it does prevent the theological confusion that arises when suffering is removed from its proper context.

We must also avoid the temptation to treat the problem of evil as if it were merely an intellectual obstacle. It is an existential challenge, one that affects the heart as much as the mind. People do not ask the question "What kind of God allows this?" from a distance. They ask it from hospital rooms, gravesides, and quiet moments of personal anguish. The question carries emotional weight, and Scripture honours this weight by preserving the voices of those who struggled with it. When we read Job, the Psalms, or the prophets, we encounter real people grappling with real pain. Their words are not theoretical reflections; they are the cries of hearts seeking God in the midst of suffering.

At the same time, Scripture teaches us that suffering cannot ultimately be understood apart from the Cross. The entire Old Testament prepares for the moment when God Himself will enter the depths of human suffering. In the Incarnation, God does not approach suffering from the outside. He approaches it from within. In the Passion, Christ takes upon Himself the full weight of human anguish. His cry from the Cross is not the cry of a distant observer; it is the cry of the Son who has entered human brokenness in order to redeem it. This is the definitive answer to the problem of suffering, but it is an answer that will be unfolded later in this book when we reach the chapters dedicated to Christ's Passion and Resurrection.

For now, it is enough to understand that Scripture does not treat suffering as something foreign to the life of faith. It treats it as something inseparable from the story of salvation. The question that haunts the human heart—"What kind of God allows this?"—is not one that Scripture ignores. It is one that Scripture embraces, carrying it through the entire arc of the biblical narrative. The answer cannot be given in a sentence because the answer is given in a story. It is the story of a God who creates, witnesses humanity's fall, calls a people to Himself, bears their sufferings, enters their condition, and transforms suffering from the inside out.

In this way, the problem of evil is not a disruption to the logic of faith. It is one of the very places where the logic of faith becomes most profound. The covenant reveals that God does not remain at a distance from human pain. He accompanies His people, guides them through trials, purifies their hearts, and prepares them for the fullness of life that He desires for them. The biblical story does not pretend that suffering is easy or that its reasons are always discernible. What it does insist upon is the unwavering character of the God who remains faithful even when circumstances appear to contradict His goodness.

As the biblical narrative unfolds, it becomes increasingly clear that the question of suffering cannot be separated from the identity of God or from the destiny of His people. The heart of the covenant is God's promise to be with His people, not merely in moments of triumph but in the very circumstances that cause them to cry out in distress. Throughout Scripture, God's closeness is often revealed most clearly when His people find themselves confronting the very realities that seem to contradict His goodness. The tension between what God has promised and what His people experience becomes a place of encounter. Far from weakening faith, this tension has the potential to deepen it.

One of the consistent features of the biblical account is that God rarely offers explanations for specific instances of suffering. Instead, He reveals Himself. This is a crucial distinction. Explanations can sometimes satisfy the intellect, but they rarely comfort the heart. Revelation, on the other hand, allows the human person to see suffering within the larger horizon of God's purpose. This does not make suffering pleasant, nor does it eliminate the grief that accompanies it. But it places suffering within a relationship—a covenantal bond that assures the believer that God remains faithful even in the darkest moments.

This becomes most evident in the New Testament, where the mystery of suffering is drawn into the very life of Christ. In the Gospels, Jesus repeatedly identifies Himself with the afflicted. He touches the sick, speaks to the oppressed, and raises the dead. Yet He also embraces suffering in His own life. The Incarnation itself is an act of divine solidarity with a world marked by pain. In His ministry, Jesus teaches His disciples that suffering will be part of the Christian life. "If anyone would come after Me, let him deny himself and take up his cross." These words do not romanticise suffering; they acknowledge its inevitability in a world marked by sin while assuring believers that suffering has a place within the path to redemption.

The Passion brings this mystery into full clarity. Christ's suffering is not accidental. It is the means by which God enters the depths of human brokenness. The Cross does not explain suffering in the conventional sense; it transforms it. Through His voluntary obedience, Jesus reveals that suffering, when united to God's will, can become the place where love is revealed most profoundly. This truth is not grasped merely by examining the external events of the Passion. It is understood by contemplating the union between the Father and the Son, a union that remains unbroken even in the midst of Christ's agony. This is why the New Testament consistently presents the Cross not as a failure or contradiction, but as the centre of God's saving work.

The Resurrection completes this transformation. In rising from the dead, Christ reveals that suffering and death do not have the final word. The wounds He bears in His glorified body testify not only to the reality of His suffering but to the fact that suffering itself has been taken up into the life of God. The Resurrection does not erase the memory of pain; it reveals pain's ultimate horizon. What appeared to be defeat becomes victory. What seemed meaningless becomes the means by which God brings about new life. This pattern—suffering followed by glory—becomes the foundation for Christian hope.

This, however, is a truth that must be unfolded gradually. While the Cross and Resurrection provide the definitive answer to the problem of suffering, they do not eliminate the need for honest engagement with the question. The early chapters of this book must respect the burden with which many readers approach the topic. It is not enough to declare that Christ has conquered suffering. The human heart must be led into this mystery step by step, beginning with the recognition that Scripture honours the question before it reveals the answer.

For this reason, our first task has been to situate the question "What kind of God allows this?" within the story of God's people. The question is not foreign to faith. It arises within faith. It is one of the recurring themes of the biblical narrative, and it is voiced by those who knew God most intimately. Job's cry, the psalmists' laments, the prophets' questions, and Christ's own words from the Cross remind us that the question is part of the path toward deeper trust. It emerges wherever human suffering meets divine promise, and it reveals the desire of the human heart to understand how God's goodness can coexist with the realities of a wounded world.

Although Scripture situates suffering within the long narrative of creation, sin, and redemption, it does not pretend that the experience of suffering becomes straightforward simply because its origin is revealed. The biblical story teaches us that suffering will remain part of our earthly condition, but it also teaches us that suffering must be approached with the mind and heart formed by God's revelation. When that revelation is forgotten or neglected, suffering becomes far more difficult to bear, because the human person instinctively seeks meaning in what he endures. Without the horizon of faith, suffering appears arbitrary. Within the horizon of faith, suffering becomes something that must be interpreted through the lens of the God who creates, promises, and remains faithful.

This recognition is especially important for the world we inhabit today. The cultural forces that shape modern life—our assumptions about comfort, our expectations of control, our diminished sense of transcendence—have dramatically altered the way people encounter pain. Much of the confusion that surrounds suffering in our age does not arise from suffering itself, but from the loss of a framework capable of interpreting it. When the imagination is no longer shaped by Scripture or by the lived faith of the Church, suffering is stripped of its context and becomes something frightening, disorienting, and seemingly purposeless. To rediscover that context is one of the essential tasks of Christian witness in the modern world.

For this reason, the chapters that follow will consider not only the biblical foundations of suffering but also the particular conditions of our time that make suffering feel more unbearable than it once did. We will explore how a culture devoted to avoiding pain has lost the capacity to understand suffering, and how the human heart, when placed under trial, reveals both its frailty and its deepest longing for God. These themes belong to the opening movement of this book, where the task is not yet to resolve the problem but to understand it—to see how suffering confronts the human person, challenges our assumptions, and draws forth questions that Scripture itself is prepared to address. Only then will we be ready to follow the biblical narrative into the mystery of God's response.

2

The Culture of Pain-avoidance

The way a culture understands suffering says a great deal about the way it understands life itself. Every generation inherits a set of assumptions—usually unstated, sometimes unexamined—about what it means to flourish as a human being. These assumptions shape how we view hardship, how we respond to pain, and how we interpret the trials that inevitably come. In recent decades, the Western world has adopted a set of expectations that would have been incomprehensible to nearly every previous age. We expect life to run smoothly. We expect discomfort to be temporary. We expect solutions to be available, professionals to manage our distress, and systems to protect us from anything that threatens our emotional or physical equilibrium. Suffering, once understood as a normal part of the human condition, is now treated as a sign that something in our world—or something in ourselves—has gone wrong.

This shift did not happen overnight. It emerged gradually as scientific and medical advances reshaped our understanding of what is possible. There is no denying the good these developments have brought. Modern medicine has alleviated countless forms of suffering, extending lifespans and improving the quality of life in ways previous generations could never have imagined. These are gifts for which we should be deeply grateful. Yet with every gift comes a temptation, and the temptation in this case is subtle but powerful: to assume that all suffering can be removed, managed, or solved, and therefore that suffering which remains must be senseless or intolerable.

The biblical worldview does not portray suffering as an aberration. Scripture treats suffering as part of life in a world wounded by sin. Redemption transforms suffering, but it does not remove it. Christ Himself warns His disciples that trials will come. The apostles speak of suffering as something to be expected, endured, and offered to God. The early Christians did not interpret suffering as a failure of faith but as part of their participation in the life of Christ. Yet this is precisely the perspective that modern culture has lost. As medical progress has advanced, the human imagination has shifted. We have come to expect the removal of pain as the normal condition of life, and in doing so we have departed from the biblical vision that formed the faith of our ancestors.

To understand the culture of pain-avoidance, we must first recognise how thoroughly the modern world has been shaped by the belief that life should be comfortable. Convenience has become the silent creed of our age. Entire industries exist to spare us from inconvenience, to streamline our experiences, to ensure that whatever we want is available quickly, efficiently, and with minimal effort. This expectation extends from the mundane aspects of daily life to the deepest dimensions of the human heart. If comfort is the norm, then discomfort becomes a disruption, and suffering becomes an intrusion. Instead of interpreting suffering through the lens of Scripture, people increasingly interpret Scripture—or ignore it altogether—through the lens of suffering.

This cultural shift has spiritual consequences. A heart shaped by the expectation of ease is easily shaken by hardship. When a society teaches people that suffering should not exist, those who suffer begin to believe that their experience is abnormal, perhaps even unjust. The biblical worldview, on the other hand, teaches that suffering is part of the story of salvation. God does not promise His people a life free from trials. He promises His presence, His grace, and His faithfulness in the midst of those trials. The loss of this worldview leaves people unprepared for the realities of life. They know how to enjoy prosperity but not how to endure adversity. They know how to celebrate success but not how to persevere through sorrow.

The pharmaceutical age has amplified these tendencies. Once again, the point is not to diminish the real blessings of medical progress. Human suffering has been relieved in extraordinary ways, and this is a sign of God's providence working through human ingenuity. Yet medicine, for all its benefits, cannot shield us from the deeper wounds of the human heart. It cannot remove grief, restore broken relationships, or reconcile us to the mysteries of life and death. When people begin to rely on medicine not only to heal the body but to shield the soul from suffering, they place upon it a weight it cannot bear.

In earlier centuries, sickness and death were woven visibly into the fabric of daily life. People prayed because they knew their dependence on God. They turned to the sacraments because they recognised that suffering could become a moment of grace. Today, medical technology often creates the illusion that we are in control. As long as treatments are available, suffering seems negotiable. But when treatments fail, when suffering persists despite our best efforts, people find themselves spiritually unprepared. They have been trained to expect a cure, and when none comes, they feel abandoned. This is not because God has changed, but because the assumptions shaping their expectations have drifted far from the biblical worldview.

The therapeutic culture reinforces this shift even further. We live in a time when emotional comfort is treated almost as a right. Any experience that disrupts our sense of psychological well-being is interpreted as a threat to be managed, corrected, or removed. The rise of therapy has offered many genuine benefits—insight, healing, and compassion for those who struggle with inner burdens. Yet the therapeutic framework often treats suffering as a problem of internal balance rather than as part of the spiritual journey. It views discomfort as something that must be resolved, not as something that might be endured in faith or offered to God.

The therapeutic mindset, unlike the biblical worldview, places the self at the centre. The primary question becomes not "What is God doing through this?" but "How can I restore my sense of equilibrium?" Without realising it, many people have adopted an outlook in which suffering is interpreted only through the lens of personal feeling. This is not the language of Scripture, where suffering is always understood within the larger covenant—the relationship between God and His people. When that covenant horizon is eclipsed, suffering loses its meaning. It becomes frightening not simply because it hurts, but because nothing greater than suffering remains to interpret it.

The culmination of this cultural shift can be seen in the rise of assisted dying. This development represents more than a moral crisis; it reveals a profound loss of confidence in the value of life itself. When a society concludes that life with suffering is no longer worth living, it has cut itself off from the entire biblical vision of human dignity. Scripture teaches that life is a gift from God, entrusted to us not because it is free from pain but because it is precious in every season. The modern impulse to end suffering by ending life arises from a worldview in which suffering has no place, no purpose, and no promise beyond itself.

But Scripture tells a different story. It presents suffering not as an obstacle to meaning but as one of the places where meaning is most deeply revealed. This does not romanticise suffering, nor does it deny the anguish it brings. Rather, it insists that suffering must be interpreted within the covenant—within the relationship that defines our identity as children of God. When this relationship is forgotten, suffering becomes intolerable. When this relationship is remembered, suffering becomes something through which God draws us into deeper trust, deeper conversion, and deeper union with Him.

A society that loses the biblical horizon begins to treat suffering as an interruption to the "real" story of life rather than a chapter within it. This shift becomes especially clear the moment we consider how people respond to trials today. When discomfort arises, the instinct is to minimise it, medicate it, or manage it. The assumption is that suffering has no significance beyond the fact that it hurts. In earlier centuries, people interpreted suffering in the light of God's providence; today, people interpret suffering in the absence of God's providence. This does not mean they have rejected God outright. It means they have absorbed a worldview in which God no longer explains life's hardships. Instead, hardships cast doubt on God.

This is why the loss of a biblical worldview is so significant. Without it, suffering becomes detached from purpose. When people no longer see themselves as part of the story God is telling, they begin to see suffering as a threat to be removed rather than as a moment to be lived faithfully. The old Christian vocabulary—words like patience, perseverance, long-suffering, sacrifice—no longer carries weight. These are not merely forgotten virtues; they are now foreign virtues. They make little sense in a culture trained to believe that happiness is immediate, comfort is normal, and hardship is a sign of failure.

The shift becomes even more striking when we examine what modern people fear most. In a world that has lost sight of eternity, suffering becomes terrifying precisely because it appears final. If there is no larger meaning, then pain becomes a kind of absolute. The soul has nowhere to place it. It becomes a burden too heavy for the heart to carry. In the biblical worldview, suffering is weighed against the promises of God, the hope of redemption, and the nearness of Christ. Without these, suffering hangs in the air with no anchor. It becomes a storm without a shoreline.

This is why the modern attitude toward death has become so fragile. Death was once understood through the lens of faith—as a passage, a judgment, a meeting with God. Today, it is often viewed solely through the lens of medicine. It appears as the final defeat of the therapeutic ideal, the moment when pain can no longer be managed or postponed. When a culture loses the hope of resurrection, it begins to view death not as a mystery to be entrusted to God but as a problem to be solved by human hands. This mindset leads inevitably toward the acceptance of assisted suicide, which presents itself as mercy precisely because suffering appears meaningless.

The logic is straightforward:

If suffering has no purpose, then eliminating suffering becomes the highest form of compassion.

If suffering has no place in human life, then a life touched by suffering begins to appear less valuable.

If suffering cannot be interpreted spiritually, then death becomes a practical solution.

This is not exaggeration; it is the cultural landscape we now inhabit. A society that has forgotten the biblical story cannot make sense of suffering. And a society that cannot make sense of suffering will try to eliminate it at any cost—even at the cost of life itself.

Yet Scripture teaches us something radically different. It teaches that suffering does not diminish human dignity; it reveals it. A person who suffers remains a person made in the image and likeness of God. A life marked by trials is still a life filled with meaning because it is held within the covenant. The saints remind us that suffering, when united to Christ, becomes a moment of profound grace. The Church insists that even in weakness, even in dependency, the human person bears a dignity that no amount of suffering can erase.

But this truth is unintelligible to a world that has lost the sense of who God is and who we are before Him. If life is defined by comfort, then suffering becomes the enemy. If life is defined by communion with God, then suffering becomes part of the pilgrimage. The modern world has embraced the former view with remarkable zeal. Everything from consumer marketing to medical technology reinforces the belief that comfort is the normal state of human existence. But comfort, elevated to an expectation, becomes spiritually dangerous. It trains the heart to collapse at the first sign of trial. It forms people who know how to avoid pain but not how to live through it.

This avoidance has a cost. When suffering is treated as an anomaly, we lose the virtues that suffering cultivates. We lose fortitude, patience, humility, compassion. We lose the ability to accompany others in their pain because we have never learned how to dwell with our own. When comfort becomes a cultural idol, the result is not greater happiness but greater fragility. People become unable to carry the ordinary burdens of life. They find themselves overwhelmed by what previous generations considered common human trials.

This is why the culture of pain-avoidance is not merely a social trend; it is a spiritual crisis. It forms hearts that cannot endure. It shapes expectations that crumble under pressure. It undermines the very virtues through which God teaches His children to trust Him. A heart that has been trained to avoid suffering at all costs will find it difficult to recognise God when suffering comes. The illusion of control will give way to confusion, resentment, or despair. This is not because God is absent but because the heart has been formed without reference to the story He is telling.

The biblical worldview, by contrast, prepares the heart for reality.

It teaches that suffering will come, not because God delights in our pain but because the world is wounded and because our salvation passes through the Cross. It teaches that God is present precisely when suffering feels most bewildering. It teaches that suffering can be redemptive, transformative, and revelatory—but only when interpreted within the covenant. The culture of pain-avoidance blinds us to these truths, leaving us spiritually unprepared and existentially vulnerable.

Once we recognise how deeply modern expectations have shifted, it becomes possible to see why suffering now unsettles people with an intensity that previous generations would have found perplexing. The problem is not that human beings suffer more today. The problem is that we no longer know what to do with suffering when it arrives. Earlier generations approached suffering within a framework shaped by Scripture, liturgy, and the life of the Church. They interpreted their trials through the Passover, the Psalms, the Cross, and the Communion of Saints. Their worldview did not eliminate suffering, but it gave suffering a place. It provided a grammar—a way to speak, pray, and hope through trials.

Modern culture has lost this grammar. We speak often about pain, but rarely about its meaning. We discuss suffering clinically or therapeutically, but not theologically. We treat it as data, not mystery. Without a theological grammar, suffering becomes mute; it becomes something we experience but cannot interpret. A mute suffering becomes a frightening suffering because the human heart needs meaning as much as it needs breath. When that meaning is absent, pain overwhelms the soul. It becomes a tide without a shoreline.

This is where the therapeutic worldview reveals its limits most clearly. The therapeutic impulse helps us explore our emotions, recognise our wounds, and seek healing for psychological burdens.

These are real goods. But when therapy becomes the primary lens for interpreting life, suffering loses its depth. It becomes a symptom to resolve rather than a season to live faithfully. The biblical worldview understands suffering as part of the journey toward maturity, conversion, and communion with God. The therapeutic worldview sees suffering primarily as an obstacle to emotional equilibrium. It is not wrong, but it is incomplete. And incompleteness is dangerous when it shapes an entire culture.

The loss of the biblical horizon also changes the way people perceive dependency. In Scripture, dependency is not a defect; it is the consequence of being a creature. We rely on God because He created us. We rely on others because we were made for communion. But when autonomy is treated as the highest good, dependency begins to look like a kind of failure. Illness, disability, aging—these become signs that a person is losing value, losing purpose, or losing control. A culture that idolises independence will inevitably struggle to see the dignity of those who can no longer care for themselves.

This helps explain why assisted dying has gained such momentum in recent decades. It is not simply a political issue. It is the logical conclusion of a worldview that cannot imagine meaning within suffering. If life's value is measured by productivity, pleasure, or autonomy, then life touched by suffering begins to appear less meaningful. The biblical worldview, however, insists on something entirely different. A life marked by suffering is not less sacred. It is often the place where God's presence becomes most vivid. The Cross of Christ stands as the definitive witness to this truth.

Yet when a culture loses the vision of the Cross, it loses the ability to understand its own trials. The Cross becomes a symbol rather than a story to inhabit. Suffering begins to feel alien, arbitrary, unnecessary. People begin to believe that a good life is a life without pain, and that death is preferable to dependency. This is one of the deepest tragedies of the modern worldview: it teaches people to fear the very experiences through which God often forms the soul most profoundly.

The consequences extend beyond the individual. When a society avoids suffering at all costs, its collective character begins to erode. Sacrifice becomes foreign. Commitment weakens. Families fracture under pressure because the virtues needed to endure hardship have never been cultivated. Marriage, parenthood, and even friendship require perseverance, but perseverance is impossible without having endured suffering. When a culture cannot face pain, it cannot sustain love. Love always carries a cost, and without the willingness to bear that cost, relationships grow brittle. The refusal to suffer becomes the refusal to love.

This cultural fragility can be seen in the way people speak about meaning. Many feel unfulfilled, aimless, or restless, yet they resist the very experiences through which meaning is forged. Meaning is not discovered by avoiding suffering. Meaning is discovered by embracing the responsibilities, sacrifices, and vocations through which God shapes the soul. When suffering is eliminated at any cost, meaning is eliminated with it. A life without trials becomes a life without depth. It becomes a life defined by consumption rather than communion.

The irony is that the more a society tries to eliminate suffering, the more anxious it becomes. When comfort is expected, discomfort becomes intolerable. When happiness is demanded, sadness becomes pathological. When success is assumed, failure becomes devastating. This is why the culture of pain-avoidance leads not to stability but to fragility. It forms hearts that are easily shaken, precisely because they have not been prepared for the realities of life in a fallen world.

The biblical worldview offers a different path. It does not minimise the pain of suffering, nor does it trivialise the anguish that people endure. But it refuses to treat suffering as an enemy to be eradicated. It teaches that suffering can be a place of encounter with God, a place of purification, a place where love is tested and strengthened. A culture that forgets this truth forgets its own soul. A culture that remembers it begins to rediscover the virtues that sustain families, communities, and hearts.

A culture that forgets this truth forgets its own soul. A culture that remembers it begins to rediscover the virtues that sustain families, communities, and hearts. For suffering has a way of exposing what comfort hides. It brings the human person back to the essentials, back to the questions that matter, back to the foundations upon which he builds his life. In times of ease, it is possible to live as though our strength were self-generated, as though our plans were secure simply because they were ours. But suffering strips away the illusion. It reminds us that our lives are not self-sufficient creations but gifts sustained by a God who speaks, who calls, and who accompanies His people through every shadowed valley.

This rediscovery is not instantaneous. It rarely arrives in a moment of clarity. More often, it unfolds slowly, the way dawn breaks gradually over a dark landscape. The heart passes through confusion before it reaches trust. It struggles against the instinct to flee discomfort and the cultural habits that teach us to interpret suffering as failure. But Scripture gives the believer a language for this struggle. It offers lament, prayer, complaint, and hope—not as contradictory impulses, but as parts of the same covenantal relationship.

The Psalms reveal this with striking honesty. They teach us that the believer can bring his anguish to God without fear of rejection. The psalmist does not conceal his pain; he names it before the Lord. He speaks of enemies who rise against him, of weakness in his flesh, of fears that trouble his soul. Yet in every lament, there is an act of trust. The psalmist cries out because he believes that God hears. He pleads because he knows God cares. He waits because he has experienced the Lord's faithfulness in every generation. This is the grammar modern culture has forgotten: suffering becomes bearable not because it is less painful, but because it is lived within a relationship that does not fail.

When suffering is understood in this way, it no longer appears as a random intrusion. It becomes something that God can use. Not something He delights in, but something He permits for reasons that surpass our comprehension yet never fall outside His providence. This is a hard truth for the modern heart, but it is a truth at the centre of the biblical revelation. The God of Israel is not a passive observer of human sorrow. He is the God who brings light from darkness, life from death, hope from despair. He is the God who speaks into the suffering of His people, not with platitudes or false assurances, but with promises rooted in His own fidelity.

Modern culture cannot grasp this because it has lost its sense of the sacred. Suffering, when stripped of transcendence, becomes purely biological or psychological. It becomes a misfortune, an error, something to be corrected rather than interpreted. But when suffering is seen through the biblical horizon, it becomes something different. It becomes a place where God reveals His presence. It becomes a moment in which the believer learns not only who he is, but who God is. It becomes a season in which faith matures, not in spite of the trial, but through the trial.

This is why the saints speak of suffering not with romanticism, but with reverence. They knew suffering intimately. They understood its weight. They felt its sting. Yet they also knew the One who met them in their trials. They discovered that suffering, far from separating them from God, became the means by which they were drawn deeper into His love. Their witness contradicts the assumptions of a culture formed by avoidance. It reveals that courage is born not from the absence of pain but from trust in the One who has conquered sin and death.

This trust is not merely emotional; it is covenantal. It is rooted in the history of God's dealings with His people. God binds Himself to Israel. He promises to be their God and to walk with them through all circumstances. This promise does not exempt them from suffering. It gives suffering a context. It frames their trials within the faithfulness of God. It assures them that the journey, no matter how dark, is never travelled alone. The believer who remembers this truth stands on solid ground even when the world around him trembles.

In a culture that prizes autonomy, this covenantal dependence appears counterintuitive. Yet it is precisely this dependence that gives the Christian the strength to endure. When a person believes he must face suffering by his own resources, the burden becomes crushing. But when suffering is borne within the covenant—within the life of prayer, the sacraments, and the communion of the Church—it becomes something God Himself sustains. The believer discovers that he is upheld not by his own resolve but by the grace that flows from the heart of the Father.

This is the wisdom the modern world has forgotten. It has replaced dependence with self-reliance, covenant with autonomy, meaning with technique. It has sought to manage pain but has forgotten how to endure it. It has tried to protect the heart by insulating it from discomfort but has unknowingly weakened the very virtues that enable the heart to stand firm. When suffering finally arrives—as it always does—the culture that promised resilience delivers fragility instead.

Yet the biblical worldview offers a different inheritance. It teaches that suffering, while painful, is not purposeless. It teaches that the believer can stand firm because God stands with him. It teaches that the heart need not collapse under the weight of trials because those trials are held within the stronger hands of divine providence. The Christian who understands this walks through life differently. He does not seek suffering, but he does not fear it. He does not interpret suffering as abandonment, but as a moment to cling more deeply to the promises of God.

And in this clinging, another truth emerges: suffering clarifies love. It removes the illusions we carry into the spiritual life. It reveals whether we love God for His gifts or for Himself. It teaches us to rely on Him not merely when His presence feels sweet, but also when His silence feels heavy. It draws out a fidelity that comfort can never foster. It forms a heart that knows how to say, with the psalmist, "Though my flesh and my heart fail, God is the strength of my heart and my portion forever."

This fidelity is the pearl modern culture does not understand. Because it avoids suffering, it cannot understand steadfastness. Because it worships comfort, it cannot understand sacrifice. Because it demands pleasure, it cannot understand joy. The world knows how to pursue gratification but not how to persevere. It knows how to chase experiences but not how to remain faithful. Suffering, paradoxically, becomes the teacher of the very virtues that make life meaningful. It trains the heart to love what is good, to endure what is hard, and to hope in what is unseen.

Suffering also reveals something about the nature of freedom that modern assumptions conceal. True freedom is not the ability to avoid all constraint. It is the capacity to choose the good even when the path is difficult. It is the inner strength that enables a person to remain faithful when his desires pull him elsewhere. Yet the avoidance of suffering weakens this interior strength. It trains the will to seek detours rather than endurance. A culture shaped by avoidance produces people who may feel free but are easily overcome by adversity. They possess choice without character, options without discernment, and desires without discipline.

Scripture, by contrast, shapes freedom through fidelity. Israel learns to trust God in the wilderness, not by escaping hardship but by walking through it. The prophets learn obedience through trials that purify their hearts. The apostles learn courage not by being spared suffering but by facing it with the grace given to them. This biblical pattern forms a different kind of human being—one who understands that freedom is not the absence of cost but the presence of love strong enough to endure it.

This truth becomes most evident when we look at the nature of the vocations God gives. Marriage, for example, requires the daily willingness to sacrifice for the good of the spouse. Parenting requires the surrender of one's own comfort for the sake of a child who depends on you completely. Priestly ministry demands a life poured out in service, often unseen and often misunderstood. None of these works of love are possible without suffering. To remove suffering from life is to remove the very structure of love itself.

Even ordinary relationships follow this same pattern. Friendships deepen not through convenience but through shared trials. Communities are strengthened not when everything runs smoothly but when they confront difficulties together. The human heart was made not for perpetual ease but for covenantal endurance. It longs for a love that does not fade, a truth that does not shift, a hope that does not collapse under pressure. Yet these are precisely the virtues that can only be forged through the willingness to face suffering with faith.

This is why the culture's attempt to eliminate suffering ultimately empties life of its deepest joys. When suffering is denied any meaning, courage becomes unnecessary. When suffering is avoided at any cost, compassion becomes optional. When suffering is seen as an intolerable burden rather than a crucible of love, the heart loses its capacity to grow. Relief becomes a substitute for redemption, and the soul becomes small in the very places it was meant to be enlarged.

But when suffering is approached through the biblical horizon, everything changes. It becomes a place where God's promises become tangible. It becomes a space where prayer gains urgency, where love gains depth, where hope gains substance. The believer begins to recognise that God is not absent in the trial. He is present in a way that comfort never reveals. The Lord meets His people not merely when they feel strong but especially when they feel weak. In this way, suffering becomes a doorway through which grace enters the heart more deeply than before.

This grace does not erase the pain, but it transforms the experience. It teaches the believer to see beyond the immediate, to perceive the hidden work of God beneath the surface of events. It unites the heart to the Cross—not as a symbol of defeat, but as the place where divine love is revealed most fully. The more a person learns to see suffering through the Cross, the more he realises that suffering is not the contradiction of God's love but the place where the mystery of that love shines with a clarity that comfort cannot produce.

For this reason, the Christian cannot allow the culture of pain-avoidance to shape his understanding of life. A worldview that denies the meaning of suffering ultimately denies the fullness of the Gospel itself. Christ did not redeem the world by avoiding suffering. He redeemed it by entering suffering, embracing it, and transforming it from within. His followers are called to walk in His footsteps, not because suffering is desirable in itself, but because love inevitably leads us to places where we must give more than we planned, endure more than we expected, and trust more than we thought possible.

This does not mean that the Christian must seek out suffering or deny the legitimate relief that medicine and compassion can provide. Scripture calls us to alleviate suffering when we can, to comfort the afflicted, to care for the vulnerable. But it also calls us to recognise that some suffering cannot be removed—and that in these moments, God does a work that no earthly remedy can accomplish. He deepens faith. He purifies love. He strengthens hope. He reveals the heart to itself and draws the soul into deeper communion with Him.

A mature Christian life is not built on the avoidance of suffering but on the willingness to live through it with faith. This willingness is not heroic self-reliance. It is humble dependence—the recognition that God is present, that His grace is sufficient, and that His promises do not fail. When the heart learns to rest in this truth, suffering loses its power to terrify. It no longer appears as an enemy but as a mystery held within the hands of a faithful God.

And this changes everything. The believer who understands suffering through the covenant is no longer swept away by fear. He becomes someone who can stand firm in the storm because his hope is not anchored in comfort but in Christ. He becomes someone who can carry others, who can love when love is costly, who can persevere when the path grows steep. His life becomes a witness to the truth that suffering does not have the final word—God does.

In the end, the culture of pain-avoidance collapses under its own promises. It offers a life without cost but delivers a life without depth. It promises comfort but produces fragility. It rejects suffering but cannot stop it. Only the biblical worldview can make sense of the reality every human being must face. Only the covenant can interpret the trials that shape the human heart. Only God can transform suffering into a place of grace.

The Christian who remembers this walks through life with a different posture. He does not deny suffering, but he does not fear it. He does not pretend to understand all its mysteries, but he trusts the One who does. And in that trust, suffering becomes not the end of meaning, but the beginning of wisdom. It becomes the place where the believer learns to say—quietly, steadily, truthfully—"The Lord is my shepherd; I shall not want," even when the valley is deep and the path is dark.

For it is precisely there, in the very places the world avoids, that

God reveals the strength of His love and teaches His children to walk by faith.

3

The Human Heart Under Trial

Suffering does something that few other experiences can accomplish: it brings the human heart face to face with itself. When pain arrives—whether in the form of loss, illness, disappointment, or fear—it has a way of stripping away the layers of distraction that normally shield us from the deeper questions of life. It presses upon the soul with an honesty that no comfort can imitate. It reveals what we trust, what we fear, what we desire, and what we avoid. In moments of ease, we assume we know our hearts; in moments of trial, the truth comes into focus with startling clarity.

Scripture understands this dynamic well. The stories of God's people are filled with moments in which suffering exposes the innermost movements of the soul. Abraham learns the depth of his faith not in the comforts of prosperity but on the mountain where he is asked to surrender the son of promise. Jacob discovers his true name not during years of cleverness but in a night of wrestling in which all his schemes are exhausted. David's heart is revealed not on the throne, but in the caves where he hides from Saul's fury. The prophets speak most truthfully not from moments of triumph, but from the crucible of injustice, exile, and rejection. Even the disciples learn who they truly are when the storm threatens their boat and fear rises faster than faith.

These stories are not preserved merely for historical interest. They show us something essential about the human condition: suffering tests the heart because suffering reveals the heart. It uncovers desires that ease allows to remain hidden. It exposes motives that comfort never challenges. It shakes loose attachments that we cling to without realising how deeply they compete with our trust in God. The heart under trial becomes the heart unveiled.

This unveiling is not pleasant, but it is necessary. The Scriptures speak of the heart as the centre of the person—the place where decisions are made, where desires are formed, where faith is either strengthened or resisted. "Guard your heart with all vigilance," Proverbs instructs, "for from it flow the springs of life." But how is the heart to be guarded if it never learns to recognise its own depths? How can desire be ordered toward God if the heart remains unaware of its own disorder? Suffering, in a mysterious but consistent way, becomes the moment in which the heart sees itself honestly.

This is one of the reasons Scripture warns against the illusion of self-sufficiency. When the heart imagines itself strong, independent, and secure, it loses the ability to perceive its need for God. It becomes inattentive to grace. It becomes complacent. But when suffering arrives, the façade of strength collapses, and the heart must confront what it has trusted all along. This confrontation can lead to despair—but it can also lead to conversion. It can reveal not only the poverty of the heart but the faithfulness of the God who calls the heart to Himself.

Suffering, then, is not merely an external challenge; it is an inward summons. It asks the soul: What do you truly desire? Comfort, or communion? Control, or covenant? Escape, or endurance? These questions cannot be answered theoretically. They are answered in the lived experience of trial. Israel learned this in the wilderness. When hunger and thirst pressed upon them, they discovered what their hearts longed for—sometimes faith, sometimes rebellion, but always truth. The wilderness did not create their desires; it revealed them.

That same dynamic continues in every human life. When suffering presses upon us, we discover desires we did not realise we carried. We learn whether our confidence in God is anchored in His promises or in the blessings He gives. We see whether our love is shaped by covenant or conditioned by convenience. We realise how easily our hearts drift toward self-reliance, how quickly they forget the fidelity of God, how subtly they cling to illusions of control. Suffering removes these illusions not to destroy the heart but to prepare it for grace.

And grace does its deepest work precisely when the heart recognises its need. This recognition is the beginning of humility—a virtue that suffering often teaches more effectively than any discipline or instruction. Humility is not self-deprecation; it is truth. It is the acknowledgement that we are creatures and not creators, dependent and not autonomous, sustained by God rather than sustained by ourselves. Suffering, when received with an open heart, leads to this truth. It brings the soul to a posture in which it can say with the psalmist, "Whom have I in heaven but You? And there is nothing upon earth that I desire besides You."

Yet the heart does not always reach this place easily. The moment of trial brings dangers as well as opportunities. When suffering presses upon us, the heart becomes vulnerable not only to grace but also to temptation. Bitterness, resentment, and self-pity rise quickly when pain unsettles the soul. These temptations are not accidental; they are distortions of the very truths suffering seeks to reveal. Instead of recognising our dependence on God, we can resent our weakness. Instead of turning toward God in trust, we can turn inward in self-accusation or outward in anger. Instead of allowing suffering to deepen our love, we can allow it to shrink our hearts.

This tension—between danger and opportunity—is the terrain on which the spiritual life unfolds. Suffering becomes the trial through which the heart must pass, and the way we respond determines whether the trial becomes a place of rebellion or a place of transformation. Scripture gives us examples of both outcomes because Scripture is honest about the human heart. It does not present suffering as automatically sanctifying. It presents suffering as the moment of choice—where the heart either turns toward God or withdraws from Him.

Suffering places the heart in a kind of sacred tension. It exposes the poverty we try to outrun and the desires we struggle to name. It brings us to the place where faith must become something more than words. The pressures that unsettle us also open the very spaces where grace can take root. When the heart is overwhelmed, it discovers that God has not abandoned it; He has drawn nearer. Suffering does not silence the covenant— it amplifies it. It teaches the soul to recognise the quiet fidelity of God in places where nothing else feels stable. The heart under trial is not abandoned to chaos. It is invited into a deeper encounter with the God who has carried His people through storms, deserts, exiles, and crosses. In that encounter, the heart begins to learn what it was made for.

The heart under trial does not enter a neutral landscape. It enters a battleground. Suffering uncovers the desires that anchor us to God, but it also exposes the impulses that draw us away from Him. When the foundations of life tremble, the heart instinctively searches for a place to stand, and the direction it turns reveals its deepest orientation. Some hearts turn toward faith. Others turn toward fear. Some turn toward trust. Others toward resentment. And still others collapse inward, unable to distinguish sorrow from despair. Scripture does not hide these reactions; it portrays them with the honesty of a Father who knows His children intimately.

One of the first movements of the heart under pressure is the tendency to retreat into bitterness. Bitterness is not simply anger; it is anger turned sour, anger allowed to ferment until it becomes a lens through which everything is interpreted. The bitter heart remembers its wounds more vividly than God's mercy. It rehearses grievances until they begin to define existence. Israel struggled with this repeatedly. When the water was bitter at Marah, when hunger gnawed in the desert, when Moses delayed on the mountain, the people allowed their frustration to harden into complaint. What began as discomfort became accusation—"Why did you bring us out here to die?" The bitterness did not reveal God's unfaithfulness; it revealed their forgetfulness.

Bitterness narrows the horizon until the heart can no longer see beyond the immediate pain. It is a contraction of the soul. It draws everything inward, suffocating gratitude and overshadowing memory. The bitter heart does not deny God outright; it simply ceases to expect anything from Him. It clings to its disappointment as if letting go would be a betrayal of experience. Yet bitterness is not truth. It is a distortion. It takes the real pain of suffering and attaches to it an interpretation that shrinks God down to the size of the heart's fear. When bitterness settles in, it becomes difficult to remember the moments in which God sustained, delivered, or forgave. The heart becomes trapped in a single chapter of its own story, unable to see that the Author has not stopped writing.

Closely related to bitterness is resentment, a more relational wound. Resentment does not simply lament suffering; it assigns blame for it. It looks outward and inward simultaneously, searching for someone to hold accountable—an enemy, a friend, a circumstance, even God Himself. The heart under resentment clings to comparison. It notices the blessings others enjoy and the burdens they escape, and it quietly asks, "Why not me? Why them?" The parable of the vineyard workers illustrates this tendency vividly. The workers who arrived early received exactly what they had been promised, yet their hearts soured when others received the same wage. The issue was not injustice. It was envy disguised as fairness, resentment dressed in the language of principle.

Resentment thrives when the heart forgets the generosity of God. Instead of seeing blessings as gifts, it sees them as entitlements. Instead of receiving graces with gratitude, it measures them against the fortunes of others. The resentful heart becomes preoccupied with the distribution of suffering rather than its meaning. It demands symmetry from a God who deals not in strict equivalence but in covenantal love. Resentment blinds the soul to the truth that God's dealings with each person are shaped with infinite wisdom, tailored to the particular story He is writing in each life. The heart that allows resentment to take root cannot perceive the personal love hidden within its own trials.

Then there is self-pity, a temptation that masquerades as honesty but leads the soul into a cul-de-sac. Self-pity is sorrow curved inward, sorrow without hope, sorrow that has forgotten prayer. It becomes a conversation with the self rather than a cry to God. Elijah's moment under the broom tree captures this with striking clarity. Exhausted, pursued, discouraged, he collapses and says, "It is enough; take my life." His anguish is real, but his vision has narrowed so completely that he can no longer see the remnant God has preserved or the mission still entrusted to him. When the angel touches him, it is not to scold but to awaken. Self-pity had closed Elijah into a small world; God breaks it open again.

Self-pity is dangerous because it feels truthful. It acknowledges pain honestly, but it stops before prayer. It recognises suffering, but it refuses surrender. It sees the wound, but it does not look for the Healer. The psalms teach a different posture—lament that opens into trust, sorrow that stretches toward God's faithfulness. "How long, O Lord?" is the honest cry of a soul in anguish, but it is also the cry of a soul that still expects an answer. Self-pity does not expect anything. It resigns itself to isolation. It allows suffering to become the final word rather than the circumstance through which God speaks.

These temptations—bitterness, resentment, self-pity—are not failures unique to the weak. They are the ordinary spiritual hazards of every soul under pressure. Scripture reveals them because Scripture understands the heart. Yet Scripture also reveals something else: suffering exposes these temptations not to condemn the heart, but to purify it. The trial that reveals our frailty also reveals God's desire to meet us precisely there. The same wilderness that uncovers Israel's distrust becomes the place where God feeds, guides, and sanctifies His people. The same storm that terrifies the disciples becomes the moment in which they learn the authority of Christ. The same cross that reveals human sin becomes the place where divine love is revealed without measure.

In this way, suffering becomes a turning point. It is the crossroads at which the heart must decide whether to fold inward or stretch outward, whether to retreat into fear or surrender to grace. The temptations that arise in suffering are not signs that faith has failed; they are invitations to a deeper faith than comfort ever requires. When the heart recognises its own reactions—not with shame, but with honesty—it begins to understand the depth of its need for God. And this recognition becomes the soil in which humility can take root.

Humility, when it emerges through suffering, is not a resignation to fate but a return to reality. It clears the fog of pride and reveals the simple truth that we are not self-made. We did not summon ourselves into existence, we do not sustain our own breath, and we do not command the course of our days. Suffering reminds us of what comfort allows us to forget—that our lives unfold within the providence of a God who knows us better than we know ourselves. When the heart bows before this truth, it is not diminished; it is liberated. The proud heart must maintain an illusion. The humble heart rests in the truth that God is God and we are His.

This humility gives rise to a second grace: dependence. Dependence is not weakness. It is the recognition that we were created to receive before we give, to trust before we act, to lean upon God before we try to stand on our own. Israel learned dependence in the wilderness, not through abundance but through hunger. The manna arrived one day at a time, never two days at once. The provision was deliberate. God was teaching His people that their survival did not come from their strategies, their skills, or their strength. It came from His word and His faithfulness. Every morning they awoke to discover that God had not forgotten them. Every evening they slept knowing they could not control tomorrow. This rhythm formed their hearts far more deeply than comfort ever could.

Dependence, then, is a grace that suffering brings to the surface. When the usual securities fall away—health, success, stability, the approval of others—the soul finds itself standing on ground it cannot command. In that vulnerability, God speaks with a clarity we often miss in easier times. The heart discovers that the promises of Scripture are not poetic embellishments; they are a lifeline. "My grace is sufficient for you." "I will never leave you nor forsake you." "The Lord is near to the broken hearted." These words take on weight precisely when the heart must lean upon them. Suffering becomes the moment in which the believer learns that dependence on God is not the last resort; it is the foundation of life.

But dependence does more than sustain. It enlarges the heart, preparing it for compassion. Compassion is not sentiment; it is the capacity to suffer with another. It is born when the heart's own wounds become places where it can recognise the needs of others. Those who have walked through affliction understand something that cannot be learned from a distance. They know how fragile strength can be, how lonely pain feels, how desperately the soul longs for even a small gesture of presence. Their own suffering becomes the vocabulary through which they learn to love more deeply.

Scripture gives us a luminous image of this in the life of Christ. He is not a distant redeemer who merely observes human suffering; He enters it. He knows hunger, betrayal, misunderstanding, exhaustion, and sorrow. The Letter to the Hebrews tells us that our High Priest is able to sympathise with our weaknesses because He has known them from within. His compassion is not abstract. It is personal, lived, embodied. And it is precisely His suffering that shapes His mercy. He does not pity from afar; He accompanies from within. When we suffer, we do not find a God who stands above our pain; we find a God who has descended into it.

The believer, conformed to Christ, learns compassion in the same way. Suffering strips away indifference. It teaches the heart to look upon others not as problems to solve but as persons to love. It trains the soul to recognise the silent burdens others carry. It allows the believer to speak words that are not merely correct but consoling, not merely true but tender. Compassion drawn from suffering becomes a kind of priesthood of everyday life—joining one's own wounds to the wounds of others, and in doing so, revealing something of Christ's heart.

This transformation does not happen automatically. Suffering offers these graces, but the heart must be willing to receive them. Humility arises when the soul stops resisting the truth of its own limits. Dependence grows when the soul turns toward God rather than away from Him. Compassion blooms when the soul allows its wounds to soften its gaze rather than harden it. These movements require openness. They require a willingness to let suffering become not a barrier to God but a doorway to His presence.

The heart that learns these lessons discovers something remarkable: suffering, though painful, becomes strangely fruitful. It becomes the place where the superficial layers of life fall away, where the soul becomes capable of love that is deeper, steadier, and more enduring. The virtues formed through suffering are the virtues that sustain faith when comfort evaporates, that uphold families when trials arise, that guide vocations when the path grows dim. A heart that has walked through trial with God becomes a heart that can carry others, because it has been carried itself.

This is why Scripture does not speak of suffering with fear, but with sobriety and hope. It knows suffering is real. It knows the pain is sharp. But it also knows that God does not waste the trials of His people. He shapes them through these trials, forming in them a strength they do not see and a depth they do not expect. When the heart yields to His work, suffering becomes not the end of faith but its refinement. It becomes the place where God reveals that His grace is not merely sufficient; it is transformative.

When suffering begins to form the soul in this way, a quiet shift takes place within the heart. What once felt like the collapse of life begins to reveal itself as the deepening of life. The believer starts to recognise that God does not work only through consolation; He also works through deprivation. There are graces that come through abundance, but there are others that can only be received when abundance fades. When the props on which we lean are removed, the heart discovers that God has been the firm ground beneath all along. This discovery rarely comes with emotional comfort. It comes with the steady realisation that God's faithfulness is not measured by our feelings but by His covenant.

This realisation awakens a kind of interior steadiness that is rare in a culture devoted to comfort. The heart that has passed through trial with God learns to trust Him not only when the path is bright but when the horizon is clouded. It learns to pray not because prayer removes the burden, but because prayer anchors the soul to the One who carries it. It learns to judge circumstances not by their immediate appearance but by the promises of God that sustain them. This steadiness is not born of naivety; it is born of encounter. It is the fruit of discovering that God remains present when everything else seems to fall away.

Such steadiness gives rise to a deeper form of courage. Courage is not the absence of fear; it is the presence of fidelity. It is the decision to remain in God's hands even when the outcome is unknown. Suffering teaches this courage because it confronts the heart with its limitations. The person who has faced his weakness with God becomes less afraid of weakness itself. He becomes more willing to act with faith, more willing to love with sacrifice, more willing to remain steadfast even when the cost is high. His courage is not bravado. It is the quiet confidence that the God who has carried him once will carry him again.

This courage, in turn, forms the foundation for hope. Hope is not optimism. It is not the expectation that circumstances will improve simply because time passes. Hope is the virtue that anchors the soul to God's future, even when the present feels unbearable. Suffering becomes the crucible in which hope is refined, because suffering forces the heart to look beyond what it can control. It stretches the soul toward a horizon that cannot be seen with earthly eyes. Hope is the fruit of trusting that God's promises do not fade in darkness. It is the assurance that He is at work even when the work is hidden. The psalmist expresses this with remarkable simplicity: "I would have despaired unless I had believed that I would see the goodness of the Lord in the land of the living." That belief does not arise in ease. It arises in trial.

The heart shaped by humility, dependence, compassion, steadiness, courage, and hope becomes capable of a depth of love that is impossible in shallow soil. Suffering, when united to grace, enlarges the capacity of the heart to love with the patience, tenderness, and endurance that mark the life of Christ. It cleanses love of possessiveness. It purifies love of pride. It strengthens love against fear. The believer discovers that love sustained through suffering becomes a testimony more powerful than words. It reveals the presence of God in a way that argument cannot. It becomes a living witness to the truth that God has entered human frailty in order to redeem it from within.

Such love is not abstract. It becomes concrete in the decisions a person makes every day: the decision to forgive when resentment whispers its logic; the decision to remain faithful when ease would be simpler; the decision to pray even when prayer feels dry; the decision to serve others even when one's own heart is wounded. These decisions are not heroic in the worldly sense. They are the ordinary acts of fidelity through which God sanctifies His people. Each small surrender becomes a thread in the larger tapestry of grace. Suffering teaches the heart to recognise these moments not as burdens but as invitations to share in the life of Christ.

This sharing is at the centre of the Christian mystery. The believer does not face suffering alone. He faces it with Christ, in Christ, and through Christ. The heart under trial discovers this not through doctrine alone but through experience. When the soul cries out in weakness, it finds a God who has borne weakness Himself. When the soul trembles in fear, it finds a God who has prayed in the garden. When the soul feels abandoned, it finds a God who has cried from the cross. This is not mere sympathy. It is union. Christ does not simply understand human suffering; He has carried it into the heart of God. And because He has entered our suffering, we can enter His strength.

In this union, the heart begins to perceive something that cannot be understood in comfort: suffering does not separate the believer from God; it deepens the communion. When the heart is stripped of illusions, it becomes capable of receiving God without distraction. When the heart is pressed, it becomes capable of loving God without condition. When the heart is wounded, it becomes capable of recognising God's tenderness with new clarity. The saints speak of this not because they enjoyed suffering, but because they discovered God within it.

This discovery does not remove the pain. It transforms the meaning. The heart under trial becomes the heart that learns—slowly, painfully, faithfully—that God does not abandon His children. He walks with them, speaks to them, strengthens them, and shapes them. Suffering becomes the place where the believer is conformed to Christ not in theory but in truth. It becomes the place where love is purified, faith is anchored, and hope becomes unshakable.

The more the heart discovers this truth, the more suffering loses its power to define the believer. It does not cease to wound, but it no longer becomes the measure of reality. God becomes the measure. His fidelity becomes the reference point. His presence becomes the anchor. When this happens, suffering takes its rightful place—not as the centre of the story, but as the circumstance in which the true centre is revealed. The believer learns to see life not through the lens of pain, but through the lens of the God who remains present within it. This shift does not deny the reality of suffering; it situates suffering within a larger truth.

This is why the heart under trial can become a place of profound clarity. The noise of life tends to scatter our attention, dividing our desires and clouding our perception. But suffering gathers the heart. It concentrates attention on what matters. It awakens questions that comfort postpones. It exposes illusions that prosperity sustains. In this sense, suffering becomes not merely a disruption but an unveiling. It shows the soul where its treasure lies. It reveals the affections that need to be surrendered and the loves that need to be strengthened. Trials become teachers—not of despair, but of authenticity.

As the heart matures through this process, it begins to recognise that the deepest work of God often occurs beneath the surface. Not in the sudden removal of difficulty, but in the slow transformation of the soul. Not in the dramatic rescue, but in the quiet fidelity that sustains a person day by day. God's grace is not always experienced as a flood. More often, it is received as a steady stream, nourishing the roots even when the branches tremble. The believer who has walked through suffering with God learns to trust this subtlety. He sees that God's work is no less real for being hidden, no less powerful for being quiet.

And something remarkable follows from this recognition: gratitude. Not a gratitude for suffering itself, but a gratitude for the God who remains present within it. Gratitude that the trial has not consumed the heart but refined it. Gratitude that suffering has not isolated the soul but drawn it deeper into communion. Gratitude that the very places of weakness have become the places where God's strength has been revealed. This gratitude does not arise at the beginning of suffering; it arises through it. It is the fruit of hindsight, the testimony of a heart that has seen God's faithfulness in the valley and now knows it in a way that ease could never have taught.

A heart formed in this way does not emerge unchanged. It becomes capable of a steadier love, a deeper trust, and a more generous compassion. It learns to bear the burdens of others with patience because it has learned how God bears its own. It learns to see past the surface of another's life and recognise the unseen struggles beneath. It becomes less quick to judge, more ready to forgive, more willing to stand beside those who suffer with the quiet conviction that God is present even when His presence is not felt. The heart shaped by suffering becomes a vessel through which God's mercy flows.

This is one of suffering's hidden gifts. When the heart opens itself to God in trial, it is not only strengthened for its own sake; it becomes a source of strength for others. Its wounds do not remain raw; they become places where grace can pass through. Its trials do not remain isolated events; they become experiences through which the believer can speak words of hope with credibility. The heart under trial becomes, in time, a heart capable of consoling, because it has been consoled. And in this, the believer participates in the mystery of Christ himself—the One whose wounds are not erased in glory but remain as signs of a love that has triumphed.

In this way, the human heart becomes the place where the mystery of suffering and the mystery of grace meet. The trial does not cease to be painful, but it ceases to be purposeless. The wounds do not cease to ache, but they cease to define. God takes what threatens to diminish the soul and uses it to enlarge the soul. He takes what seems to weaken the believer and uses it to deepen faith. He takes what seems to scatter desire and uses it to clarify desire. The heart that passes through trial with God discovers that suffering does not have authority over its destiny. God does.

And when that truth settles deeply within the soul, suffering is no longer the shadow that darkens life. It becomes the place where light enters through cracks that pride once sealed. It becomes the place where the believer learns that God is not simply present in moments of triumph but intimately present in moments of trial. It becomes the place where the heart realises that its deepest identity is not forged by pain but forged by the God who guides it through pain. The trial becomes, in time, a testimony: the heart has been pressed, but not crushed; wounded, but not abandoned; shaken, but not severed from the God who holds it.

The human heart under trial is not left to endure alone. It is met by the God who knows what it is to suffer, who knows what it is to weep, who knows what it is to entrust Himself to the Father in the darkness. In that encounter, the heart learns what it was made for: a love stronger than fear, a faith steadier than circumstance, and a hope that no suffering can extinguish. Suffering, in the hands of God, becomes the place where this truth is etched not only into belief but into being. And when the heart recognises this, it discovers that even in the trial, it is being prepared for glory.

4

At the Threshold of Mystery

Suffering has carried us to the threshold of a deeper question. We have looked closely at the human heart—its fears, its longings, its temptations, its surprising capacities for grace—and the picture that emerges is unmistakable. The human person cannot explain himself. Our wounds reveal our need, but they do not reveal the meaning. Our trials expose our poverty, but they do not unveil their purpose. The heart cries out not simply for relief but for understanding—an understanding that does not arise from the heart itself. If suffering uncovers our hunger for God, then only God can satisfy the hunger it exposes.

This is where the journey bends inward toward the mystery from which all things come. The human experience of suffering, as honest and unfiltered as it is, remains incomplete until it is gathered into the story God has spoken from the beginning. The heart seeks an answer larger than psychology, deeper than culture, older than the world itself. It seeks a word that does not originate in human longing but in divine love. Every lament, every plea, every trembling act of trust stretches toward a truth that precedes us—toward the God who has revealed Himself not in abstractions, but in history, covenant, flesh, and blood.

The more we listen to the ache within us, the more we recognise that suffering cannot be understood from the inside out. It must be understood from the outside in—from the God who has chosen to enter the very wounds that confuse us. If the heart is the place where suffering is felt, Scripture is the place where suffering is interpreted. The story of God is not a detour from the human story. It is the only horizon wide enough to hold it. The only light strong enough to illumine it. The only truth deep enough to redeem it.

The questions that rise in suffering—Where is God? Why is this happening? What does this mean? —do not remain unanswered. They echo across a landscape shaped by creation, covenant, exile, promise, incarnation, cross, and resurrection. The heart that has been stripped bare by trial does not stand before God in theory. It stands before the One whose voice spoke the world into being, whose mercy shaped a people, whose Son entered history with wounded hands and a human soul capable of sorrow.

If suffering teaches us anything, it is that the human heart was made for a story greater than itself. And it is only by entering that story—God's story—that the heart begins to recognise the meaning of its own.

II

The Story God Tells

5

Genesis And The Wound Of The World

Creation is the first gospel. Before Scripture speaks of sacrifice or covenant, before it recounts the trials of Israel or the sorrows of Christ, it opens with a world that is whole. The Bible begins not with chaos but with order, not with conflict but with communion. This is not accidental. Revelation begins by revealing the world as God meant it to be, because without that vision the meaning of suffering can never be understood. Suffering is a wound, but a wound presupposes health. Pain signals rupture, but rupture presupposes harmony. The story of suffering, if it is to be understood, must begin not in Genesis chapter three, where the wound is inflicted, but in Genesis chapter one, where the world is spoken into being with a rhythm of goodness that moves like a litany across the first days of creation.

"In the beginning, God created the heavens and the earth." These words are not simply an introduction to the narrative; they are the key to everything that follows. They anchor the reader in the truth that the world is not a cosmic accident, nor a random convergence of forces, nor an indifferent arena where life blindly struggles to survive. The world is willed. It is chosen. It is spoken into existence by a God whose word does not merely command but gives life. Creation is the outward expression of divine generosity—a generosity that delights in giving being to what is not God, and in drawing that creation into relationship with Himself.

The order of creation reflects this generosity with clarity and precision. Light is called forth before the luminaries that will later govern it. Waters are separated to create space for life to flourish. Land emerges, plants sprout, stars take their places, creatures fill sky and sea, and the earth begins to hum with vitality. But the pinnacle of this order arrives when God forms humanity. "Let us make man in our image, after our likeness." These words reveal the deepest truth about the human person. We are not merely part of creation; we are the creatures through whom creation speaks. We are not merely alive; we are called to communion. The image of God is not a decorative feature. It is a vocation. It is the invitation to know God, to love God, and to reflect His life within the world.

This original state—this harmony of creation, humanity, and divine presence—is essential for understanding suffering. For in this beginning, suffering is absent not because humanity possesses power, but because humanity is ordered. The relationship between God and the human person is rightly aligned. The relationship between man and woman is marked by unity rather than rivalry. The relationship between humanity and creation is marked by stewardship rather than struggle. This is what the Fathers of the Church would later call "original justice," the integrity of a world that knows its Creator and rests in His love.

It is crucial to grasp this because suffering, in all its forms, is a disruption of this integrity. Physical pain, emotional grief, moral confusion, and even death itself are not part of the world as God made it. They are intrusions—foreign elements that do not belong to creation's original design. This means that suffering is not a divine invention. God does not craft suffering as a tool or mechanism for the human story. Suffering enters only when something fractures, when something in the created order turns away from the God who sustains it.

That fracture is recorded with stark simplicity in Genesis 3. The serpent's subtlety, the woman's hesitation, the man's silence—these elements introduce a drama that will echo through every generation. Humanity is tempted to see God not as Father but as rival. The divine command, given to preserve freedom, is reinterpreted as a boundary that restricts it. The promise of likeness is grasped prematurely, as though it could be seized apart from communion. In this act, the harmony of creation collapses. The rupture is not merely moral; it is ontological. It tears at the fabric of the human person, the unity of the human family, and the relationship between humanity and creation itself.

The immediate consequences reveal the depth of this rupture. The serpent's triumph is short-lived; his apparent victory becomes the occasion for divine judgment. But before judgment is spoken, something else emerges: fear. "I heard the sound of You in the garden, and I was afraid." Humanity's first response to sin is not rebellion but terror. The experience of God's presence, which once brought delight, now brings dread. The rupture inside the human heart distorts its vision of God. Love gives way to suspicion. Communion gives way to hiding. The human person, made for relationship, now flees from the One who formed him.

This interior rupture spreads outward. The relationship between man and woman is strained by blame. The relationship between humanity and creation is marked by toil. The relationship between life and death is altered by mortality. Every form of human suffering—spiritual, emotional, relational, physical—can be traced to this moment. The Fathers called it the "wound of nature," and it affects everything we experience. Suffering is not the random unfolding of natural forces. It is the echo of a world that has drifted from its Creator.

Yet it is here, in the very moment of humanity's fall, that the depth of God's mercy is unveiled. The judgments spoken in Genesis 3 are not condemnations of cruelty; they are the necessary descriptions of a world now misaligned. But within these judgments, something astonishing is spoken: a promise. "I will put enmity between you and the woman, and between your seed and her seed; he shall bruise your head, and you shall bruise his heel." This line, known as the *Protoevangelium*, is not merely a prediction. It is the first announcement of redemption. Before humanity is sent out of the garden, God declares that the wound will not have the final word. The fracture opened by sin will be healed by grace. The suffering introduced by disobedience will be transformed through the obedience of Another.

This is the hinge upon which the entire story of suffering turns. We did not invent suffering, nor did God. Suffering is the shadow that follows sin. But God, in His mercy, chooses to enter the shadow. He does not remove the wound immediately, for redemption is not a reversal but a restoration. He promises a Redeemer—not a distant remedy, but a person, a Son, born of a woman, who will take the wound into Himself and heal it from the inside. The promise is whispered in Genesis, but it reverberates across every page of Scripture.

The world we inhabit is shaped by this wound. Every grief we encounter, every hardship we endure, every sorrow we witness is a reminder that creation is no longer as it was. But every longing for healing, every act of faith, every hope that refuses to die is a reminder that the promise spoken in the garden still stands. The wound is real, but so is the promise. And the promise is older than the wound.

The promise spoken in the garden is not merely a faint thread running through the fabric of Scripture; it is the warp upon which every thread is woven. From the moment humanity steps outside Eden, the world becomes a place marked by contradiction—a place where beauty and brokenness coexist, where longing and loss live side by side. The wound of the world is not abstract. It touches soil and soul, families and nations, bodies and hearts. The rupture is cosmic in scale, yet painfully intimate. It reveals itself in the toil of labour, the strain of relationships, the ache of grief, and the fear of death. But Scripture does not present this wound as chaos without meaning. It presents it as the arena in which God's mercy begins its work.

Genesis shows us that suffering is not the arbitrary punishment of an offended deity. It is the lived experience of a creation now misaligned from its Source. The harmony between God and humanity is disrupted, and that disruption reverberates outward. The ground that once yielded its fruit with ease now resists. The communion that once united Adam and Eve now faces tension and mutual incomprehension. Even the natural world reflects the fracture; the dust from which humanity was formed becomes the dust to which humanity must return. Sin reaches into the very matter of creation, introducing a disorder that only grace can heal.

Yet even as suffering enters, God refuses to abandon His creation to its wound. The God of Genesis does not retreat into distant transcendence. He approaches humanity with questions—not to gather information, but to draw His children out of hiding. "Where are you?" is not the inquiry of a confused God; it is the lament of a Father who refuses to let shame have the final word. God does not allow sin to silence relationship. His questions become invitations—calls to honesty, vulnerability, and ultimately to repentance.

This movement of God toward His wounded children becomes the pattern repeated throughout salvation history. The world is fractured, yet God's presence presses into the fracture. The wound is deep, yet God chooses to dwell within the world rather than above it. Even the act of clothing Adam and Eve is a gesture of tenderness. They attempt to cover their shame with fig leaves; God covers them with garments that speak of care, dignity, and protection. Judgment is spoken, but mercy enfolds it. The exile from Eden is real, but the exile is not abandonment. It is the beginning of a journey that will lead, in time, to a new creation.

The suffering that flows from the Fall is therefore neither meaningless nor final. It is the condition of a world in process—a world waiting for the promise that was spoken in Eden to be fulfilled. The enmity between the serpent and the woman is not merely a curse; it is a declaration of war in which God Himself takes the side of His children. The promise of "her seed" reveals that redemption will be personal, familial, embodied. The wound came through disobedience; the healing will come through obedience. The rupture came through grasping; the restoration will come through self-giving love.

Seen in this light, suffering becomes something more than the evidence of humanity's fall. It becomes the stage upon which God will reveal the depth of His love. For if sin introduced disorder into the world, it is God's own presence within the world that will restore it. The story that begins in Genesis 3 is not a story of despair. It is the story of a God who refuses to leave His creation in its brokenness. The curse contains a promise, and the promise contains the shape of salvation.

To understand the weight of this promise, we must see how the wounded world shapes every human experience. The griefs we carry, the fears that unsettle us, the injustices that provoke us, the tears that fall in silence—all of these are echoes of the loss of Eden. They are reminders that the world is not as it should be, and that our hearts are not as they were created to be. Yet, at the same time, our yearning for healing, our hunger for justice, our longing for wholeness, and our hope for redemption are echoes of the promise spoken in the same moment that suffering began. The wound and the promise live side by side, and the human heart feels both with equal intensity.

The narrative of Genesis teaches us to see suffering through this double lens. We are not meant to deny the wound or to pretend the rupture is insignificant. Scripture does not shy away from the gravity of sin or the consequences that flow from it. But neither are we meant to interpret suffering as proof that God has stepped away from His creation. The very first pages of the Bible insist that suffering must be understood within a relationship—a relationship that God refuses to sever, even when humanity attempts to hide from Him. The wound is real, but it is held within the embrace of a God who has already begun to heal it.

This means that the story of suffering is inseparable from the story of love. The wound of the world exposes our need for God, but the promise reveals God's desire for us. The rupture shows the consequences of turning away, but the mercy shows the heart of the One who calls us back. Suffering is not God's design, but it becomes the place where God's design for redemption is unveiled. The drama of salvation begins not after the Fall, but within it. The darkness of Genesis is the canvas upon which the first strokes of divine light appear.

When we return to the beginning of Scripture, we discover that suffering does not raise the question, "Where is God?" so much as it reveals the deeper truth, "God is coming." The Creator who walked with Adam in the cool of the garden will one day walk again among His people, not only in the shade of trees but beneath the weight of a cross. The promise whispered in Eden is the seed of the story that will unfold across generations. And the wound that began there will one day be healed by the One who bears our sorrows and carries our griefs.

The world outside Eden reveals the truth Genesis has already taught us: suffering is not an illusion, nor is it a divine invention. It is the lived experience of a creation that remembers what it was made for and yet feels, in every fibre of its existence, the distance from its original harmony. The groaning of creation that St. Paul describes is already present in Genesis. Thorns and thistles grow from soil that once yielded fruit without resistance. Labor becomes toil. Childbearing, meant to be the joyful flowering of life, is overshadowed by pain. Death, which is the greatest contradiction of the Creator's intention, enters as an intruder. The human story is marked by a tension that neither resignation nor rebellion can resolve.

But Genesis never allows us to interpret this tension apart from God's presence. The world may be wounded, but it is not abandoned. The Creator who shaped humanity from the dust does not relinquish His claim over the world or over His children. Even Cain—whose hands are stained with his brother's blood—does not escape God's pursuit. The ground cries out with a voice Abel can no longer use, and God hears it. He confronts Cain not with indifference but with questions meant to awaken a conscience that has fallen silent. The mark placed upon Cain is not a symbol of rejection but of protection; even in judgment, God shields the sinner from the violence of a world now spiralling into disorder.

This divine persistence continues as the chapters unfold. Humanity multiplies, but so does wickedness. Violence spreads, corruption deepens, and the very fabric of society becomes a reflection of the fracture introduced in Eden. Yet God's response is never the cold wrath of a distant ruler. His grief over the world's condition is described in words that reveal a Father's heart—"the Lord was grieved… and His heart was filled with pain." The flood, though severe, is not a gesture of contempt; it is a cleansing. It is the divine refusal to allow evil to become the dominant logic of creation. And when the waters recede, God begins again with a covenant, binding

Himself to humanity with promises of fidelity even though the wound of sin remains.

This covenantal approach is the thread that keeps Genesis from becoming a tragedy. The world is wounded, but the wound is held inside a relationship. God repeatedly enters the story, not as a spectator but as a participant—calling, questioning, blessing, promising. He does not undo the Fall by erasing freedom. Instead, He begins to heal the world through a series of covenants that anticipate a redemption deeper than the wound itself. Each covenant—Noah, Abraham, Isaac, Jacob—becomes a reminder that God's answer to the wound of the world is not abandonment but intervention.

Suffering, seen through this divine persistence, becomes something more than the raw fact of a broken world. It becomes a reminder that God's love is older than our wounds. The world bears the marks of sin, but it also bears the marks of God's mercy. Every covenant tells us that suffering will not have the final word, because the God who speaks creation into being continues to speak His promises into the very places where creation has been marred. The God who formed the world does not relinquish it to darkness. He calls it back to Himself, piece by piece, heart by heart, generation by generation.

When we read Genesis with this lens, suffering begins to take on a different light. It is not simply the evidence of disobedience; it is the place where the longing for restoration becomes unmistakable. The ache for Eden lingers in every human heart. We may not articulate it, but we feel it—in our desire for justice, in our grief over loss, in our yearning for peace, in our hope for redemption. These desires are not illusions. They are echoes. They are the resonance of the original harmony, the memory of what we were made for and the longing for what God has promised to restore.

This longing is what keeps suffering from collapsing into despair. It is the evidence that the human heart was not created for a world in which pain is the final word. Even in sorrow, the heart remembers joy. Even in grief, the heart remembers love. Even in death, the heart remembers life. These memories, woven into our very being, are signs of the divine image—signs that the wound is not the whole story. The wound is real, but it is not the end.

Genesis allows us to see suffering not as the contradiction of God's goodness, but as the condition into which God has chosen to reveal His goodness more deeply. The world is not healed yet, but the healing has begun. The promise spoken in Eden has already set the story in motion. And every moment of suffering becomes, in some way, an invitation to remember that promise. The rupture that introduced suffering into the world also introduced the hope that God Himself would one day enter the rupture and restore what sin has broken.

This is why the early chapters of Genesis, though marked by sorrow, are never without light. From the garden to the flood, from Babel to the call of Abraham, God's presence is constant. His voice interrupts silence. His mercy interrupts judgment. His promise interrupts despair. The wound of the world becomes the context in which God reveals the endurance of His love. And it is within this wounded world that the story of redemption begins to unfold—a story shaped not by human strength but by divine fidelity.

The more we sit with Genesis, the more we realise that suffering forces us to return to the beginning not to find an explanation that satisfies curiosity, but to rediscover the God who speaks order into chaos and promise into fear. The world is wounded, but the wound is not beyond the reach of the One who formed it. Every ache of the human heart is an echo of Eden, and every hope is a whisper of the promise that the God who began the story will also bring it to its fulfillment.

The wound of the world does not remain confined to the first chapters of Genesis. It stretches across the entire landscape of human history, shaping the stories of nations and the destinies of families. Yet the remarkable truth revealed in Scripture is that God chooses to enter this wounded world not with distant pronouncements, but with personal promises. The drama of salvation unfolds not in abstraction, but in the particular lives of men and women who encounter God in the midst of their own struggles. This is why the narrative turns from the universal tragedy of Eden to the particular story of a wandering man named Abram. The shift is deliberate: the healing of the world begins with a conversation, a call, a covenant.

When God speaks to Abram, the wound of the world is already deep. Humanity has scattered across the earth. Violence has multiplied. The pride of Babel has revealed the human desire to grasp greatness without receiving it from God. Yet into this confusion, God speaks a word of blessing: "Go… and I will bless you." The promise given to Abram is nothing less than God's answer to the wound introduced in Eden. If the Fall fractured creation through disobedience, God will begin to restore creation through a man who trusts Him enough to obey. The blessing is not limited to Abram; it is destined for "all the families of the earth." The wound is universal, and the remedy will be universal—but it begins in the heart of one man learning to walk by faith.

This covenantal pattern reveals something essential about the nature of suffering. The world does not return to harmony by human ingenuity or moral effort. It returns through relationship—through God binding Himself to His people, and His people responding with trust. Suffering entered when humanity grasped at autonomy; healing begins when humanity returns to dependence. Abram does not heal the wound, but his faith becomes the channel through which God's promise moves forward. The story of suffering is inseparable from the story of covenant because suffering reveals the human need for God, and covenant reveals God's desire to draw near to humanity even in its wounded state.

As the covenant unfolds through Abraham, Isaac, and Jacob, we see the wound of the world mirrored in their lives. Abraham endures the sorrow of barrenness, the anguish of uncertainty, the test of offering Isaac. Isaac experiences famine, conflict, and the ache of family division. Jacob wrestles with fear, exile, and the consequences of his own deceit. But in each life, suffering becomes a place of revelation. God is not distant from their trials. He speaks in them. He guides through them. He transforms them. The wound does not disappear, but grace begins to move through it in ways that prepare the world for a greater healing yet to come.

The story of Joseph brings this truth into even sharper focus. Betrayed by his brothers, sold into slavery, falsely accused, and forgotten in prison, Joseph embodies the depth of the world's brokenness. Yet he also reveals the mysterious logic of God's providence—how God can work through suffering without causing it, how God can redeem evil without endorsing it. Joseph's words to his brothers capture the heart of the entire biblical worldview: "You meant evil against me, but God meant it for good." This is not a denial of the wound. It is the revelation that the wound is not sovereign. God remains Lord even in the places where human sin seems to dominate. Suffering becomes the stage upon which God's fidelity is displayed with unmistakable clarity.

What we learn from these patriarchs is that suffering is not merely an explanation of the past; it becomes a preparation for the future. The trials they endure shape the identity of a people who will one day be called to trust God through even greater afflictions. The famine that drives Jacob's family to Egypt is not an accident. It is part of a story in which God's presence remains constant even when His people cannot perceive it. The exile into Egypt foreshadows an exodus; the darkness anticipates dawn. The wound of the world remains, but the promise continues to advance.

Through these narratives, Genesis teaches us how to read the world as believers. Not with naïve optimism, pretending the wound is small, and not with despair, believing the wound is final, but with covenantal vision—a vision that sees both the fracture and the faithfulness. The pain is real. The disorder is real. But the promise is louder than both. The God who spoke the world into being continues to speak within its brokenness, shaping a people through whom He will reveal the fullness of His mercy.

This means that every human experience of suffering carries within it a hidden thread that reaches back to the garden and stretches forward toward redemption. The world is not as it was created to be, yet God has refused to leave it in its wounded state. From Adam to Noah, from Noah to Abraham, from Abraham to Joseph, the story unfolds with increasing clarity: suffering is the condition of a world awaiting deliverance, but God is already at work within it. He is not waiting for the wound to heal before He draws near. He draws near in order to heal the wound from the inside.

This is why the early pages of Scripture are indispensable for understanding suffering. They reveal the origin of the wound, the depth of its consequences, and the determination of God to bind Himself to a world that has turned away from Him. The wound is ancient, but so is the love that heals it. The fallenness of creation is real, but it is not the foundational truth. The foundational truth is the goodness of the God who made the world, who sustains it, and who refuses to abandon it to the consequences of sin.

Genesis does not explain suffering by reducing it to a concept. It situates suffering within a relationship—a relationship that precedes the wound and will outlast it. And the more deeply we understand this relationship, the more clearly we see that suffering is not the end of the story. It is the place where the story of redemption begins to shine.

6

Israel And The School Of Affliction

If Genesis teaches us that suffering enters the world through a wound, the story of Israel teaches us that suffering becomes the classroom where God forms His people. It is in Israel's history that we see a remarkable truth take shape: affliction does not merely accompany the covenant—it becomes the very environment in which the covenant is understood, remembered, and lived. God does not shield His people from trials; He fathers them through trials. Israel learns who God is not when life is easy, but when life is stripped bare, when comfort fades, when faith must walk without seeing.

This pattern begins with Abraham. His life unfolds like a series of holy interruptions, each one demanding trust in the face of uncertainty. God calls him to leave his homeland without explaining where he will go. God promises descendants while his wife remains barren. God leads him into foreign lands where famine threatens his survival. And when the long-awaited son is finally born, God asks Abraham to offer him on the mountain. These are not arbitrary sorrows. They are moments in which Abraham learns the nature of the covenant—learns that the God who calls him is the God who provides, even when the path appears impossible. Abraham's suffering becomes the soil in which faith takes root. Without trial, he might have admired God; through trial, he learns to trust Him.

The pattern continues in the life of Jacob. If Abraham shows us the suffering of obedience, Jacob shows us the suffering of transformation. His life is marked by conflict, deception, exile, and fear. Yet beneath these struggles lies the steady hand of God shaping a man who must learn to receive rather than grasp. The turning point comes when Jacob wrestles with the mysterious figure at the ford of the Jabbok. The struggle lasts until daybreak. Jacob emerges limping—wounded, yet blessed. His limp becomes the reminder that blessing is not seized; it is given. His new name, Israel, declares a truth that will define the nation: "He who wrestles with God." The people descended from Jacob will learn, again and again, that faith involves struggle, that relationship with God requires perseverance, and that wounds can become signs of grace.

Then we meet Joseph, whose story brings the mystery of affliction into even sharper relief. Sold by his brothers, falsely accused, thrown into prison, Joseph endures a depth of injustice that would crush most men. Yet Scripture does not portray him as abandoned. Again and again, the narrative repeats the quiet refrain: "The Lord was with Joseph." Divine presence does not remove the suffering; it accompanies him within it. And through this companionship, God works a grace that Joseph could never have foreseen. The very events intended to destroy him become the means by which God saves entire nations from famine. Joseph's final words to his brothers capture the heart of Israel's theology of suffering: "You meant evil against me, but God meant it for good." These words reveal a vision of providence that neither denies evil nor despairs before it. They affirm that God can weave grace into the fabric of human wrongdoing without ever becoming the author of the wrong.

This same pattern extends beyond individuals to the nation as a whole. Israel's identity is forged not in palaces or marketplaces, but in the wilderness. The wilderness becomes the school of the covenant. It is there, among barren landscapes and uncertain tomorrows, that Israel learns the character of God. They learn that God provides bread where no bread should exist. They learn that God brings water from rock. They learn that faith requires patience, perseverance, and obedience. They learn that complaining cannot substitute for trust. The wilderness strips Israel of illusions. It teaches them that freedom does not mean escaping suffering but learning to walk with God through suffering. The generation that left Egypt filled with excitement soon discovers that salvation must be lived, not merely received.

Israel's history continues in this rhythm: affliction, prayer, deliverance, renewal. In the time of the judges, in the rise and fall of kings, in the warnings of the prophets, God remains faithful even as His people falter. Again and again, the Scriptures show us that Israel does not learn God's heart in moments of triumph. She learns it in exile, mourning by the rivers of Babylon. She learns it in the anguish of Hannah, who pours her soul before the Lord and discovers that God hears the cry of the afflicted. She learns it in the wanderer David, who hides in caves and deserts, discovering that God's anointing is tested long before it is enthroned. She learns it through prophets who carry burdens heavier than their own strength, speaking God's word through tears.

Affliction becomes the thread that runs through the garments of Israel's story. It purifies desire, shapes identity, and reveals the difference between true worship and comfortable idolatry. God uses suffering not to harm His people but to draw them deeper into the relationship He has initiated. Israel does not suffer outside the covenant; she suffers inside it. And because she suffers inside it, her afflictions never become meaningless. They become invitations—

sometimes painful, sometimes bewildering, always transformative.

What sets Israel's story apart is not the presence of suffering, but the presence of God within the suffering. The nations around Israel suffer as well, but their suffering drives them toward despair or superstition. Israel's suffering drives her to prayer. It pushes her toward the God who binds Himself to her in covenant fidelity. It teaches her to ask questions honestly, to lament boldly, to repent sincerely, and to hope stubbornly even when circumstances seem to contradict every promise. This is why Israel becomes, in the words of the prophets, a people who "know the Lord." Not merely a people who know about Him, but a people who have encountered Him in the deepest places of their history.

The lives of Abraham, Jacob, Joseph, Hannah, David, and the prophets form a tapestry in which God's purpose becomes visible. Their afflictions are not random. They are woven into a story that reveals the character of God and the vocation of His people. Israel learns that suffering is not the absence of God but the opportunity for God to reveal Himself more fully. In trial, the heart is purified. In waiting, faith is strengthened. In lament, hope is refined. The school of affliction does not destroy Israel; it forms her. It prepares her for the greater works God will accomplish in the centuries to come.

Israel's story does not unfold as a tale of uninterrupted blessing. It unfolds as a pilgrimage punctuated by trials—trials that reveal the heart of God and the heart of His people. This becomes especially clear when we look at the figure of Hannah. Her suffering is quiet, domestic, and deeply personal. She is not a patriarch or a prophet. She is a woman who longs for a child, who endures the sting of mockery, who carries her sorrow in silence until she can no longer bear it. Yet Hannah's prayer becomes one of the most powerful scenes in Scripture. She goes to the house of the Lord and pours out her soul—not with eloquence, but with honesty.

Her tears teach Israel something essential: suffering is not merely endured; it is offered. Her lament becomes liturgy. Her silence becomes intercession. And when the Lord answers her prayer with the birth of Samuel, Hannah understands that affliction has not been wasted. It has formed her heart for a deeper obedience. She gives her son back to God, not out of compulsion, but out of love born from suffering. Her story shows that affliction can enlarge the heart, preparing it for a vocation it would never have embraced without passing through sorrow.

This theme of suffering preparing a person for greater fidelity reaches its fullest Old Testament expression in the life of David. Scripture calls him "a man after God's own heart," yet his path to kingship is anything but glorious. David spends years fleeing from Saul, hiding in caves, living as a hunted man. He knows what it means to be betrayed, misunderstood, and alone. These afflictions do not diminish him; they refine him. In the wilderness, David learns the difference between grasping and receiving. He refuses to seize Saul's life, even when he has every opportunity. His suffering becomes the place where he learns that kingship is a gift, not a prize. Authority is responsibility, not privilege. The heart that will one day shepherd Israel is shaped first in exile, where God shepherds David through darkness.

David's psalms reveal that his suffering was not simply external; it was deeply interior. He faced fear, guilt, abandonment, and spiritual desolation. Yet he brought these experiences to God in prayer. The psalms show us a man who refuses to hide his afflictions from the Lord, who refuses to pretend that faith eliminates pain. Instead, David teaches Israel to cry out with raw honesty: "How long, O Lord?"; "Why do You hide Your face?"; "Out of the depths I cry to You." These prayers become the heartbeat of Israel's spiritual life. Through David, the psalms become the inspired school of lament, shaping the language of every generation that seeks God in sorrow.

Where David's suffering reveals the testing of a king, the prophets reveal the suffering of those who must speak God's word to a reluctant people. Isaiah's vision overwhelms him; Jeremiah's calling burdens him; Ezekiel's symbolic actions exhaust him. Their afflictions are not punishments but participations. They share in the grief of God over His people. Through them, Israel learns that suffering does not only come from the world's injustice; it also comes from bearing God's message in a world that resists it. The prophets carry the weight of God's own heartbreak. Their suffering becomes revelation—not of their weakness, but of divine love that refuses to abandon Israel, no matter how far she strays.

In all these stories—Abraham's waiting, Jacob's wrestling, Joseph's injustice, Hannah's longing, David's exile, the prophets' burdens—we see a single pattern: suffering is the crucible in which God forms hearts capable of covenant fidelity. Each trial strips away self-reliance, deepens desire for God, and reveals the difference between false idols and the living God. Israel becomes a people who know that the Lord is not to be sought only in triumph, but in tears; not only in victory, but in vulnerability; not only in prosperity, but in the places where the soul tastes its deepest need.

This is why the Scriptures never sanitise Israel's afflictions. They record the failures, fears, doubts, and detours with striking honesty. The Bible does not hide the fact that suffering often provokes questions, confusion, and even protest. Yet these responses are not condemned. They are drawn into prayer. Israel does not silence her pain; she brings it before the Lord. Her history teaches us that suffering is not a sign that God has abandoned His people. It is the place where God teaches His people to seek Him with all their heart.

This leads us to one of the most profound gifts God gives Israel: the psalms. In the psalms, Israel receives not just permission to lament, but a language with which to do it. God Himself teaches His people how to speak to Him in affliction. He gives them inspired words for their anguish. This is not merely therapeutic; it is covenantal. It means that lament is not a break in the relationship—it is an expression of it. When Israel cries, she does so as a child crying to her Father. And when the Father hears, His answer may come in deliverance, or in endurance, or in a renewed sense of His presence. But the relationship remains intact. The psalms teach us that faith is not the absence of suffering; it is the courage to bring suffering into the presence of God.

Israel's story becomes, in this way, the story of every believer. Affliction is not the enemy of faith. It is one of its greatest teachers. The God who formed Israel through suffering continues to form hearts in the same way—gently, firmly, patiently, through trials that reveal His faithfulness and our dependence. The school of affliction is not an elective course in the spiritual life. It is the classroom where discipleship is learned. Israel walked this path before us, and through her story, we learn that suffering can become a place of encounter, purification, and grace.

The psalms occupy a unique place in Israel's formation because they gather every thread of the nation's suffering and weave it into worship. They do not offer explanations so much as invitations—inviting the afflicted to step into a relationship deeper than their wounds. The psalms refuse to let suffering remain private or silent. They lift it into the presence of God. This is why they remain the prayerbook of the Church: they teach believers how to stand before God not merely when life is whole but precisely when it feels broken.

Consider the rhythm of lament that echoes through so many psalms. "My God, my God, why have You forsaken me?" This is not blasphemy. It is faith refusing to surrender in the darkness. "How long, O Lord?" This is not impatience. It is hope stretching toward a horizon that has not yet appeared. "Out of the depths I cry to You." This is not despair. It is the soul discovering that even the depths belong to God. These cries reveal something profound about Israel's spirituality: suffering never silences relationship. Even when God seems distant, the psalmist keeps speaking to Him. The conversation continues, and in that continuation, faith is purified.

Many of the psalms begin with lament but end with praise. This movement is not emotional volatility; it is theological realism. The psalmist does not ignore his pain. He lays it bare. But as he speaks honestly to God, something changes within him. He remembers the Lord's faithfulness in the past. He recalls the covenant promises. He reflects on God's steadfast love. And slowly, the darkness lifts—not because circumstances have changed, but because the heart has been reoriented. Affliction becomes the doorway through which the soul encounters the God who saves.

This pattern—lament leading to renewed trust—is central to Israel's understanding of suffering. It teaches that God is not a distant observer but an active participant in the life of His people. It teaches that faith is not a shield against sorrow but a path through it. It teaches that hope is not rooted in circumstances but in the character of God. The psalms reveal that suffering is not an interruption of Israel's relationship with God. It is part of that relationship, a place where fidelity is tested and deepened.

Israel's prophets deepen this vision by showing that suffering can also be prophetic. Isaiah sees the sin of the people and feels it as a wound. Jeremiah weeps over Jerusalem and becomes known as the "weeping prophet." Ezekiel bears symbolic burdens—lying on his side, eating measured food, acting out the exile—to reveal the seriousness of Israel's spiritual condition. Their suffering is not incidental to their mission; it is integral to it. They carry within their hearts a share of God's grief over sin. Their afflictions become a lens through which Israel can see the pain of a God whose love has been rejected.

The prophets' experience reveals a truth that Israel would slowly come to grasp: suffering does not only reveal the weakness of the human heart. It reveals the love of God's heart. God is not indifferent to Israel's afflictions. He enters into them. He speaks through them. He uses them to call His people back to Himself. Through the prophets, Israel learns that suffering is not simply about endurance; it is about conversion, purification, and renewal. The prophetic voice becomes the voice of God pleading with His people to return, promising that their wounds will not have the last word.

This promise becomes especially vivid in the experience of exile. Exile is the collective affliction of a nation that has turned away from God. Yet even in exile, God does not abandon His people. He speaks through Jeremiah, assuring them that "I know the plans I have for you… plans for welfare and not for evil." He speaks through Ezekiel, promising to give them "a new heart and a new spirit." He speaks through the psalms of exile, where the tears of God's people become seeds of future joy. The exile becomes the ultimate demonstration that suffering can be disciplinary without being destructive. God disciplines His people not to punish them but to restore them.

By the time Israel returns from exile, she has learned something she could not have learned in any other way: suffering can purify the heart, strip away idols, deepen longing, and awaken hope. Israel learns to pray with greater sincerity, to worship with greater humility, to obey with greater resolve. Her affliction becomes her education in faithfulness. The school of suffering prepares her to recognise God's presence in ways she never would have recognised in comfort.

Through this long history, Israel becomes not simply a people who endure suffering, but a people who interpret it. She learns to see affliction not as a meaningless burden but as a moment in the covenant story—a moment when God's faithfulness and human frailty meet. She learns that suffering can be preparation for mission, purification of desire, or discipline born from love. But she also learns that suffering can be brought to God in prayer without fear. Israel's God is not offended by tears. He receives them as offerings.

This is why Scripture insists that God is "near to the broken hearted." Israel discovers that nearness not by escaping affliction but by encountering God within it. The stories of the patriarchs, the psalms of lament, the trials of the prophets—all reveal a God who walks with His people through every valley. Suffering becomes the place where Israel learns the depth of divine love, the seriousness of divine justice, and the steadfastness of divine mercy.

Israel's journey through the school of affliction shows that suffering does not merely test the covenant; it strengthens it. Affliction teaches Israel to trust, to repent, to hope, and to love. It teaches her that God is not only the Creator who formed the world but the Redeemer who enters its wounds. And through this long education, Israel becomes a people capable of bearing the weight of God's promises—a people who know that suffering, far from contradicting the covenant, becomes one of the ways God draws His children deeper into it.

Israel's history shows that suffering is not a random intrusion into the life of God's people. It is woven into the rhythm of covenant life. But this does not mean Israel glorifies suffering for its own sake. The Scriptures are clear: affliction is never presented as a good in itself. It becomes good because of what God does within it. The goodness comes from God's presence, not from the pain. Israel clings to this truth even when her circumstances appear to contradict every promise she has received. She holds onto God not because she understands the meaning of her suffering, but because she knows the One who accompanies her through it.

At the heart of this understanding lies a conviction that God is faithful. Israel's suffering often comes from her own disobedience, but God does not turn away. He disciplines, but He does not abandon. He corrects, but He does not reject. Even in the darkest moments—when the temple burns, when prophets are mocked, when the people are carried off in chains—God continues to speak through His messengers, assuring Israel that her story is not over. Suffering becomes the moment when Israel hears the call to return, the invitation to renew the covenant, the promise that God will restore what has been lost.

One of the most striking features of the Old Testament is how often Israel's greatest revelations come in times of affliction. In the desert, she receives the Law. In exile, she receives the promises of a new covenant. In persecution, she hears the words of prophets whose visions reach across centuries. Affliction becomes the time of divine speech. When the noise of comfort fades, the voice of God becomes clearer. Israel's suffering peels away the layers of distraction, revealing what truly sustains her: the word of the living God.

This is why the Scriptures are unafraid to portray Israel at her most vulnerable. They show her confused, frightened, repentant, and hopeful—all within the same breath. They show her oscillating between faith and fear, trust and complaint. Yet they also show that God remains patient with His people. He guides her slowly, like a father teaching a child to walk. He allows her to stumble, but He does not let her fall beyond His reach. The school of affliction is not designed to crush Israel. It is designed to mature her.

The psalms capture this maturity in poetic form. They trace the movement of a heart that has learned, through suffering, to see life through covenantal eyes. Some psalms cry out in anguish, others praise with joy. Many begin with lament and end with confidence. All reveal a relationship so honest that it refuses to hide anything from God. In the psalms, Israel speaks to God with a boldness that comes from intimacy. She knows that God welcomes her questions, receives her tears, and honours her trust. Her lament becomes an act of faith because it assumes that God is listening.

Psalm after psalm shows the same rhythm: suffering presses the soul down, prayer lifts the soul up, and God's faithfulness meets the soul in the space between. This rhythm becomes the pulse of Israel's spiritual life. It teaches that suffering is not the boundary of hope but the birthplace of deeper hope. The psalms insist that the human cry is heard in the heavens. They insist that God bends low to listen to the oppressed, that He rescues those who call upon Him, that He binds up the broken-hearted. Israel's suffering becomes bearable not because it disappears, but because she discovers that she does not bear it alone.

This truth shines especially in the moments when Israel reaches the limits of her strength. When she cannot rely on her own plans or power, she learns to rely on God. When she faces enemies too strong for her, she learns that deliverance comes from the Lord. When she experiences devastation beyond her understanding, she learns that God's purposes reach further than her vision. Suffering teaches Israel humility, dependence, and trust—virtues that shape her identity far more deeply than prosperity ever could.

Israel's afflictions also purify her desires. They expose the idols she has created, the false securities she has embraced, the illusions she has entertained. When these are stripped away, what remains is the simple, powerful truth that God alone is her portion. "Whom have I in heaven but You?" the psalmist asks. "And there is nothing upon earth that I desire besides You." These words are not spoken from comfort but from affliction. They arise from a heart that has discovered, through suffering, that God's presence is more precious than anything the world can offer.

The prophets echo this discovery in their call to repentance. They warn Israel against trusting in kings, alliances, wealth, or idols. They remind her that these cannot save her in the day of trouble. Only God can. Their message is not one of doom but of mercy. They speak harshly because the stakes are high. They speak tenderly because

God's heart is tender. They reveal that suffering can be a doorway to renewal—a moment when God invites His people to return with their whole heart.

Everything in Israel's story—her patriarchs, her psalms, her prophets, her exiles—points toward a single truth: suffering is not a detour in the covenant journey. It is part of the journey. It becomes the place where God forms His people, instructs them, purifies them, and prepares them for the fulfillment of His promises. Israel does not seek suffering, but she does not flee from the lessons it brings. She learns to trust the God who walks with her through every trial, who speaks into every sorrow, who restores what has been broken.

Israel's school of affliction forms a people capable of faithfulness. A people capable of hope. A people capable of love that endures. Through her suffering, Israel learns to recognise the God who never abandons, never forgets, never breaks His covenant. Her wounds become the places where His faithfulness shines most clearly. Her trials become the testimony that God is near to those who seek Him, even when they seek Him through tears.

Israel's long journey through affliction ultimately shapes her into a people who understand that suffering is not merely a human experience—it is a theological one. It reveals who God is, who we are, and what the covenant truly means. Through her trials, Israel discovers that the God who calls her is not a distant architect of history but a Father who walks with His children. He leads them by cloud and by fire. He disciplines them with patience. He restores them with mercy. Nothing in Israel's suffering escapes His providential care. Nothing is wasted.

This conviction becomes the anchor that holds Israel through every storm. Whether she suffers because of her enemies, because of her own sins, or because of the mysterious trials that accompany life in a fallen world, Israel learns that the Lord remains faithful. Suffering exposes her frailty, but it also reveals His steadfast love. Again and again, she discovers that affliction is not the end of the covenant story—it is the context in which the covenant becomes real. God does not love His people only in moments of peace. He loves them in famine, in exile, in fear, in darkness, in tears. He loves them not because they are strong but because He is strong for them.

This covenantal vision transforms the meaning of suffering. It becomes purification rather than punishment. Preparation rather than abandonment. Discipline given in love rather than wrath poured out in anger. Israel learns that God shapes His people as a potter shapes clay—through pressure, through fire, through time. Her experiences teach her that God uses affliction to turn hearts away from idols, to draw them back to Himself, to deepen their desire for His presence. Suffering becomes the moment when the covenant moves from the page to the heart, from law to love, from duty to devotion.

This is why Israel's prayers never end with despair. Even when she cries from the depths, she refuses to let go of hope. Her laments may be fierce, but they are never final. They rise from the soil of trust—a trust planted by God Himself. Lament is the cry of a child who knows she has a Father. Israel may weep, but she weeps toward God, not away from Him. Her tears become the water in which faith grows.

And in those tears, Israel discovers that God Himself shares in her afflictions. The prophets reveal a God who feels the weight of Israel's sorrow, who speaks of His love in the language of wounded longing: "How can I give you up?"; "My heart recoils within me"; "Is Ephraim My dear son?" These are not metaphors. They are windows into the heart of the living God. Israel's suffering becomes the mirror in which she glimpses God's own compassion—a compassion that carries her through every trial.

By the end of the Old Testament story, Israel has become a people who understand that suffering can be endured because suffering is not empty. It is held within the hands of the God who formed her. It is shaped by His wisdom. It is accompanied by His presence. It is destined for His purposes. This is not romanticism; it is the realism of faith. Israel knows the wilderness, the exile, the sword, the famine, the longing for deliverance. Yet she also knows the God who meets her in each of these places, transforming sorrow into wisdom and weakness into trust.

Israel's school of affliction forms not merely individuals but an entire nation capable of receiving the fullness of God's revelation. A people capable of hope even when hope seems unreasonable. A people capable of prayer even when prayer feels unanswered. A people capable of waiting for the promises of God even when the wait is long. Through suffering, Israel learns to recognise God's voice when He speaks and God's hand when He acts.

The covenant forged in joy is sustained in sorrow. The God who delivered Israel from Egypt also accompanies her through every trial that follows. He teaches her that affliction does not eclipse His faithfulness; it reveals it. He shows her that suffering is not a contradiction of His promises but the place where His promises take root. And through generations of trial, Israel becomes a people who know that the Lord is not merely the God of the mountaintop but also the God of the valley.

Israel emerges from the school of affliction with a wisdom that shines across the pages of Scripture: suffering does not have the last word. God does. Affliction may shape the journey, but covenant shapes the destination. The trials Israel endures do not define her. The God who sustains her does. And everything she learns in her suffering becomes part of the story that reveals Him to the world.

7

Christ The Man Of Sorrows

From the moment Israel learned to cry out in affliction, her Scriptures turned their gaze toward Someone who would one day carry those cries within Himself. The prophets spoke of Him in fragments—sometimes in shadows, sometimes in blazing clarity. He would be a Servant who suffers, a Shepherd who is struck, a King who is rejected, a Prophet who is pierced, a Priest who gives His life for His people. When the fullness of time arrived, these threads wove together in the person of Jesus of Nazareth. And in Him, suffering itself entered a new horizon, because in Him, God stepped into the wound of the world.

Christianity makes a claim so astonishing that we often forget how shocking it truly is: the God who created the universe chose not to remain distant from human suffering. He did not stand above it. He entered it. Every ancient religion wrestled with the problem of suffering, but only one dares to say that God has borne suffering in His own flesh. Only one proclaims a God who weeps. Only one offers a God who can say, without metaphor, "I have been pierced." Israel longed for deliverance; she never imagined that deliverance would come through a Deliverer who Himself would become afflicted.

The Gospels introduce Jesus not merely as a teacher or healer, but as the One who embodies the story of Israel in His very life. He is the Son called out of Egypt, the Beloved in whom the Father is well pleased, the Servant upon whom the Spirit rests. He gathers around Himself a renewed Israel—twelve disciples for twelve tribes. He gives the Sermon on the Mount as a new law on a new mountain. Yet throughout His ministry, there is an unmistakable undercurrent: all of this leads to suffering. He speaks of it often, but few understand. "The Son of Man must suffer many things." "The Son of Man will be delivered into the hands of sinners." "The Son of Man will be lifted up."

These are not predictions of defeat. They are revelations of identity. To understand why Jesus must suffer is to understand who He is. He is the Word made flesh, and the Word enters a wounded world prepared not only to heal but to bear the wound. He is the Bridegroom who loves His bride unto the end, even when the end leads through betrayal and abandonment. He is the Shepherd who finds the lost sheep not by calling from afar, but by entering the thickets where it bleeds. He is the Lamb whose offering is not taken from Him but given freely. Jesus does not suffer in spite of being God. He suffers because of the way God loves.

This is the truth that begins to dawn as we watch His earthly life unfold. When He touches the leper, He does not recoil from impurity; He draws it into His own holiness. When He heals the sick, He does not avoid their pain; He carries it. When He raises the dead, He does not deny mortality; He prepares to enter it. The Gospel does not portray Jesus as a healer who keeps suffering at arm's length. It portrays Him as a healer who walks straight into the valley where human sorrow collects like cold morning mist. He does not offer comfort from a distance. He becomes our comfort by taking our suffering upon Himself.

In the Old Testament, Israel learned that God is close to the broken hearted. In Jesus, that closeness takes flesh. The God who once spoke through prophets now speaks through wounds. The God who once accepted sacrifices now becomes the sacrifice. The God who once called Israel His firstborn now becomes the Firstborn who carries Israel's failures, fears, and tears on His shoulders. This is why the early Christians found in Isaiah's prophecy the clearest portrait of Jesus: "a Man of Sorrows, acquainted with grief." The Servant does not merely observe sorrow. He knows it. He shares it. He descends into its depths so no one must walk those depths alone.

This descent reaches its climax on the road to the Cross. At every step, Jesus reveals that His mission is not to escape suffering but to transform it. He enters Gethsemane, the garden where the human heart trembles before death, and He allows sorrow to weigh upon Him until His sweat becomes "like drops of blood." He prays not to avoid the Father's will but to embrace it. In the wrenching honesty of His prayer—"My soul is sorrowful, even unto death"—we see that Jesus does not approach suffering with stoic detachment. He approaches it with a heart fully human, fully vulnerable, fully open to the cost of love.

What happens next is not an accident of history. It is the revelation of God's heart. Jesus is arrested, abandoned, mocked, scourged, crowned with thorns, and condemned. None of these sufferings are arbitrary. Each reveals something essential about the love that does not turn back. He accepts betrayal to heal betrayal. He endures false accusation to redeem sinners who hide behind lies. He shoulders the cross to bear the weight we cannot carry. Every wound becomes a word spoken by the Word-made-flesh, proclaiming the depth of divine compassion.

At Calvary, the meaning of suffering is forever changed. The place of execution becomes the place of revelation. The cross, an instrument of torture, becomes the throne from which the love of God is displayed in its fullest clarity. And here, in this moment that stands at the centre of salvation history, we encounter the truth that Christianity has proclaimed from the beginning: the Cross is not the failure of God's plan. It is the fulfillment of it. It is not the collapse of hope. It is the birth of hope. It is not a contradiction of God's love. It is its clearest expression.

At the foot of the Cross, the world sees only tragedy. The onlookers see a failed prophet. The soldiers see a criminal. The religious leaders see a threat removed. But heaven sees something entirely different: the love of the Father meeting the suffering of the world in the body of His Son. What appears as defeat becomes the moment when divine love is poured out without reserve. The Cross is not God turning away from the world. It is God entering the world's deepest darkness with a love stronger than death.

The Gospels describe the crucifixion with a simplicity that invites contemplation. They do not sensationalise the violence. They do not dramatize the agony. They present Jesus suspended between heaven and earth, arms stretched wide, offering Himself for the salvation of His people. In this silence, we are invited to behold a mystery no words can fully contain. The One who spoke galaxies into existence now speaks forgiveness from a place of pain. The One who breathed life into Adam now breathes His last. The One who formed Israel in the wilderness now allows Himself to be led outside the city, carrying the burden of the world.

It is here—at the very moment when human suffering reaches its most brutal expression—that the heart of God is revealed. The Cross is not divine cruelty inflicted upon an innocent victim. It is the self-giving love of the Trinity made visible. Jesus offers His life to the Father in the Spirit. The Father receives the offering with infinite love. The Spirit unites the offering to every human cry for mercy. This is not a story of a Father punishing a Son. It is the story of God giving Himself completely, holding nothing back. The Cross becomes the icon of divine generosity—a generosity that enters suffering not to glorify it, but to redeem it from within.

When Jesus cries out, "My God, My God, why have You forsaken Me?", He is not expressing despair. He is praying the opening line of Psalm 22, a psalm that begins in anguish but ends in triumph. In that single cry, Jesus gathers the lament of every wounded heart. He speaks for the abandoned, the grieving, the betrayed, the forgotten, the suffering poor, the victims of injustice. He speaks for Israel. He speaks for humanity. He enters the place where God seems absent in order to reveal that God is present even there. What appears to be forsakenness becomes revelation: there is no human darkness into which God will not descend.

This is why the early Church proclaimed the Cross not with embarrassment, but with boldness. In a world that saw crucifixion as the ultimate symbol of shame, Christians saw it as the ultimate symbol of love. They saw that Jesus did not come to explain suffering from a distance. He came to carry it. He came to transform it. He came to open a way through it that leads to life. The Cross becomes the place where suffering is no longer meaningless, where sin is no longer victorious, where death is no longer final. Everything humanity fears—pain, guilt, loneliness, death—Jesus takes upon Himself so that none of these realities can separate us from the love of God.

This is the moment when suffering itself is redefined. Before the Cross, suffering could easily be interpreted as punishment, failure, or abandonment. After the Cross, suffering becomes something different. It becomes a place of communion. Not a place of explanation, but a place of encounter. Suffering becomes the space where the disciple meets the Master, where the heart learns to love with the love that has been poured out upon it. The Cross becomes the template for

Christian hope—a hope that is not built on ideal circumstances but on the God who enters our circumstances and fills them with His presence.

Christian hope is not optimism. It is not the expectation that life will always go well or that suffering will always make sense. Christian hope is rooted in a Person—the One who hung upon the Cross and rose from the grave. Hope begins at the foot of the Cross because the Cross reveals that God is faithful even when everything else fails. If God has gone this far—if He has taken on flesh, entered our sorrow, borne our sin, embraced our death—then nothing can separate us from His love. Hope is not the denial of suffering. It is the conviction that suffering cannot defeat the God who has conquered it from the inside.

This is why Christian hope must always remain cruciform. Without the Cross, hope becomes sentimental. It becomes fragile. It becomes a wish projected into the future rather than a truth anchored in history. But with the Cross, hope becomes unshakeable. It becomes a certainty grounded in the love that has already endured the worst the world can offer. The wounds of Christ do not fade in His risen body. They remain as eternal signs of a love that has entered suffering and emerged victorious. Those wounds are the pledge of hope for every believer who suffers.

In the face of the Cross, we discover that suffering no longer has the power to isolate. It draws us into communion with the One who knows suffering from the inside. We discover that our wounds can be joined to His wounds, our sorrows to His sorrow, our crosses to His Cross. And in that union, something extraordinary happens: suffering becomes a place where love can grow. It becomes a moment when our hearts, stripped of illusion and pride, learn to lean on the God who has bent low to meet us.

The Cross stands at the centre of Christian faith because it stands at the centre of human experience. Every human being knows suffering. But only in Christ do we discover that suffering is not a dead end. It is a door—a narrow door, to be sure, but one that opens into the heart of God.

If the Cross reveals the heart of God, it also reveals the truth about the human person. We often imagine that suffering isolates, divides, or diminishes us. At Calvary, we discover the opposite. The Cross is the place where humanity is gathered, not scattered. Jesus is lifted up not only to offer Himself to the Father, but to draw us to Himself. He enters the depths of human suffering so that no one who suffers needs to think, even for a moment, that they suffer alone. The fellowship of the Cross becomes the foundation of the fellowship of the Church. We are united in the One who has carried our griefs.

When we contemplate the Man of Sorrows, we are not looking at an outsider to suffering. We are looking at the One who has walked every path of human sorrow. He knows the loneliness of betrayal. He knows the sting of injustice. He knows the terror of abandonment. He knows the weakness of the body and the agony of death. Nothing human is foreign to Him, except sin; and precisely because He is sinless, He can carry sin's consequences with perfect love. The Cross does not remove suffering from the Christian life. It transforms suffering into a place of communion with Christ.

This transformation begins with a simple but profound truth: suffering looks different when love is present. The Cross is not the spectacle of a cruel Father demanding satisfaction. It is the self-giving love of the Son, offered freely, joyfully, even in agony. Jesus does not drag His cross. He embraces it. Not because the pain is good, but because the love is real. He knows that by carrying the cross, He carries us. He knows that by entering death, He will destroy it. He knows that by bearing the world's sin, He will open the world to forgiveness.

This is why the early Christians never separated the Cross from glory. They saw the Cross as victory—not the kind of victory the world celebrates, but the victory of love overcoming hatred, truth overcoming lies, humility overcoming pride. The Cross unveils the deepest logic of the Gospel: the way up is down, the way to life is through death, the way to glory is through obedience. Jesus reveals that suffering, when united to love, becomes fruitful. It becomes redemptive. It becomes a seed that falls into the earth and bears much fruit.

This truth challenges every human expectation. We assume that suffering destroys meaning. Jesus shows that suffering can reveal it. We assume that pain separates us from God. Jesus shows that pain can draw us nearer to Him. We assume that suffering is a sign of failure. Jesus shows that suffering is the place where love proves itself faithful. He teaches not by explanation but by example. From the Cross, He shows us that God is never closer to us than when we feel most forsaken.

This is why Christian hope cannot be understood apart from the Crucified. Hope that does not pass through the Cross is not hope—it is illusion. It collapses under the weight of real loss. Christian hope endures precisely because it is rooted in a God who has entered the worst of human suffering and transformed it from the inside. When Jesus breathes His last, darkness covers the land. Yet in that darkness, something begins to shift. The veil of the Temple is torn. The earth trembles. The centurion confesses, "Truly this man was the Son of God." The very moment of death becomes a moment of revelation. In the apparent defeat, the true identity of Jesus shines forth.

In this moment, we begin to understand why the Cross stands at the centre of the Christian life. It is not merely an event from the past. It is the enduring sign of who God is. And who is He? He is the God who loves unto the end. He is the God who bears our sorrows. He is the God who enters suffering so that suffering can never again be a place without Him. The Cross becomes the moment when human suffering is gathered into divine love. No longer is suffering the mark of isolation. It becomes the place of meeting—where human frailty encounters divine compassion.

This is why the saints, generation after generation, have found in the Cross a source of consolation rather than fear. They saw what the world could not see: suffering united to Christ becomes fruitful. It becomes a participation in His redemptive love. It becomes a way of offering oneself to God, not in resignation but in trust. When we suffer in union with Christ, our suffering is no longer meaningless. It becomes a prayer. It becomes a gift. It becomes an echo of the love that once hung upon Calvary.

At the heart of it all is the stunning truth that God is not distant from human sorrow. He has taken it into Himself. The Cross stands as the indestructible sign that suffering does not have the last word. Love does. And because love has taken flesh and entered suffering, every sorrow we carry can become a place where God draws near, heals, strengthens, and transforms. The Man of Sorrows is not simply the one who suffered. He is the one who redeems suffering. He turns the world's darkest hour into the hour of salvation.

When we look upon the Crucified, we are not gazing at a distant event but at the living centre of God's revelation. The Cross tells us not only what God has done but who God is. He is the God who loves to the point of suffering. He is the God who enters the depths that we fear most. He is the God who chooses to be with us where we are weakest, not where we imagine ourselves strong. And in this choice, the meaning of human suffering is forever altered. It no longer stands outside the story of salvation. It becomes the place where salvation touches our lives most intimately.

This is why the Church has always insisted that the Cross is not merely an example. It is an event that changes the world. Jesus does not die simply to inspire compassion or moral improvement. He dies to conquer the forces that hold humanity captive. Sin, death, and the fear of death—these are the tyrants that enslave the human race. Jesus enters their territory not as a victim but as a victor disguised in weakness. He allows death to touch Him so that He may break its power from the inside. What appears to be surrender is divine strategy. What looks like helplessness is hidden strength. The Cross reveals a God who saves not by avoiding suffering but by absorbing it.

This revelation is central to Christian hope. Hope is not wishful thinking. It is not the belief that suffering is an illusion or that life will eventually organise itself into something pleasant. Hope is rooted in the certainty that God has acted in history. That He has entered the human condition. That He has carried its burdens. That He has overcome its darkness. The wounds of Christ are not healed over or erased in His risen body. They remain as signs of victory. They remain as windows into the divine heart. They remain as the promise that our own wounds can be taken up into His.

This is the paradox of Christian hope: suffering, when united to Christ, becomes a pathway to deeper life. Not because suffering itself is good, but because Christ fills it with His presence. Without Christ, suffering narrows the world, darkens the mind, and burdens the heart. With Christ, suffering can purify desire, deepen trust, strengthen love, and open the soul to a grace it might never have known in comfort. The Cross does not romanticise suffering. It redeems it. It shows that God can bring life out of death, goodness out of evil, hope out of despair.

In this light, every Christian is invited to see his or her own suffering differently. The Cross does not take away the pain of illness, loss, betrayal, or grief. But it reveals a companionship deeper than pain. We do not suffer at a distance from God. We suffer in the presence of a God who has chosen to suffer with us. The Cross becomes the assurance that no darkness is impenetrable, no valley is God-forsaken, no wound is beyond His reach. When we lift our eyes to the Crucified, we see that God's love is not defeated by suffering. It is displayed within it.

This truth begins to shape the Christian heart in countless ways. It teaches us to trust when trust feels impossible. It teaches us to persevere when circumstances seem overwhelming. It teaches us to forgive when forgiveness feels too costly. The Cross becomes the measure of love: not a love that avoids pain, but a love that is willing to bear it for the sake of another. And as we learn from the Crucified, our own suffering can become a place where the love of God is made visible in us. Not because we seek suffering, but because we seek Christ within it.

The Cross also reveals the cost of redemption. God does not save the world with a word from heaven. He saves it with a Word made flesh, a Word who bleeds, a Word who cries out, a Word who descends into death so that death may lose its claim over the human heart. Redemption is not cheap. It is costly. It is paid for in wounds. Yet the cost is not imposed upon the Son; it is embraced by Him. The Father does not force the Son to die. The Son freely offers Himself in love. The Cross is not divine division. It is divine unity—the Father giving the Son, the Son offering Himself, the Spirit strengthening the sacrifice. The Trinity moves as one in the work of redemption.

This is why Christian hope is cruciform. It is shaped by the Cross because it flows from the Cross. It is hope that looks suffering in the face and refuses to be conquered by it. It is hope that acknowledges the reality of pain without surrendering to despair. It is hope that draws its strength from the love revealed on Calvary—a love that endures, a love that saves, a love that goes to the very limits of human sorrow and transforms those limits into places of grace.

When the Christian gazes upon the Cross, he sees not only what Christ has suffered but what Christ has accomplished. He sees a love strong enough to enter every human wound. He sees a victory that does not erase suffering but redeems it. He sees a God who bears our sorrows so that our sorrows may become a path to Him. This is the heart of Christian hope: that suffering, because it has been touched by God, is no longer the final word over human life.

If we allow the Cross to speak on its own terms, a final truth emerges—one that reshapes every Christian understanding of suffering: the Crucified Christ does not merely reveal God's love in suffering. He reveals that God's love is stronger than suffering. The Cross is not the endpoint of the story, nor is it the cancellation of the promises God made to Israel. It is the moment when those promises pass through fire and come forth purified. The love that began in covenant fidelity now shines with a clarity the world has never seen. At Calvary, we do not witness the weakness of God. We witness His strength—a strength expressed not in domination, but in self-giving.

This strength, revealed in apparent weakness, anchors the entire Christian life. It means that no believer walks into suffering without the companionship of the One who has walked there first. It means that sorrow does not cut us off from God; it draws us nearer to Him. It means that the very places where we feel most vulnerable can become the places where grace flows most freely. Suffering becomes a place of encounter not because suffering is good, but because Christ is there. The Man of Sorrows stands at the centre of every human loss, bearing the weight we cannot bear, illuminating the darkness that would otherwise overwhelm us.

This truth becomes a source of profound consolation. Life will bring afflictions—some expected, others sudden, all of them unwelcome. Illness, grief, betrayal, exhaustion, failure—none of these are foreign to the Christian life. But the Cross teaches us that none of them are foreign to God. In Christ, God has taken these sorrows into His own life. He has sanctified the very places where we feel weakest. He has opened a way through suffering that leads not to despair but to communion. The path may be narrow, but it is marked by the footprints of the One who goes before us.

This is why the saints speak of suffering not only with sobriety but with reverence. They are not naïve. They know the bitterness of tears. They know the weight of affliction. But they also know the nearness of Christ in those moments. They know the grace that flows from union with the Crucified. They know that suffering, when offered in love, can become a participation in the redemption of the world. This participation does not compete with Christ's sacrifice. It flows from it. The Cross makes space for the disciple to share, in a small way, in the love that saved humanity.

Christian hope, then, is not built on the avoidance of suffering. It is built on the presence of Christ within suffering. This hope does not deny the reality of pain. It refuses to let pain have the final authority. It does not ignore the terrors of death. It proclaims that death has been entered, endured, and conquered by the God who loves us. It does not eliminate the uncertainty of life. It anchors life in a love that is certain.

Standing before the Cross, every believer faces a choice: to trust the God who suffers for us, or to turn away because His love does not fit our expectations. The Cross challenges our assumptions about what divine power looks like. It challenges our desire for quick answers and easy explanations. It forces us to confront the truth that God's way of healing the world does not bypass suffering—it passes through it. But in that passing-through, suffering loses its tyranny.

At the Cross, suffering becomes something it could never have been on its own: a place of revelation. A place of communion. A place of hope. The Man of Sorrows reveals a God who chooses to bear the burdens we cannot lift, who transforms wounds into channels of grace, who turns the darkest hour into the dawn of salvation. Through Him, suffering becomes a chapter of the story, not its conclusion.

This is why the Church has never ceased to return to Calvary. Every liturgy, every sacrament, every prayer echoes the love revealed there. The Cross remains the measure of divine fidelity and the anchor of human hope. It tells us that God has not abandoned the world. He has entered it with a love stronger than sorrow, stronger than sin, stronger than death.

The One who hangs upon the Cross is not merely a suffering man. He is the God who bears our sorrows. And because He has borne them, we need never fear that suffering will have the final word. The final word belongs to love—wounded, poured out, victorious.

8

The Resurrection And The Rewriting Of Pain

The story of salvation does not end in darkness. It passes through darkness, but it does not remain there. The same Scriptures that speak with searing honesty about suffering also speak with unshakable confidence about what God does *after* suffering has done its worst. When the Gospels tell us that "on the first day of the week, while it was still dark," Mary Magdalene went to the tomb, they are describing more than a moment in time. They are describing the condition of the human heart. Suffering brings every soul to a place where it is "still dark." A place where loss feels final. A place where silence feels permanent. A place where the future feels buried.

But the Gospel insists on a truth the world never expects: the darkness is not final. The tomb is not sovereign. Death does not get the last word. When Mary arrives at the tomb and finds the stone rolled away, she discovers that God has acted in a way no human imagination could have anticipated. The Resurrection is not simply a reversal of suffering. It is the re-creation of the world. It is not the denial of death. It is the defeat of death. It is not the erasing of wounds. It is the glorification of wounds.

THE RESURRECTION AND THE REWRITING OF PAIN

This is the first great surprise of the Resurrection: Jesus rises with the marks of the nails still visible in His hands, the spear-wound still open in His side. He does not hide these wounds. He shows them. He invites Thomas to touch them. He allows His disciples to see that the very instruments of suffering have become signs of victory. The wounds that once spoke of violence now speak of love. The wounds that once declared death now declare life. The wounds that once marked the end of hope now become the beginning of new hope.

This alone reshapes the entire meaning of human suffering. In every other worldview, suffering either remains a problem to be solved or a burden to be endured. In the Resurrection, suffering becomes something different: it becomes transformable. Christ does not rise *in spite* of His wounds. He rises *with* His wounds—and because of this, every wound offered to Him in faith can be taken up into His glory. This is why the risen Christ does not erase the story of Good Friday. He rewrites it. He does not undo the Cross. He unveils its meaning.

The disciples struggle at first to grasp this. They had expected a Messiah who would conquer without suffering, who would triumph without loss, who would reign without wounds. They imagined glory as the absence of pain. Jesus reveals glory as the transformation of pain. The Resurrection teaches them, and teaches us, that suffering in union with God is never wasted. It is gathered, redeemed, and brought into the light of eternity. Nothing surrendered to God is lost. Nothing borne in love is forgotten. Nothing buried in faith remains in the ground.

This is why Christian hope is not optimism. Optimism depends on circumstances. Hope depends on Christ. Optimism fades when suffering intensifies. Hope grows stronger. Optimism expects improvement. Hope expects fidelity—God's fidelity. Optimism looks for silver linings. Hope looks for the risen Christ. Christian hope is a theological virtue because it anchors the soul not in probabilities but in promises. Not in what we see, but in what God has done. Not in the avoidance of suffering, but in the transformation accomplished through suffering by the One who has conquered death.

In this light, the Resurrection becomes the lens through which every Christian reads the story of his own life. Without the Resurrection, suffering looks like a tomb. With the Resurrection, suffering becomes a seed. Jesus Himself uses this image when He says, "Unless a grain of wheat falls into the earth and dies, it remains alone; but if it dies, it bears much fruit." The mystery becomes clear: what feels like burial may in fact be planting. What feels like loss may be preparation for growth. What feels like the end may be the hidden beginning of something new.

This truth does not make suffering easy. It makes suffering meaningful. It assures us that God does not lead His people into darkness in order to abandon them there. He leads them through darkness to show that His light is stronger. That His life is greater. That His mercy is able to reach into places no one else can reach. The Resurrection reveals that God is faithful not only in joy but in sorrow, not only in strength but in weakness, not only in life but in death.

The dawn of the Resurrection is the dawn of Christian hope. It shines gently but decisively across the landscape of every fear and every wound. It shows that the story of suffering is not closed. It can be rewritten by the God who brings life out of death, healing out of brokenness, and glory out of wounds. The light that broke over the garden tomb now breaks over every human heart that dares to believe that Christ is risen—not in theory, not in symbol, but in truth.

The disciples did not understand this mystery immediately. When they first encountered the risen Christ, they were filled with fear, confusion, and astonishment. Their world had been shattered on Friday, and Sunday's revelation felt almost too great to trust. They had watched Him suffer the full brutality of human sin. They had seen

His body taken down from the Cross, lifeless. They had seen the tomb sealed. And now He stands before them—alive, glorified, bearing the marks of His sacrifice. The One they feared they had lost forever now speaks their names.

In these encounters, Jesus does more than prove He has risen. He teaches them what *His* Resurrection means for *their* suffering. To the disciples on the road to Emmaus, He opens the Scriptures and shows that the Messiah "had to suffer" before entering His glory. He does not treat suffering as an unfortunate detour in the divine plan. He explains it as the path through which redemption unfolds. He shows them that the wounds of the world have been absorbed into His own Body—and that by entering into suffering, He has broken suffering's power to define the story of humanity.

When He appears in the Upper Room, His first words are "Peace be with you." These are not casual words. They are the announcement that the world has changed. Peace is not the absence of conflict; it is the presence of the risen Christ. The apostles had locked themselves in out of fear. Jesus enters not only through the door they had barred but through the fear that had chained their hearts. The Resurrection does not erase the trauma of Good Friday. It places that trauma within a new horizon. It reveals that God's fidelity is stronger than human betrayal, that His life is more enduring than human death, that His love is deeper than human sin.

And then comes Thomas—the apostle who embodies the honest questions of every believer. He wants to see the wounds. He wants to touch them. He wants to know that the suffering was real and that the victory is real. Jesus does not rebuke him. He invites him: "Put your finger here… see My hands." The invitation is astonishing. The glorified Christ does not hide the memory of pain. He holds it out as proof of love. He asks Thomas not merely to believe in the Resurrection, but to understand that the wounds have been transformed, not erased.

This is the mystery at the heart of Christian hope: what is given to God in suffering is not discarded; it is transfigured. Christ does not rise into a world untouched by sorrow. He rises into the same world—but now He carries within His resurrected Body the permanent signs of God's victory over sin and death. His wounds become sacraments of hope, constant reminders that no wound suffered in union with Him is meaningless. The world's cruelty does not have the power to write the final chapter. God does.

The Resurrection unveils a truth that Israel hinted at but could never fully see: suffering is not a tomb for those who belong to God. It is a seed. A seed buried in trust, watered with tears, warmed by divine love, destined to rise in ways unseen. Jesus Himself uses this image in the Gospel of John. "Unless a grain of wheat falls into the earth and dies, it remains alone." Death seems like isolation. But Jesus continues: "If it dies, it bears much fruit." In the Resurrection, this becomes more than a parable. It becomes the pattern of redemption, the pattern of discipleship, the pattern of life.

This redefines how a Christian reads every sorrow. Illness is not simply deterioration; it can become a place where grace deepens. Betrayal is not simply harm; it can become a place where forgiveness takes root. Loss is not merely absence; it can become a place where longing learns to look toward eternity. The Resurrection teaches that suffering does not need to be denied or trivialised to be transformed. It needs to be brought to Christ. Once it is placed in His hands, it undergoes a change we could never accomplish on our own. It becomes part of a story larger than our pain.

Christian hope grows out of this soil. It is not optimism—it does not depend on predictions or probabilities. It is the virtue that anchors the heart in the certainty of God's promises. Hope is theological because its origin is God. Its content is Christ. Its sustenance is grace. Hope looks at the wounds of the world and refuses to believe they are final. Hope looks at the empty tomb and understands that God's faithfulness reaches beyond every grave. Hope looks at the risen Christ and knows that love is stronger than death.

This kind of hope does not free us from suffering. It frees us *within* suffering. It allows us to walk through sorrow without surrendering to despair. It gives courage to endure when endurance feels impossible. It whispers that the night will not last forever, that dawn is coming, that the God who raised Jesus from the dead will raise all who belong to Him. The Resurrection becomes the promise that no faithful suffering is wasted, no tear is unseen, no sacrifice forgotten.

The disciples' fear did not vanish instantly. Their wounds remained. Their memories of Friday did not disappear. But everything they carried was now bathed in the light of Easter. They knew that the world's worst hour had become the hour of salvation. They knew that the darkest place in human history had been filled with the light of divine love. They knew that if Christ could transform His Cross, He could transform theirs. And so they walked into the world—not as men who had avoided suffering, but as men who had seen suffering rewritten.

The Resurrection places every believer before a truth that is at once bracing and beautiful: God does not promise a life without suffering, but He promises that suffering will never have the final word. The empty tomb stands as the decisive declaration that suffering is not an ultimate destination. It is a passage. A threshold. A place where God prepares His people for glory. When Christ rises, He reveals not only His own victory but the pattern by which every life joined to His will be raised.

This is why the early Church proclaimed the Resurrection with such urgency. They did not preach it as a distant hope. They preached it as a living reality capable of rewriting the present. When Peter stands before the crowds at Pentecost, he does not speak as a man still crushed by Friday's grief. He speaks as one who has seen the risen Lord and now understands that every sorrow, including his own betrayal, has been caught up into redemption. "This Jesus whom you crucified," he declares, "God has raised up." The announcement is not merely historical. It is theological. It means the story has changed.

For the apostles, the Resurrection reinterprets not only Christ's suffering but their own. What once felt like failure now becomes the soil of transformation. What once filled them with shame now becomes an occasion for mercy. What once threatened to extinguish their faith now becomes the fire that strengthens it. The Resurrection teaches them that God wastes nothing—not sin, not sorrow, not fear, not loss. Everything surrendered to Him can be redeemed.

This is why the New Testament writers speak of suffering with a confidence that can seem startling to modern ears. Paul writes that "the sufferings of this present time are not worth comparing with the glory to be revealed." He does not deny the pain of affliction. He does not ask believers to pretend that suffering is pleasant. He simply knows that suffering cannot thwart the purposes of God. It cannot halt the progress of grace. It cannot diminish the inheritance promised in Christ. Paul understands suffering not as a detour, but as a participation in the path Christ Himself walked from death into life.

Peter speaks in the same way. Writing to Christians facing persecution, he does not offer strategies for escape. He offers the logic of the Resurrection. "After you have suffered a little while," he promises, "the God of all grace… will Himself restore, confirm, strengthen, and establish you." The promise does not rest on human resilience. It rests on the fact that Christ is risen. Because Christ has passed through suffering into glory, the believer can endure suffering with hope. Not with stoic resolve, not with denial, but with the quiet certainty that God is at work in ways unseen.

THE RESURRECTION AND THE REWRITING OF PAIN

This does not diminish the reality of pain. It deepens the reality of hope. The Resurrection does not ask us to minimise sorrow; it asks us to place sorrow within the horizon of eternity. When a seed is buried in the ground, it looks like an ending. But the one who knows the reality of growth understands that the burial is preparation. In the same way, suffering often looks like burial. Yet the Resurrection teaches that in God's hands, burial becomes planting. It becomes the moment when the life of grace begins to take root in a new way.

This is why the saints speak of their sufferings not as obstacles to holiness but as occasions for deeper union with God. They do not seek suffering for its own sake. They seek Christ. And they have discovered that Christ often meets His disciples most intimately in the very places where the world sees only loss. They have learned that the One who rose from the tomb also raises hearts weighed down by grief. They know that every cross borne with faith becomes a place of encounter.

The risen Christ teaches His disciples that glory is not the absence of wounds but the transformation of wounds. When He appears to them, they see not a return to the past but the beginning of the new creation. His Body is the first fruits of the world restored. His wounds are the first signs of a redeemed humanity. His presence is the pledge that death has been conquered and that every sorrow entrusted to Him will be gathered into that victory.

Christian hope grows from this revelation. It is the sure expectation that God will finish what He has begun. Hope anchors the soul not in what is visible but in what has been promised. It sees suffering and does not flinch. It sees death and does not yield. It sees the wounds of Christ and understands that nothing surrendered to God is ever wasted. The Resurrection teaches us that even when life feels buried, God is at work bringing forth something new.

For this reason, the Resurrection becomes the lens through which the believer reads every chapter of his life. It teaches that grief is not abandoned. It is held. Pain is not forgotten. It is transformed. Tears are not signs of failure. They are seeds of a future harvest. The Risen Christ stands at the centre of human history and declares that God has entered every place where sorrow tries to reign. The world's story no longer ends in death. It ends in life.

The Resurrection does not offer an escape from the world. It offers a new way of living within it. The disciples, once fearful and hidden, now step into public life with a courage unexplained by human strength. Their boldness is not a personality shift; it is a theological revelation. They have seen the Lord alive. They have witnessed the first light of the new creation. And because of this, the world's threats no longer hold the same power. Suffering, once feared as the great extinguisher of hope, is now seen as a doorway through which the power of God becomes visible.

This transformation is especially clear in the way the early Christians spoke about death. In the ancient world, death was the final sovereign. It ended stories. It sealed destinies. It silenced every hope. But for the Christian, death becomes something profoundly different. It becomes the moment when the believer is most fully united with Christ. It becomes the moment when the promise of resurrection becomes personal. Death is not a cliff. It is a threshold. And the One who has passed through it now stands on the other side, calling His people into life.

Yet this hope is not limited to the end of life. It reaches into every sorrow of the present. The Resurrection teaches the Christian to look at suffering not only in light of eternity but in light of God's active presence now. The risen Christ does not wait for the end of time to bring healing. He begins His work in hearts even as they ache. He begins to rewrite stories even while the wounds are fresh. He begins to bring light into places where darkness has settled for years. The

Resurrection is not only future; it is present. It is the power by which God renews His people daily.

Paul expresses this reality when he says, "Though our outer self is wasting away, our inner self is being renewed day by day." He does not deny that the body grows weak or that life carries wounds. But he knows that a deeper work is unfolding beneath the surface. Every trial borne with faith shapes the soul. Every sorrow entrusted to Christ plants a seed of grace. Every sacrifice offered in love becomes a participation in the life of the risen Lord. This is the hidden rhythm of resurrection life: outward decline, inward renewal; earthly loss, heavenly gain; present tears, future glory.

The Resurrection allows Christians to hold two truths at once. First: suffering is real and painful. Second: suffering is not ultimate. These truths do not cancel each other. They form the tension within which Christian hope grows. The world resolves the tension by denying one truth or the other. It either romanticises suffering or denies suffering. It either clings to despair or manufactures shallow optimism. The Christian does neither. He stands at the Cross with full honesty, and he stands at the empty tomb with full faith. He refuses to lie about the world's brokenness. And he refuses to forget God's victory.

This balanced vision gives depth to Christian compassion. When believers accompany others in their suffering, they do not offer clichés. They offer Christ. They offer presence, patience, and prayer. They offer the hope that sorrow does not define the destiny of those who belong to God. They offer the truth that Christ has already gone ahead into every darkness. They offer the assurance that even when healing is delayed or denied in this life, it is guaranteed in the life to come. The Resurrection grants Christians the ability to sit with the suffering without being crushed by their grief and without fleeing from their pain.

In this way, the Resurrection reshapes the entire moral and spiritual life. It teaches the believer to measure reality not by what is visible but by what God has promised. It gives meaning to sacrifice. It strengthens perseverance. It sustains fidelity when circumstances are harsh. It guards the heart from the temptation to despair. It teaches the soul to wait—not with resignation, but with expectation. To wait as the farmer waits for harvest. To wait as Israel waited for redemption. To wait as the apostles waited for the Spirit. To wait with the certainty that the God who raised Jesus from the dead is faithful.

Hope becomes, in this way, a discipline of the heart. It must be practiced. It must be nourished. It must be guarded against the corrosive voices of fear, cynicism, and self-reliance. The Resurrection trains the believer to resist the lie that suffering has the final say. It teaches him to interpret his trials through the lens of God's victory. It invites him to believe that, in God's hands, even the things that feel like endings may become beginnings. Even the things that feel like burial may become planting.

This is why early Christians could rejoice in the midst of affliction. Their joy was not emotional cheerfulness. It was spiritual clarity. They saw what suffering could become when united to Christ. They saw what God had done with the worst evil ever committed—the Crucifixion. They saw that God does not simply repair the world; He renews it. He brings life out of death. He brings glory out of wounds. He brings grace out of sorrow. And once this truth entered their souls, nothing could dislodge it.

The Resurrection is the guarantee that nothing surrendered to God will ever be wasted. Every act of forgiveness, every tear shed in faith, every hidden sacrifice, every silent endurance, every cross borne in love—all of it becomes part of the great work God is accomplishing in His people. When Christ rose, He did not only conquer death. He conquered the meaninglessness that suffering once seemed to carry. He gave the world a new grammar, a new horizon, a new hope.

The Resurrection also reveals something profound about the nature of God's fidelity. He does not merely restore what was lost. He brings forth something greater. He does not simply return life to its previous form. He raises it into glory. This is why the New Testament speaks of "a new creation." The phrase is not metaphorical. It is the theological declaration that Christ's risen Body is the beginning of a world renewed, a humanity healed, a creation restored. The Resurrection is not an appendix to the Gospel. It is the heart of it. Everything that God has promised, everything Israel longed for, everything the prophets foretold—finds its fulfillment in the risen Christ.

For the believer, this means that suffering is never the end of the story. Whatever we surrender to God can be taken up into this new creation. Whatever seems to die in our hands can live again in His. Whatever grieves us today may become the very place where God's glory is revealed tomorrow. This is the logic of resurrection: what is buried in faith rises in grace. The seed that falls into the earth does not vanish. It yields a harvest.

This truth gives the Christian a unique strength—a strength that does not depend on circumstances or temperament. It is the strength that comes from knowing that God has already gone ahead into every future, every fear, every unknown. The risen Christ stands not only at the end of time but at the centre of every moment. He is the One who says, "Behold, I make all things new." Not some things. Not future things only. All things. Even the wounds we carry. Even the sorrows we cannot explain. Even the losses that break our hearts.

And so the Resurrection becomes the anchor of Christian endurance. It is what allows a mother to mourn her child with tears that are real but not hopeless. It is what allows the sick to pray for healing without despair when healing does not come. It is what allows the betrayed to forgive, the lonely to persevere, the discouraged to rise again. The

Resurrection is the assurance that the God who brought light out of darkness at creation and life out of death at Calvary will not fail to bring good out of every trial endured in faith.

This hope does not make suffering easy. It makes suffering meaningful. It does not eliminate pain. It transforms it. The Christian still feels the weight of sorrow, but he feels it differently. He carries it not as a burden that crushes but as a cross that leads somewhere. He carries it knowing that Christ walks with him. He carries it knowing that the story is not finished. He carries it knowing that what begins in tears may end in glory.

The risen Christ teaches us to read our lives as He taught the disciples to read the Scriptures: with the understanding that the path to glory runs through sacrifice. What feels like loss may be preparation. What feels like defeat may be the soil of renewal. What feels like death may be the beginning of resurrection. This is not wishful thinking. It is the pattern God Himself has revealed by raising Jesus from the dead.

And so, the Christian learns to live with a posture of expectation. Not naïve optimism, but theological hope. The expectation that God is at work even where we cannot see Him. The expectation that grace is growing like a seed hidden beneath the earth. The expectation that the risen Lord is shaping a future that reflects His victory. The expectation that what we commit to Him—our wounds, our fears, our tears—will be gathered into His resurrected life.

This expectation is not easy. But it is possible because Christ is risen. The One who kept His wounds in glory now keeps His promise to His people. He goes before them. He walks with them. He intercedes for them. He strengthens them. He holds their stories in His hands. He gathers their suffering into His own. He rewrites what sin and sorrow tried to erase. He transforms wounds into witness, grief into grace, loss into life.

THE RESURRECTION AND THE REWRITING OF PAIN

The Resurrection does not only reveal that Christ lives. It reveals that Christ reigns. He reigns as the Lamb who was slain. He reigns as the Firstborn from the dead. He reigns as the One who holds the keys of death and Hades. He reigns as the Shepherd who leads His flock through valleys that once inspired terror. He reigns as the Lord who lifts His wounded hands in blessing over a world still aching for redemption.

And this is why the Resurrection is the heart of Christian hope. It is the promise that no suffering endured in union with Christ will end in darkness. It is the assurance that the Cross is not a tomb but a threshold. It is the proclamation that love is stronger than death, grace stronger than sin, and God's fidelity stronger than every wound the world can inflict. The Resurrection rewrites the meaning of human pain because it reveals the destiny of the human heart: to share in the glory of the One who rose bearing our sorrows, and who will never cease to make all things new.

9

When the Victory Becomes a Vocation

The Resurrection does not close the story of suffering; it opens a new one. When Christ rises from the dead, the victory He reveals is not a private triumph. It is the beginning of a life He intends to pour into His people. The empty tomb is not only the vindication of Jesus. It is the foundation of the Church. And because the Church is His Body, the pattern of His life becomes the pattern of her life. If He passed through suffering into glory, then those who belong to Him will pass along the same path. This is the unbroken logic of the New Testament, the logic that binds Easter morning to the life of every believer.

The disciples learn this slowly. In the days after the Resurrection, they remain astonished, joyful, and overwhelmed. They rejoice in the presence of the risen Christ, yet they have not yet understood the full consequence of His rising. Jesus must teach them still. He must open the Scriptures again. He must breathe the Spirit upon them. He must send them out. Only then will they grasp that the glory they behold is not meant to be admired from a distance; it is meant to be lived from within.

This is why Jesus appears to them repeatedly, not merely to prove that He is alive, but to shape them into a people capable of carrying

His mission. The Resurrection is the moment when God entrusts His victory to human hands. It is the moment when the life of the new creation takes root in a community. The same power that raised Jesus from the dead does not remain locked in the past. It is poured out upon the apostles. It becomes the breath of the Church. It becomes the grace that enables ordinary men and women to live the extraordinary mystery of union with Christ.

Pentecost makes this truth unmistakable. When the Holy Spirit descends, the apostles are transformed. Fear gives way to courage. Uncertainty gives way to proclamation. A faith once carried in secret becomes a faith announced to the world. But even more importantly, the Spirit reveals the shape of this new life: it is cruciform. The apostles preach a risen Christ, yet they do so with the full knowledge that following Him will cost them everything. The Spirit does not remove the Cross from their future. He gives them the strength to carry it.

This is the moment when the meaning of suffering changes forever. It is no longer simply the plight of a fallen world. It becomes the way the Church participates in the mystery of Christ. Suffering, once a sign of defeat, becomes a sign of fidelity. The apostles rejoice when they are found worthy to suffer for His Name. They do not seek hardship, but they do not fear it. They understand now that suffering joined to Christ is not sterile. It is fruitful. It becomes a means by which the grace of God flows into the world.

From this point forward, the Church becomes the place where the Resurrection and the Cross meet in the lives of believers. She becomes the community in which suffering is not hidden but sanctified. She becomes the home where human weakness becomes the stage for divine strength. She becomes the school where love is purified, courage is formed, and sacrifice becomes the language of communion. The Church does not explain suffering away. She carries it. She carries it because her Lord carried it, and she carries it with the confidence that His victory will be hers.

This is why the saints become so central to the Christian story. They are not anomalies. They are not exceptions. They are the clearest expressions of what the Church is meant to be. In them, the pattern of Christ's life becomes visible again. Their holiness is never detached from the Cross. Their joy is never superficial. Their faith is never sentimental. They see the world as it truly is—a world redeemed by a God who has taken suffering into His own heart. And because they see this clearly, they embrace the Cross not as an enemy, but as a gift. Not because pain is good, but because love is worth its cost.

The saints are the ones who perceive reality in its deepest dimension. They recognise that suffering does not diminish the dignity of the human person; it reveals it. It reveals what a person treasures. It reveals what a person hopes for. It reveals whether a person belongs to himself or to God. The saints show us what happens when suffering is not avoided or resented, but entrusted to the One who can transform it. Their lives become a commentary on the Gospel, written not in ink but in endurance. They show us that the Resurrection is not a doctrine to be memorised but a power to be lived.

This becomes especially clear in the martyrdoms that shape the early Church. Men and women who had once been ordinary become radiant with courage. They stand before emperors and executioners without fear, not because they are strong, but because they belong to Christ. Their suffering becomes a testimony that death no longer reigns. Their blood becomes the seed of the Church because it flows from a hope stronger than death. They bear witness that suffering united to Christ does not extinguish life; it bears fruit in ways the world cannot fathom.

And where martyrdom is not given, other forms of sacrifice take root. The daily endurance of illness, the long patience of parenthood, the hidden fidelity of marriage, the tireless labour of priests and religious—these too become places where holiness is forged. The saints teach us that suffering does not need to be dramatic to be redemptive. It needs only to be offered. It needs only to be lived in union with the One whose Cross has become the source of all grace.

In this way, the Church becomes the living continuation of Christ's Paschal mystery. She does not merely remember the Cross. She shares it. She does not merely proclaim the Resurrection. She lives it. And because she does, the world continues to see in her the mystery of divine love at work—love that suffers, love that sacrifices, love that redeems.

This is the movement that Part III will enter. It will not revisit the explanations given earlier. It will turn our attention to the people who have lived these truths with their whole being. It will explore the way the saints embraced suffering not with despair, but with clarity—because they understood that suffering, when joined to Christ, becomes a chisel in the hands of God. It shapes the soul. It enlarges the heart. It makes room for a love that the world cannot give.

Before we look to them directly, we stand at the threshold where doctrine becomes flesh. The Resurrection has told us what God has done. The Church will now show us what God continues to do. The saints will show us what happens when the fire of divine love meets the frailty of human life. And in their stories, we will discover that the mystery of suffering does not end with understanding. It ends with transformation—a transformation that allows the believer to say, with confidence and hope, that every cross carried in faith becomes a place where the risen Christ is found.

III

The Church, the Saints, and the Fire

10

Why The Saints Embrace The Cross

The saints are not strange exceptions in the Christian story. They are not spiritual athletes who happen to enjoy hardships or mystics who simply feel less pain than the rest of us. They are not people who went looking for suffering as if suffering itself were a virtue. Nothing could be further from the truth. The saints embraced the Cross for one reason: they loved the Lord who carried it. They saw in Christ's Passion the deepest revelation of who God is and who they were called to become. And because they loved Him, they wanted to follow Him wherever He led—even into the places where love demands sacrifice.

From the outside, this can seem puzzling. The modern mind looks at the lives of the saints and sees contradictions. It sees people who endured illnesses without complaint, injustices without bitterness, humiliations without resentment. It sees men and women who gave up comfort, reputation, and sometimes even life itself. And it whispers, sometimes with suspicion and sometimes with pity, "Why would anyone choose such a path?" But this question reveals more about our assumptions than theirs. It assumes that suffering is always meaningless. It assumes that the highest good is comfort. It assumes that love should cost nothing. The saints thought differently because

Christ taught differently.

Jesus never pretended that following Him would be easy. He never promised a life protected from pain. In fact, He promised the opposite. "If anyone would come after Me, let him deny himself, take up his cross daily, and follow Me." These words are not spiritual decoration. They are the structure of Christian discipleship. They are the invitation into a life shaped by love that is willing to give itself completely. The saints did not hear these words as a threat. They heard them as a gift—the gift of becoming like Christ.

They understood something that many overlook: the Cross is not a symbol of defeat. It is the place where divine love is revealed in its fullest form. At Calvary, God shows that love is not mere sentiment but self-giving. Love is not fragile. Love is strong enough to bear the weight of the world's sin. Love is not fearful. Love is willing to go where suffering tries to reign. When the saints looked at the Cross, they did not see cruelty; they saw clarity. They saw reality. They saw that love—true love—always carries a cost. And they saw that Christ had carried that cost first.

This is why the saints embraced the Cross. Not because they were enamoured with pain, but because they were captivated by love. They believed that union with Christ was worth any sacrifice. They believed that suffering joined to Him became a place of grace. They believed that the wounds they carried in faith would one day shine with the same glory that radiated from His risen Body. Their embrace of the Cross did not come from emotional fervour or human endurance. It came from a vision formed by the Gospel: that Christ's path is the only path that leads to life.

But this vision did not arise from naïveté. The saints were not immune to sorrow. They felt the sting of loss, the weight of illness, the pain of betrayal. They wept. They struggled. They doubted. But in all of this, they discovered what modern culture often misses: suffering reveals the truth of the heart. It reveals what we trust. It reveals what we value. It reveals whether our faith rests on circumstances or on Christ Himself. This is why suffering has a purifying power. It strips away illusions. It exposes false loves. It draws the soul into a deeper dependence on God.

When the saints speak about suffering, they are not romanticizing it. They are describing what grace accomplishes in the depths of the soul. They are describing how suffering, when united to Christ, becomes a chisel in the hands of God—shaping, refining, and enlarging the heart. They speak of suffering as a fire because fire purifies. They speak of trials as a school because trials teach. They speak of the Cross as a gift because it leads to communion.

This clarity is what distinguishes the saints from the world around them. They saw reality through the lens of Christ's Passion and Resurrection. They saw that suffering is not the end of the story but the place where God begins His deepest work. They saw that the Cross is not an interruption to the spiritual life; it is the pathway into it. They saw that God does not waste a single tear offered to Him in faith. They saw that love, when tested by suffering, becomes stronger—not weaker.

The modern world often fails to see this because it has forgotten the meaning of sacrifice. It assumes that love should be effortless and that suffering is always a threat. But the saints knew that love matures through fidelity, and fidelity often requires endurance. They knew that the virtues that sustain relationships, families, and vocations are forged in the fires of difficulty. They knew that suffering embraced in bitterness destroys the heart, but suffering embraced in faith enlarges it.

This is why the saints appear so luminous. They are not radiant because their lives were easy. They are radiant because they allowed grace to transfigure their suffering. They discovered that the Cross does not diminish a person; it deepens him. It teaches humility by revealing our dependence. It teaches compassion by opening our eyes to the pain of others. It teaches patience by purifying desire. It teaches hope by anchoring the soul in the God who raises the dead.

In this way, the saints become living commentaries on Scripture. Their lives echo the mystery of Christ. They show that the Gospel is not an idea but a life—a life shaped by sacrifice and crowned with glory. They show that belief without fidelity is fragile, but fidelity grounded in the Cross is unshakable. They show that love capable of suffering is love capable of enduring.

And so we turn to them not to admire from a distance but to learn how to follow Christ more deeply. The saints show us what happens when a life is surrendered to God. They show us what suffering can become when it is joined to Christ. They show us that the Cross is not the burden of a few extraordinary Christians—it is the vocation of every disciple.

The saints teach us that what matters is not the presence of suffering, but the *direction* of suffering. Suffering can turn a heart inward on itself or outward toward God. It can harden a person or soften him. It can make him bitter or make him holy. The saints are those who allowed suffering to lead them deeper into the life of Christ. They discovered that the Cross, when accepted with faith, becomes a meeting place—a place where God draws near, where the soul learns to trust, where love is purified.

This is why suffering never isolated the saints. It united them. It united them to Christ, and through Christ, it united them to the world they served. Their suffering was never self-absorbed. It was intercessory. They carried their trials with an awareness that God was doing something in them and through them. Even the most hidden afflictions became a way of participating in Christ's redeeming love. Their willingness to endure did not make them withdrawn. It made them generous. Their pain did not turn them inward. It turned them outward, toward God and toward others.

But the saints did not come to this understanding easily. Each of them had to pass through moments of confusion, nights of the soul, and trials that stretched them beyond their strength. What made them saints was not the absence of struggle, but the perseverance of faith. They learned to cling to Christ when every earthly support failed. They learned to surrender their wills when their desires collided with God's timing. They learned to pray not for escape, but for endurance. They learned to trust that God was present even when He seemed silent.

Consider the way they speak of suffering. St. Thérèse, with her little way of simplicity, teaches that even the smallest trials—misunderstandings, inconveniences, hidden sacrifices—can become holy when offered to God. She does not glorify pain; she glorifies love. She shows that suffering embraced with humility becomes a way of loving God with a purity that nothing else can produce. In her witness, we learn that the Cross is not always dramatic. Sometimes it is the quiet acceptance of the ordinary difficulties that slowly shape the soul into the image of Christ.

St. John of the Cross offers another dimension. He speaks of the dark night not as abandonment but as purification. In the darkness, the soul learns to love God for His sake, not for the consolations He gives. The night strips away spiritual pride, false security, and all the ways we cling to our own understanding. It is painful, yes. But it is the pain of healing—the withdrawal of every lesser support until the soul rests on God alone. John does not teach that suffering is good. He teaches that the soul, purified by suffering, becomes capable of a deeper union with God.

Padre Pio adds yet another witness. He bore physical suffering, spiritual trials, and misunderstanding with remarkable patience. His life shows that suffering can become a form of intercession—a way of standing in the gap for others. He did not carry his wounds privately. He carried them for the sake of those entrusted to him. His acceptance of hardship became a channel of grace for countless souls. He teaches us that the Cross, when embraced in love, becomes a gift offered for others, not merely endured for oneself.

And then there is Maximilian Kolbe, whose martyrdom reveals the extremity of Christian charity. In the horror of Auschwitz, he stepped forward to take the place of another man condemned to die. Kolbe's act was not driven by a fascination with suffering. It was driven by love. It was the fruit of a life shaped entirely by the pattern of Christ. He shows us, with breathtaking clarity, that the Cross is not about pain—it is about self-gift. It is the willingness to give one's life for another, just as Christ gave His life for the world.

These saints, different in personality and vocation, share one truth: suffering becomes fruitful when it is united to Christ. Their lives reveal that the Cross does not diminish the human person. It enlarges him. It expands his capacity to love. It stretches his heart beyond self-interest. It deepens his compassion. It frees him from the illusion that life is meant to be comfortable. And it anchors him in the reality that life is meant to be holy.

The saints embraced the Cross because they understood what it accomplishes. They knew that suffering endured with Christ is never wasted. They knew that the Cross is the furnace where faith is tested, purified, and strengthened. They knew that holiness does not grow in perfect conditions but in the soil of sacrifice. They knew that love matures most deeply where it is most tested. And they knew that Christ Himself meets His disciples in these very places—not as a distant observer, but as the companion who carries the heavier end of the Cross.

The world sees this and is bewildered. It thinks the saints are extreme. It thinks their sacrifices are unnecessary. It thinks their endurance is misguided. But the world sees only the surface. It does not see the joy that flows from union with Christ. It does not see the freedom that comes from detachment. It does not see the peace that takes root in a heart shaped by grace. The saints see what the world does not: suffering is not the enemy of love. It is the place where love becomes real.

The saints show us that the Cross is not a detour in the Christian life; it is the path itself. They did not arrive at holiness by avoiding struggle. They arrived there by allowing struggle to draw them deeper into the mystery of Christ's love. And this is where their witness becomes essential for every believer—because they reveal that the Cross is not an obstacle to union with God. It is the very means by which that union unfolds.

At the heart of their vision is a truth woven throughout Scripture: God forms His people through adversity. Israel learned this in the wilderness. David learned it in exile. The prophets learned it in rejection. The apostles learned it in persecution. The saints simply continue this pattern in the life of the Church. They read their trials through the same lens God used to shape His people throughout salvation history. They recognised that suffering is not a sign of divine absence. It is often the place where God is most present, refining the heart and strengthening faith.

This is why the saints never interpreted their hardships as punishment. They interpreted them as participation. They saw their trials as a way of sharing in the life of Christ, who learned obedience "through what He suffered." They knew that discipleship means imitation, and imitation must include the Cross. Not because God delights in seeing His children suffer, but because love, when purified, becomes more capable of receiving His grace. The saints embraced suffering because they trusted the One who allows it. They knew His purposes are always for good, even when the path is shrouded in mystery.

When we look closely at their lives, we discover something striking: the saints did not become less human through suffering—they became more human. Their trials did not shrink their hearts; they expanded them. Their wounds did not close them off; they made them more open to the needs of others. Their crosses did not harden them; they made them tender. This is the paradox at the centre of Christian holiness: when suffering is joined to Christ, it produces not despair but compassion, not bitterness but mercy, not resignation but hope.

This transformation was not automatic. It required a continual turning toward God, especially in the moments when suffering threatened to overwhelm them. The saints prayed in their trials, not merely to be delivered from them but to be faithful within them. They asked for the grace to endure, the grace to trust, the grace to love. They sought not escape from suffering but union with Christ through it. This prayerful surrender became the seed of their holiness. It was in these hidden, interior acts of trust that their souls were shaped by the Cross.

The saints also teach us that suffering embraced in faith becomes a form of wisdom. They saw life with remarkable clarity because their trials stripped away illusions. They saw the world's promises for what they are—temporary, fragile, unable to satisfy. They saw the human heart for what it is—hungry for God, restless until it rests in Him. They saw Christ for who He is—the One who enters every sorrow, transforms it from within, and leads His people through it into glory. The saints were not escapists. They were realists—spiritual realists who understood the true landscape of the soul.

This is why their writings and testimonies carry such authority. They do not speak from theory. They speak from experience—experience that has been purified by the Cross and illuminated by the Resurrection. Their words have weight because their lives bear witness to the truth they proclaim. They show us that suffering does not need to be interpreted through the lens of fear. It can be interpreted through the lens of faith. And that shift in interpretation changes everything.

For the saints, the Cross was never an object to admire from afar. It was a pattern to adopt. They believed Jesus meant what He said when He invited His disciples to take up their crosses daily. They understood that this invitation was not a call to gloom but a call to love. The Cross reveals love that is willing to give, willing to endure, willing to sacrifice. When the saints embraced the Cross, they were embracing the form of love revealed by Christ—a love that saves.

Yet their embrace of the Cross never made them gloomy or severe. Quite the opposite. They are the most joyful people in the Church's history. Their joy did not come from a life free of suffering. It came from a life united to Christ. They discovered that joy does not depend on circumstances but on communion. It is the fruit of a heart anchored in God. Their joy was not fragile. It endured because it was rooted in the One who conquered death. They show us that joy, far from being opposed to suffering, often grows precisely through it.

This is why the saints become such powerful witnesses in every age. They remind us that holiness is possible. They show us that suffering does not need to paralyse faith or extinguish hope. They demonstrate that grace can reshape even the most painful experiences. And they invite us to see our own trials not as barriers to God but as pathways toward Him.

The transformation we see in the saints is not the result of temperament or personality. It is the result of grace received in a heart willing to be shaped. They were not born with a special capacity for suffering. They were born with the same frailties, fears, and limitations we all carry. What distinguishes them is not strength of will, but depth of surrender. They allowed God to work where nature faltered. They entrusted their wounds to the One whose own wounds had become channels of glory. And because they entrusted themselves to Him, He shaped them into reflections of His own love.

This is why the saints become so essential to the Church's understanding of suffering. They show us what God can accomplish in a soul that refuses to let suffering become self-absorption. They reveal that holiness is not a flight from the world's pain but a transformation of it. Their lives are sacraments of hope—signs that even the darkest trials can become places where the presence of Christ is encountered. They stand as witnesses that suffering, when joined to Him, becomes not a barrier but a bridge.

The saints also remind us that suffering is not simply endured. It is interpreted. And the interpretation makes all the difference. When suffering is interpreted through the lens of fear, it becomes a threat. When interpreted through the lens of pride, it becomes a grievance. When interpreted through the lens of Christ, it becomes a participation. The saints interpret their trials through the Gospel. They see their suffering as a share in Christ's own offering, a moment when their lives can be conformed more deeply to His. This is not romanticism. It is realism—the realism of faith that sees God's hand where others see only loss.

Their ability to do this springs from a profound intimacy with Christ. They knew Him not as an idea, but as a presence. They encountered Him in prayer, in silence, in the sacraments, and in the ordinary events of life. This intimacy gave them confidence in His love. They trusted that He would not lead them into suffering without leading them through it. They trusted that whatever He allowed, He allowed for their good. They trusted that the Cross they carried was already carried by Him. This trust did not remove pain, but it removed fear. It allowed them to walk the path of suffering with peace.

This peace was not passive. It was active, resilient, and alive. The saints carried a calm that did not come from resignation but from conviction. They believed what the Resurrection proclaimed: that death is not final, that suffering is not sovereign, that love is stronger than every wound. This conviction gave them courage to endure trials that would have crushed others. It made them free—free from the fear of loss, free from the fear of humiliation, free from the fear of death. Their freedom was the fruit of the Cross.

And because they were free, they could love. They could love with a generosity that astonished the world. They could forgive when forgiveness seemed impossible. They could serve when service required sacrifice. They could give themselves without calculation. Their suffering did not diminish their love. It purified it. It stripped away the layers of self-interest and pride that so often limit human affection. The saints embraced the Cross because it taught them to love as Christ loves—completely, freely, and without reserve.

This is perhaps the most striking aspect of their lives: suffering made them more loving. In a world that assumes suffering only damages, the saints become a contradiction. They are not diminished. They are enlarged. They become more compassionate, more patient, more understanding. Their own wounds make them gentle toward the wounded. Their own tears make them attentive to the tears of others. Their own trials make them wise in the ways of the heart. They show us that suffering does not have to make a person smaller. It can make him greater—greater in charity, greater in humility, greater in hope.

And because they loved, they became fruitful. Their lives bore the kind of fruit that cannot be measured in achievements or recognitions. Their fruit was the transformation of souls, the renewal of communities, the strengthening of the Church. Their fruit was the hidden work of grace that unfolded quietly but powerfully through their fidelity. The saints embraced the Cross because they knew it was the place where grace flows most abundantly. They knew that

God accomplishes His greatest works through hearts that are willing to give themselves completely.

The saints stand before us as living proof that suffering does not nullify the Christian life. It deepens it. They show us that holiness is not the absence of struggle but the presence of Christ in the midst of struggle. They teach us that suffering carried with Christ becomes fruitful, meaningful, and redemptive. They invite us not to fear the Cross but to follow the One who carried it before us.

The saints reveal a truth that stands at the heart of the Christian mystery: the Cross does not end with suffering. It ends with love. And because it ends with love, it becomes the place where God accomplishes His greatest work. The saints show us that this work begins not when life is easy, but when life is difficult. It begins when the soul stands before the undeniable reality of its own weakness and chooses, despite everything, to trust in the strength of God. It is in that moment—when the heart yields in faith—that suffering begins to change. It ceases to be a burden carried alone. It becomes a participation in something infinitely larger than the self.

This participation is the key to everything. The saints did not endure suffering by relying on their own endurance. They endured it because they allowed their suffering to be taken up into the suffering of Christ. They believed that He was with them in every trial, not as a distant observer, but as the One who had walked the path before them. Their suffering became a place of communion, a place where the life of Christ was poured more deeply into their souls. And because this communion shaped them from within, their lives began to resemble His.

When we look at the saints, we see this resemblance everywhere. We see it in their patience during affliction, in their gentleness toward those who harmed them, in their perseverance when they had every reason to give up. We see it in the way their lives bear the marks of Christ—not in literal wounds, but in the unmistakable imprint of sacrificial love. Their stories echo the Gospel because their hearts were shaped by the same mystery that shaped the life of Jesus.

This resemblance is not accidental. It is the fruit of the Cross. The saints did not become holy in spite of suffering. They became holy through suffering. Not because suffering has power on its own, but because Christ has power in suffering. The Cross becomes the place where divine love meets human frailty, where the grace of God works most deeply, where the soul learns to surrender, trust, and love. The saints embraced the Cross because they discovered what it accomplishes—not only in the world, but in the heart.

And this is the great invitation that their lives extend to us. The saints do not stand before us as unattainable ideals. They stand before us as reminders of what God desires to accomplish in every believer. They show us that the path of holiness is not for a select few. It is for all who belong to Christ. The Cross they carried is not theirs alone. It is the Cross Christ gives to each of His disciples, tailored to the contours of each life, designed for the good of each soul.

The saints teach us that when suffering comes—and it will come—our task is not to run from it, but to bring it to Christ. To place it in His hands. To trust that He will use it. Suffering becomes unbearable when we carry it alone. It becomes transformative when we allow Him to carry it with us. The saints embraced the Cross because they discovered that Christ was present in it, and that His presence turned every trial into a place of grace.

Their witness stands as a challenge to the modern world, which seeks comfort without cost and meaning without sacrifice. The saints reveal a different vision—one in which love is measured not by how little it suffers, but by how much it gives. They show us that a life without sacrifice becomes shallow, but a life shaped by the Cross becomes radiant. Their joy, their peace, their holiness—all of it flows from the mystery of a love that does not flee suffering but transforms it.

In their lives, we see what it means to follow Christ fully. We see that suffering is not an obstacle to holiness but a catalyst for it. We see that the Cross is not the enemy of joy but its foundation. We see that the saints did not embrace suffering for its own sake; they embraced the One who sanctified it. And because they did, their lives shine with a clarity that draws every generation toward the truth of the Gospel.

The saints embraced the Cross because they knew Christ embraced them. Their suffering became a place where His love was revealed, where their souls were refined, where their hearts became capable of a love that reflects His own. This is the mystery at the heart of Christian discipleship. The Cross, when carried with Christ, becomes the place where human love is united to divine love. It becomes the furnace where the heart is purified. It becomes the path that leads to resurrection.

And so this chapter stands as a threshold. The saints have shown us what suffering becomes when grace enters it. They have shown us what it means to share in the life of Christ. They invite us to see the Cross not as a burden to be feared but as a gift to be received. Not because suffering is good, but because God's love is greater. And it is that love—revealed in the saints, poured out in the Church, anchored in the Cross—that prepares us for the mystery of redemptive suffering that unfolds next.

11

Redemptive Suffering And Participation In Christ

There are few phrases in Catholic life more familiar—and more misunderstood—than the simple counsel, "Offer it up." For many, the words sound like a dismissal, a way of silencing complaint or avoiding honest emotion. For others, it feels like a pious cliché, a spiritual band-aid placed over wounds that run far deeper than any phrase can reach. But in the heart of the Church, and in the pages of Scripture, this simple expression carries a meaning far richer and far more demanding than most people realize. To "offer it up" is not an escape from suffering. It is a vocation within suffering. It is the invitation to join our trials to the redeeming love poured out by Christ on the Cross.

The entire Christian vision of redemptive suffering begins here: with Christ. Not with our endurance, not with our courage, not with our ability to cope. Everything begins with the Passion of the Lord. The Cross is not one event among many in His life—it is the centre of His mission, the place where the covenant reaches its fulfillment, the hour in which He offers Himself entirely to the Father for the salvation of the world. When Jesus suffers, He does not merely endure evil. He transforms it. He takes what sin has unleashed and offers it in love, turning suffering into sacrifice, pain into offering, death into life.

And this is precisely where the heart of Christian participation is found. Christ's sacrifice is complete, perfect, and sufficient. Nothing can be added to what He has accomplished. Yet in the mystery of grace, He invites His people to share in what He has done. He does not save us from a distance. He saves us by drawing us into His own offering. This is the covenant pattern woven throughout the whole of Scripture. God accomplishes His work, and then He invites His people to join Him in it. He forms Noah, Abraham, Moses, David—not because He needs them, but because love desires participation. And in the fullness of time, He forms a new people in Christ, a people who share in His life, His mission, and yes, even His suffering.

This is the meaning of St. Paul's astonishing words: "I rejoice in my sufferings for your sake, and in my flesh I complete what is lacking in Christ's afflictions for the sake of His Body, the Church." Paul is not claiming that Christ's sacrifice was insufficient. He is claiming something else entirely: that by grace, his own sufferings have been united to Christ's and therefore participate in the work Christ is still unfolding in the world. Paul does not see his trials as interruptions to ministry. He sees them as ministry. His sufferings are not obstacles to his mission. They have become part of the mission because they have been taken up into Christ.

This is the heart of redemptive suffering. It is not about creating value through pain. Pain, on its own, is destructive. Suffering, on its own, wounds. But suffering offered to God becomes something different. It becomes prayer. It becomes intercession. It becomes participation in the redeeming love of Christ. The Cross is not simply an event we admire. It is a mystery we enter. The saints understood this. Paul understood it. The early Church understood it. This is why suffering becomes not a reason for despair, but an invitation to communion.

And yet, this teaching cannot be grasped unless we begin where the Church always begins: with baptism. In baptism, we are united to Christ's death and resurrection. We are grafted into Him like branches into a vine. His life becomes the life of His people. His Spirit becomes the breath of their souls. His mission becomes theirs. And because of this, His offering becomes the pattern of their lives. Baptism is not a symbol. It is a reality. It means that the believer does not suffer alone. He suffers in Christ. He suffers with Christ. He suffers as a member of the Body joined to its Head.

This is why the Church can speak of "participation" in Christ's Passion. It is not a poetic metaphor. It is a sacramental truth. Our sufferings, when united to Him, are taken up into His own act of offering. They do not compete with His Cross; they are drawn into it. They do not supplement His sacrifice; they are transformed by it. Grace does this. Grace takes the raw material of human pain and shapes it into something that resembles Christ's own self-gift to the Father. In the hands of grace, suffering ceases to be a dead weight. It becomes a living offering.

But this participation must be understood rightly. It does not mean that we become redeemers parallel to Christ. It means we become instruments through which His redemption reaches others. God allows His people to share in His work not because He lacks anything, but because He desires to involve His children in the very life of His Son. This is the logic of love: it seeks union. It seeks collaboration. It seeks communion. And so Christ gives His people the privilege of joining their sufferings to His own, allowing their crosses to become places where His grace flows into the world.

When the Church speaks of "co-redemptive" suffering, this is what it means—*co* not as equal, but as "with." The Redeemer draws His people into His redeeming love. He does not erase their trials; He invests them with purpose. He does not remove their crosses; He teaches them to carry them with Him. He does not promise a life without suffering; He promises a life in which suffering becomes a path to union.

This is why the saints speak so boldly about the Cross. They do not glorify pain. They glorify the grace that transforms pain. They glorify the union that suffering offers. They glorify the love that suffering can express. They lived what Paul preached: "present your bodies as a living sacrifice." A living sacrifice is not an idea. It is a life—your life, my life, shaped by the same pattern that shaped Christ's.

Redemptive suffering is not a theory. It is the mystery of love at work in the heart of a disciple.

The heart of redemptive suffering is not human strength—it is divine union. Everything depends on union. Without union with Christ, suffering isolates. It narrows the soul. It breeds resentment or despair. But when suffering is joined to the suffering of Christ, it is caught up into a love that is stronger than death. That union changes everything. It does not always change the circumstances. It does not remove the wound. But it changes the meaning of the wound. It changes the direction of the suffering. It changes what suffering becomes in the hands of God.

This is why redemptive suffering must be approached through Christology before psychology. The modern world tries to resolve suffering through methods that are, at best, therapeutic but not transformative. Christ does not teach us how to escape suffering. He teaches us how to offer suffering. He teaches us how to let suffering become a place where love is proved, where trust is deepened, and where the heart becomes conformed to His own Heart.

The most decisive truth the New Testament teaches about suffering is found in the pattern of Christ's life: He loved the Father through suffering. He obeyed the Father through suffering. He fulfilled the mission of the Father through suffering. "Although He was a Son, He learned obedience through what He suffered." These words from the Letter to the Hebrews do not mean that Christ lacked obedience before His Passion. They mean that obedience reached its fullness through His Passion. Suffering became the place where love was completed.

This is what the saints understood so clearly. They saw in the sufferings of Christ the shape of their own vocation. Holiness is not achieved by escaping the Cross but by carrying it. Love matures under weight. Faith grows under pressure. Hope ripens in darkness. The Cross reveals this truth, not as an abstract principle, but as the living form of divine love. Every believer who shares in Christ's life must also share in His pattern of love.

And this is why redemptive suffering is not peripheral to the Christian life. It is central. Christ does not redeem the world by teaching or by miracle alone. He redeems the world by offering Himself. His suffering becomes a sacrifice because His suffering becomes a gift. And in the mystery of grace, the believer's suffering can also become a gift—not a gift that saves, but a gift that participates in the saving love of God.

To understand this, we must recognise that suffering is never neutral in Scripture. It always pushes the heart in one of two directions: toward God or away from Him. Suffering either hardens the heart or purifies it. It either diminishes love or deepens it. This is why suffering has such significance in the Christian life. It reveals where we stand before God. It uncovers the foundations on which we have built our lives. And when these foundations are weak, suffering exposes the cracks so that grace can rebuild what sin has fractured.

When suffering is embraced with faith, something remarkable happens. The soul is not simply enduring. It is responding. It is answering Christ. It is placing its trust in Him, not because He removes the cross, but because He carries it with us. Trust becomes the act that transforms suffering into offering. When the believer says, "Lord, I give this to You," suffering moves from the realm of pain to the realm of sacrificial love. It becomes prayer. It becomes worship.

This is why the Church insists that suffering can become meritorious—not because pain earns anything, but because love offered in union with Christ participates in His saving work. Grace elevates the soul. It allows the believer to stand within the mystery of the Cross. Nothing in Christian life is more intimate than this union. Prayer unites us to Christ's mind. Charity unites us to Christ's heart. But suffering unites us to Christ's Passion.

Yet this union must be understood with theological clarity. The believer does not redeem himself. The believer does not redeem others by his own suffering. Christ alone is Redeemer. But the Redeemer draws the redeemed into His redeeming work. This is the marvel of the Gospel: God allows His children to share in what He accomplishes. The Cross is not only the source of salvation; it becomes the pattern of participation. The believer is not a spectator. He is a participant, called to share in the mystery that saved him.

Paul says it plainly: "We are heirs of God and fellow heirs with Christ, provided we suffer with Him, in order that we may also be glorified with Him." To be an heir with Christ is to share not only His glory but His path. The path includes suffering, but suffering is not the destination. It is the way love is tested and proven. It is the way the heart is shaped for glory.

In this light, the phrase "offer it up" emerges as something far more profound than a spiritual cliché. It becomes a summary of the entire Christian mystery. It becomes the Church's way of saying: Bring your suffering to Christ. Join it to His sacrifice. Let it become part of His offering to the Father. Let your wounds touch His wounds, not to diminish His, but to allow His love to transform yours.

This participation is not automatic. It requires intention. It requires surrender. It requires an interior act of the will—a spiritual offering made in faith. This is why the saints were so deliberate in uniting their sufferings to Christ. They did not wait for pain to become meaningful by itself. They made it meaningful by joining it to the One who gives all things meaning.

In this union, suffering becomes not only bearable but fruitful. It becomes a source of grace—not because suffering has power, but because Christ has power, and suffering is the place where Christ's power is often most vividly revealed.

The more deeply we enter this mystery, the clearer it becomes that redemptive suffering is not an individual achievement but a supernatural gift. Participation in Christ's Passion is grace from beginning to end. It is grace that stirs the heart to trust. It is grace that moves the will to offer. It is grace that unites the soul to Christ. And it is grace that allows the suffering of one believer to bear fruit in the life of another, just as the suffering of the Head bore fruit in the life of His Body. The Cross has not lost its power. It continues to work, and it works through those who are joined to Christ.

This is why the Church speaks so carefully about cooperation with grace. It is not that we contribute something Christ lacks. It is that Christ chooses to accomplish His work through His Body. He chooses to make our lives instruments of His mercy. He chooses to make our willingness a vessel for His love. In the covenant, God binds Himself to His people, and then He binds His people to His mission. He does not act without them. He acts through them. This is not a limitation of His power but an expression of His love. The God who could redeem the world alone desires to redeem it with His children at His side.

This truth illuminates one of the great paradoxes of the Christian life: suffering, when united with Christ, becomes fruitful not only for the one who suffers, but for the entire Body of Christ. When

Paul rejoices in his sufferings "for your sake," he is expressing the covenant solidarity that defines the Church. The believer's suffering, offered in faith, becomes a channel of grace for others. It strengthens, consoles, purifies, intercedes. God uses the wounds of His people as instruments of mercy. This is the logic of the Body of Christ, where no member suffers alone and no act of love remains isolated.

This raises an important question: How can suffering—even when willingly offered—become an act of love? The answer is found in the interior life of Christ. When Jesus suffered on the Cross, He did not simply endure pain; He freely offered Himself. His suffering became redemptive because His suffering became a gift. Every moment of His Passion was suffused with love—love for the Father, love for the world, love for the men and women whose sins He bore. The gift was not measured by the intensity of pain, but by the intensity of love. Pain, in itself, is not an offering. Pain offered in love becomes sacrifice.

This is the pattern of redemptive suffering. It is not the pain that redeems. It is the love that transforms the pain into offering. This truth rescues the doctrine from every distortion. Redemptive suffering is not a glorification of pain. It is a glorification of love. It is the proclamation that love can enter suffering and change its nature. Love can lift suffering from the realm of tragedy into the realm of sacrifice. Love can join our wounds to the wounds of Christ, allowing His redeeming work to shape our lives and touch the lives of others.

This is why the saints never praised suffering for its own sake. They praised the love that suffering made possible. They praised the union that suffering created. They praised the grace that suffering opened within the soul. When St. Thérèse of Lisieux spoke of suffering as her "daily bread," she was not extolling pain. She was extolling the opportunity to offer herself with Christ to the Father. When St. John of the Cross described the "dark night," he was not romanticizing spiritual desolation. He was unveiling the path by which God purifies the soul for union. When Padre Pio bore the stigmata, he was not celebrating wounds. He was celebrating the souls those wounds helped bring to Christ.

Every saint expresses the same truth in a different key: suffering becomes redemptive when it becomes love. The Cross is the shape of that love. And the believer who enters that shape finds not misery but meaning. He finds not emptiness but purpose. He finds not despair but hope. Suffering offered in union with Christ becomes a seed of grace. It bears fruit in ways the believer may never see in this life, yet fruit that God promises to bring forth in His time.

This brings us to a critical point: the Eucharist. Nowhere does the union of suffering and sacrifice become clearer than at the altar. In every Mass, Christ's perfect offering is made present. The one sacrifice of Calvary is not repeated; it is re-presented. And the faithful are invited to unite their lives to that offering. The altar becomes the place where the believer's crosses, carried throughout the week, can be joined to the Cross of Christ. It is here that suffering is consciously lifted into the hands of God. It is here that pain becomes prayer. It is here that the believer learns that his trials are not wasted. They are taken up into the offering that saves the world.

In this sacramental context, the phrase "offer it up" finds its deepest meaning. It means placing our suffering on the altar of Christ. It means letting the priestly sacrifice of Jesus transform our wounds into a participation in His redeeming love. It means recognising that the Cross we carry is not separate from the Cross He carried. It is His grace that allows our suffering to become an offering. It is His Spirit that moves our hearts to unite our pain to His. It is His presence in the Eucharist that makes our small sacrifices part of His infinite one.

This is the mystery of participation in Christ's Passion. It is not about endurance alone. It is about union. It is not about pain alone. It is about love. It is not about suffering alone. It is about grace. When the believer offers his suffering to God, he is not performing a private act. He is entering the very heart of the Christian mystery. He is stepping into the pattern Christ established. He is standing within the covenant, where God uses the weak to shame the strong, the wounded to heal the broken, and the suffering to carry His mercy into the world.

When we begin to see suffering through this sacramental lens, something in the heart shifts. The believer stops asking only, "Why is this happening to me?" and begins asking, "How can this be offered with Christ?" These two questions stand worlds apart. One leaves the soul turned inward, trapped within the limits of its own pain. The other turns the soul outward and upward, into the larger story God is telling—a story not of escape but of redemption. The change does not come through stoicism or denial. It comes through faith, the faith that knows Christ has entered every place where human suffering can reach.

This is the faith Paul lived. He never pretended that suffering was easy. He never minimized its agony. He never claimed that trial and hardship should be welcomed for their own sake. But he did believe—deeply, fiercely—that suffering joined to Christ bears fruit for the Kingdom. When he wrote to the Philippians about sharing "the fellowship of His sufferings," he was describing the most intimate communion available to the soul. Fellowship—koinonia—means participation, sharing, union. Paul understood that the Christian life is not merely imitation of Christ; it is communion with Christ. And that communion reaches its deepest expression when the believer bears the Cross with the One who first carried it for all.

This is the theology the Church has guarded across the centuries. God does not ask His children to carry crosses alone. He asks them to carry crosses *with Him*. This is why redemptive suffering is not a burden imposed but a grace bestowed. It is grace that allows the believer to say, "Lord, take this and use it." It is grace that gives the heart courage to offer what it does not understand. It is grace that enables the soul to trust that its suffering—unwelcome, painful, confusing—can become a place where God reveals His love in ways that comfort never could.

When suffering is joined to the Cross, it begins to reflect the shape of that love. The believer does not become heroic. He becomes surrendered. He does not become strong in himself. He becomes strong in Christ. Modern culture tells us that strength means self-reliance, the ability to bear burdens without help. Scripture tells us the opposite. True strength is dependence on God. True strength is the willingness to lean on the One who carries the heaviest part of the cross. True strength is the humility that allows grace to do for us what we cannot do for ourselves.

This humility is essential, because suffering always tempts the soul to retreat into itself. It tempts us to interpret pain as abandonment, silence as absence, trial as evidence that God has stepped back. But redemptive suffering reveals the opposite. Christ is never closer to a soul than when that soul stands where He once stood—before a cup that cannot pass, before a cross that must be carried, before a suffering that demands trust instead of explanation. He does not ask the believer to understand. He asks the believer to unite. And union, not comprehension, is what brings grace.

This brings us to a crucial truth: redemptive suffering is not primarily about feeling. It is about fidelity. It is about remaining in the covenant even when emotion collapses. It is about choosing to love God when consolation disappears. It is about standing with Christ in the place where He stood alone. The saints knew this well. They understood that suffering often brings dryness, heaviness, confusion. They understood that grace does not always feel like grace. Yet they also understood that fidelity offered in darkness is one of the greatest gifts the soul can give to God.

When a believer says, "Lord, I remain yours," even when the heart cannot feel His presence, that act becomes a profound participation in Christ's Passion. This is the hidden offering—the offering no one sees except the Father who "sees in secret." It is the offering Christ Himself made in Gethsemane. And it is the offering the Church invites every believer to make when suffering arrives.

In this light, redemptive suffering becomes not only a theological concept but a practical path. It teaches the soul how to pray when words fail. It teaches the heart how to trust when understanding vanishes. It teaches the believer how to live within the covenant even when the covenant feels costly. This is not abstract spirituality. It is the daily shape of Christian discipleship. The Cross is not an event we remember once a year. It is the pattern of life for every believer. And that pattern is not imposed by a harsh God. It is given by a loving God who desires to share His life with His children.

This is why the Church has always spoken of suffering as a participation, not a punishment. Punishment isolates. Participation unites. Punishment pushes the soul inward. Participation draws the soul into the life of Christ. Punishment ends in fear. Participation ends in communion. When suffering is seen as punishment, it becomes intolerable. When suffering is seen as participation, it becomes a mystery that can be lived, endured, and even offered with hope.

This hope does not erase the Cross. It illuminates it. Hope does not deny the reality of pain. It reveals the presence of God within it. Hope does not pretend that suffering is good. It proclaims that God can bring good from suffering. And this hope is not optimism. It is not the refusal to face reality. It is the confession that Christ is Lord of reality, including the places where reality hurts the most.

Hope rooted in the Cross leads to one of the greatest truths of redemptive suffering: nothing offered to God is wasted. No tear, no trial, no wound—nothing is lost when it is placed in the hands of the

Redeemer. The Cross guarantees this. Christ gathered every sorrow, every injustice, every wound into His offering. He allowed the worst of human suffering to become the place where divine love triumphed. And when the believer joins his suffering to Christ's, he steps into that triumph—not by removing pain, but by allowing grace to transform it.

The Cross teaches us that suffering is never the final word. Love is. And because love is the final word, the suffering borne in love becomes part of the very work Christ continues to accomplish through His Body, the Church. This is why the saints were convinced that suffering offered to God takes on a supernatural fruitfulness. They were not speaking metaphorically. They were describing a mystery as real as the sacraments themselves: when a believer offers his suffering to God, God receives it, sanctifies it, and pours it out again as grace for the world.

This truth stands at the heart of Christian intercession. We pray for others not only with our words but with our lives. Our sacrifices, our fasts, our hidden acts of fidelity—all of these become intercessory offerings when united to Christ. Suffering becomes one of the most powerful forms of this intercession. When the believer takes the pain that could have turned inward and instead turns it Godward, that act becomes a channel of mercy. It becomes a way God strengthens others, heals wounds, converts hearts, protects families, and draws souls closer to Himself.

This should never be romanticised. Suffering remains suffering. It wounds, it confuses, it tests the heart deeply. But the moment suffering is offered, it moves from the realm of isolation into the realm of communion. It becomes part of the mystery of the Church— one Body, many members, all united in Christ. Paul understood this with profound clarity. He knew that his trials, endured for the sake of the Gospel, were not merely personal burdens. They were offerings that strengthened the communities he loved. His chains became a blessing for others because they were united to Christ.

This is the difference between suffering endured and suffering offered. Suffering endured may build endurance. Suffering offered builds the Kingdom. It becomes an act of priesthood, not the ordained priesthood of the altar, but the baptismal priesthood that every Christian shares. The believer, united to Christ the High Priest, offers his life—its joys and its sorrows—as a spiritual sacrifice. This is what Peter calls the vocation of the "royal priesthood": to proclaim the works of God not only through speech, but through a life shaped by sacrificial love.

The Eucharist reveals this most clearly. At every Mass, the priest prays that God will accept "the sacrifice of our hands," a phrase that includes not only bread and wine, but the entire life of the faithful—every cross, every trial, every suffering. When the believer consciously places his suffering on the altar of Christ, the offering becomes more than endurance. It becomes worship. It becomes the believer's share in the one sacrifice that saves.

In this sense, redemptive suffering is nothing less than the believer's participation in the Paschal Mystery. The Paschal Mystery is not simply Christ's death and resurrection. It is the pattern of dying and rising that Christ invites His people to share. When suffering is offered in union with Him, it becomes a Paschal act—a dying with Christ that prepares the soul for rising with Him. This is why suffering offered in love always bears hope within it. The seed that dies in the soil is the seed that bears fruit. Christ has shown us this. The saints have lived it. And the believer who offers his suffering learns it from within.

This does not mean that every trial will feel meaningful. It does not mean that suffering will always be accompanied by consolation. Often, the opposite is true. The offering must sometimes be made in darkness, in dryness, in confusion. Yet even then, the act itself becomes a place of profound union with Christ. He prayed His most costly prayer—"Not My will, but Yours be done"—in agony, not in sweetness. The believer who echoes that prayer shares in the very heartbeat of the Son.

This is the covenant God has established with His people. He does not promise a life free from suffering. He promises that suffering will never be wasted. He promises that every cross carried with Christ becomes a seed of grace. He promises that love offered in trial becomes part of His redeeming work. And He promises that the believer who unites his suffering to Christ will not only share His Cross but His resurrection.

This is why the Church insists that redemptive suffering is not merely a doctrine. It is a way of life. It is the vocation of the baptized. It is the privilege of those who belong to Christ. It is the mystery by which God draws ordinary men and women into the extraordinary work of salvation. No suffering is too small when united to Christ. No suffering is too hidden. No suffering is ever forgotten. The Redeemer takes what is offered and uses it far beyond what the believer can imagine.

In the end, redemptive suffering reveals the deepest truth of the Christian life: God draws His people into His own love by drawing them into His own sacrifice. The Cross is not a detour on the path to holiness. It is the path. And the believer who walks that path with Christ discovers a love stronger than fear, a hope deeper than sorrow, and a union more powerful than suffering itself.

Christ has redeemed the world by His Cross.

And by grace, He invites His people to share in the mystery of that redemption—not as spectators, but as participants, not as passive recipients, but as living offerings, united to Him who loved us to the end.

12

Suffering, Love, And The Human Vocation

Love is the oldest truth in creation. It is the first word God speaks over the world when He calls it good, and it is the last word He speaks through His Son when He gives Himself upon the Cross. Everything God does—everything He commands, everything He reveals—flows from this one reality: God is love. But Scripture also reveals something more. Love is not simply affection or sentiment. Love, in its deepest form, always carries a cost. Love gives. Love sacrifices. Love pours itself out. And because love pours itself out, love suffers.

This is not because suffering is valuable in itself, but because the giving of oneself is costly, and love—true love—never holds itself back. We see this from the very beginning. When God creates humanity in His image, He forms them capable of love: capable of communion, capable of gift, capable of giving their hearts to one another and to Him. To be made in the image of a God who is self-giving means that human love must share that same shape. And the shape of that love is cruciform. Not because God delights in suffering, but because love delights in giving.

We need to recover this truth, especially in an age that has torn love away from sacrifice. The modern world speaks easily of love, but only the kind that feels pleasant, affirming, or convenient. When love costs something—when it demands patience, fidelity, perseverance, or forgiveness—modern culture hesitates. It pulls back. It calls the cost unfair, or unhealthy, or unnecessary. Yet Scripture never separates love from sacrifice. The entire biblical story is the story of a God who gives Himself. And every vocation God calls forth—marriage, priesthood, parenthood, the Christian life itself—participates in that same rhythm: love that gives, love that bears, love that suffers for the sake of the beloved.

This is why suffering is woven into the fabric of every authentic human calling. Not because suffering is a punishment, but because love is a gift. And gifts cost something. The world tries to convince us that a good life is a life without sacrifice. Scripture teaches the opposite. A good life is a life given. A meaningful life is a life poured out. A holy life is a life shaped by the same love that brought the Son of God to the Cross. When love is separated from sacrifice, it collapses into sentiment. When sacrifice is separated from love, it collapses into cruelty. But when love and sacrifice remain united—when the heart gives itself freely, even when it hurts—that is where the deepest truth of human vocation is revealed.

This is why Christ teaches His disciples that anyone who would follow Him must "take up his cross." He does not speak of suffering as an unfortunate burden. He speaks of it as the shape of discipleship. The cross is not a symbol of pain; it is a symbol of love. The cross reveals what love looks like in a fallen world. Love remains faithful even when betrayed. Love continues to give even when rejected. Love continues to bless even when wounded. The Cross is the clearest revelation of the Father's heart, not because suffering reveals God, but because suffering reveals how far God will go for love.

And this truth extends to every vocation we live. Whether we speak of the covenant of marriage, the grace of the priesthood, the daily sacrifice of parenthood, or the life of charity embraced by every Christian, the pattern remains the same. Love demands self-gift. Self-gift demands sacrifice. And sacrifice always involves suffering. But this suffering is not empty. It becomes the place where love matures, deepens, and bears fruit.

This is why the story of vocation can never be told without the Cross. Marriage grows through sacrifice. Parenthood grows through sacrifice. The priesthood is founded on sacrifice. The Christian life itself begins at baptism—a sacramental dying and rising with Christ. Every vocation God gives carries within it the imprint of His Son's offering. Every call to love is a call to give oneself. And every giving of oneself draws the heart closer to the One who gave Himself first.

Yet this truth is often lost in a culture that avoids suffering at any cost. We speak of freedom as if it means doing what we want. Scripture speaks of freedom as the ability to give ourselves in love. We speak of happiness as the absence of pain. Scripture speaks of happiness as communion with God, even when pain remains. We speak of fulfillment as the pursuit of comfort. Scripture speaks of fulfillment as the offering of the heart. When love is reduced to emotion, suffering becomes nonsensical. But when love is understood as self-gift, suffering becomes the place where love becomes real.

This is why suffering is not the enemy of vocation. It is the test of it. Suffering reveals whether love has taken root or whether it remains shallow. Suffering reveals whether we seek our own comfort or the good of the other. Suffering reveals whether we are willing to give ourselves or whether we hold back. The Cross does not replace love; it reveals love. And every vocation is a path on which that revelation must take place.

Marriage, parenthood, priesthood—these are not merely states of life. They are cruciform paths, marked by the same pattern that defined the life of Christ. When spouses remain faithful through difficulty, when parents give themselves tirelessly for their children, when priests pour out their lives for the sake of their people, the world sees a reflection of the love that brought salvation. These vocations become sacraments not only in the liturgical sense but in the human sense: signs of divine love made visible through human sacrifice.

But the truth runs deeper still. These sacrifices do not merely imitate Christ's love. Through grace, they participate in it. The love poured out in marriage, the love poured out in parenting, the love poured out in the priesthood—these are not separate loves. They are the ways Christ extends His love into the world through His people. When the believer gives himself in love, he is drawn into the life of Christ, whose entire mission was self-gift.

This is the heart of vocation. Before it is a task, before it is a duty, it is participation. God invites His children into the mystery of His own life, a life of love poured out. And because His love is cruciform, our participation in that love will always involve sacrifice. It will involve suffering. But it will also reveal the deepest truth of who we are. We were made to love. And because we were made to love, we were made to give ourselves. And because we were made to give ourselves, we were made to carry the Cross—not as a burden, but as the shape of love.

If love is the deepest calling of the human heart, then sacrifice is the deepest expression of that calling. This is why every authentic vocation—every way in which a person gives his life to God—is shaped by the Cross. Not because God desires His children to suffer, but because love, when it is real, gives itself away. The Cross is the clearest revelation of this truth. It is the form love takes when it refuses to stop short of total gift. Christ does not love halfway. He does not love until it is inconvenient. He loves to the end. And in loving to the end, He reveals what human love is meant to become.

We see this most clearly in the vocation of marriage. Scripture does not describe marriage as a contract between two individuals but as a covenant sealed by sacrifice. The covenant between husband and wife echoes the covenant between Christ and His Church. "Husbands, love your wives, as Christ loved the Church and gave Himself up for her." This is the heart of marital love: a self-gift that reflects the Bridegroom who laid down His life. Marriage is not sustained by emotion alone. It is sustained by sacrifice—by the daily choosing of the other above oneself, by the willingness to bear one another's burdens, by the readiness to forgive when wounds cut deep. The Cross stands at the centre of marriage not as a threat, but as a promise: the promise that love can endure, heal, uphold, and redeem.

Parenthood makes this truth even more visible. There are few forms of love more demanding, more exhausting, or more costly. A parent's life is marked by interruption, sleepless nights, constant worry, and uncounted sacrifices. And yet, in this crucible of self-giving, love grows with a strength that astonishes the soul. A parent learns what it means to pour out one's life for another—not because the child earns it, but because love seeks the good of the beloved. In the parent's sacrifice, the Cross becomes tangible. The heart that sacrifices becomes capable of a deeper tenderness, a deeper patience, a deeper joy. Parenthood teaches the soul that suffering for another is not the loss of life, but the very shape of giving life.

The priesthood, too, reveals the cruciform nature of vocation. A priest is not called merely to perform sacred functions. He is called to become a living sacrifice. His life is offered for the sake of the people entrusted to him. He bears their burdens, listens to their wounds, intercedes for their souls, and gives himself in service day after day. The priest's life is profoundly Eucharistic—not only because he offers the sacrifice of Christ, but because his own life becomes an extension of that sacrifice. The altar is not the only place where he offers himself. His entire existence becomes an offering: a life taken, blessed, broken, and given for others. This is the priest as Christ's visible icon—the Shepherd who lays down his life for his sheep.

But this cruciform pattern is not limited to marriage, or parenthood, or priesthood. It is the pattern of every Christian vocation. Whether a person is called to contemplative life, to a hidden life of service, to work in the world, or to a life marked by illness or limitation, the fundamental truth remains the same: love matures under sacrifice. A vocation flourishes when the heart is willing to give itself. God calls each person to a way of life in which love can be offered, and every offering will carry some cost.

This truth stands in stark contrast to the expectations of our age. The culture of self-preservation teaches that the good life is the painless life. It promises fulfillment without sacrifice, intimacy without commitment, and meaning without responsibility. But a life without sacrifice becomes empty, not full. It becomes brittle, not strong. When a person avoids suffering at all costs, he avoids the very path where love grows. Relationships fracture because no one is willing to bear the weight of another. Commitments evaporate because no one is willing to endure difficulty. Hearts become fragile because they have never been stretched by the cost of loving.

Love without sacrifice cannot endure. It cannot weather the storms of life. It cannot sustain a covenant. It cannot form a family. It cannot build a Church. The absence of sacrifice creates an absence of depth. And the absence of depth creates an absence of communion. When sacrifice disappears, love collapses—not because suffering is desirable, but because love cannot grow without giving.

The biblical vision of vocation restores this lost truth. It shows that suffering embraced in love is not a threat to happiness but its foundation. The Cross is not opposed to joy. It prepares the heart for joy. Sacrifice is not the enemy of fulfillment. It is the path to fulfillment. When a person gives himself generously—whether as spouse, parent, priest, or disciple—he discovers the paradox at the heart of the Gospel: the more the heart gives, the more it becomes itself. The heart expands. The soul deepens. The image of Christ becomes clearer within.

This is the mystery of human vocation. God invites His people into a life where love and sacrifice converge. He invites them to share His own life, a life poured out for the redemption of the world. And because His love is cruciform, the love of His people will be cruciform as well. Not as a burden imposed from without, but as a participation embraced from within. Suffering does not define vocation. Love defines vocation. But love, when it is true, will always bear a cross.

The more we understand this cruciform pattern of vocation, the more the entire Christian life begins to make sense. God does not call His people to love in abstraction. He calls them to love in ways that cost them something. And because He calls them to love concretely, He calls them to suffer concretely. Not because He delights in their pain, but because He delights in their transformation. The sacrifice that love demands becomes the means by which the human heart is formed into the likeness of Christ. Just as the clay must be shaped, pressed, and moulded, so the heart must be shaped by the weight of giving.

This is why the saints speak of sacrifice not with dread, but with reverence. They know that sacrifice is not the end of love—it is the beginning of mature love. They know that when the heart gives itself generously, it discovers its true capacity. They know that when love is tested, it becomes stronger, purer, more deeply rooted in God. The childlike sentiment that begins love must grow into the mature fidelity that sustains it. And fidelity, by its very nature, requires the willingness to suffer for the sake of the beloved.

This truth appears everywhere in Scripture. Abraham's trust in God is revealed not in comfort, but in trial. Joseph's fidelity is revealed not in ease, but in imprisonment. David's heart is purified not on the throne, but in exile. Israel learns the covenant not in prosperity, but in the wilderness. The prophets speak not from safety, but from persecution. And Christ Himself reveals the fullness of divine love not in miracle alone, but on the Cross. In Scripture, suffering is never the opposite of vocation. It is the place where vocation is clarified, purified, and fulfilled.

And this clarifying effect of suffering touches every relationship we live. In marriage, spouses discover their deepest love when they carry one another through weakness. When illness comes. When disappointment cuts deep. When forgiveness must be extended again and again. In those moments, love is not destroyed by suffering; it is revealed. It becomes clear that vows are not merely spoken—they are lived. The words "in good times and in bad" take flesh. The promise to give oneself becomes real.

In parenthood, suffering reveals love with even greater intensity. The sleepless nights, the endless concerns, the sacrifices no one sees—these become the school where the heart learns to love with endurance. A parent's love becomes courageous precisely because it is costly. It charges ahead into difficulty, not because the difficulty is attractive, but because the child is loved. The Cross becomes visible in ways that are immediate and raw. It strips away illusions and reveals the core of the human vocation: to give one's life for those entrusted to us.

In the priesthood, the cruciform shape of love becomes explicit. A priest stands before his people not as a manager or a technician, but as a man configured to Christ the High Priest. His life must be poured out. His heart must be open. His sacrifices must be hidden and unceasing. He bears the weight of sins that are not his own, the burdens of souls entrusted to him, the griefs of families, the wounds of the broken. He learns that the only priesthood worth having is one shaped by the Cross. The altar teaches him to live what he celebrates:

a life offered, not preserved.

But it is not only priests, spouses, and parents who walk this path. Every Christian vocation—every life called into the mystery of God's love—is shaped by the Cross. Whether a person lives in the cloister or in the workplace, whether he is called to solitude or to service, whether he is marked by health or by illness, the pattern remains the same. God calls each person to a life in which love becomes visible. And love becomes visible when it is given. It becomes visible when it bears another's burden. It becomes visible when it remains faithful even when the cost rises.

This is why a life without sacrifice becomes brittle. It may be filled with comfort, but it is empty of depth. It may be protected from pain, but it is deprived of meaning. A person who avoids sacrifice avoids the very experiences that awaken compassion, strengthen fidelity, and enlarge the heart. Without sacrifice, relationships remain shallow. Commitments remain tentative. The heart remains untested. And untested hearts remain fragile.

The tragedy of our age is that it mistakes fragility for freedom. It teaches that the self must be preserved at all costs, that one's comfort is sacred, that boundaries must shield the heart from every inconvenience. But in shielding the heart from sacrifice, the culture also shields the heart from love. It forms people who long for communion but who cannot endure the cost of communion. It forms people who desire intimacy but who flee the responsibilities that make intimacy possible. It forms people who hunger for meaning but who resist the very sacrifices that give meaning its substance.

Scripture reveals a different path. It shows that a heart stretched by sacrifice becomes capable of love. It shows that the soul strengthened by endurance becomes capable of communion. It shows that the person who gives himself discovers who he truly is. Christ teaches this with a clarity that cannot be softened: "Whoever loses his life for My sake will find it." This is not a threat. It is a promise. The life poured out is the life fulfilled. The heart that loves sacrificially is the heart that finds joy.

This is the call of every Christian vocation: to let love become sacrificial in order that it may become divine. When the believer gives himself in love—in marriage, in family life, in service, in prayer, in the hidden sacrifices of daily fidelity—he participates in the self-giving love of Christ. His suffering does not diminish his life. It deepens it. His sacrifices do not deplete him. They enlarge him. His willingness to carry the Cross does not weigh him down. It roots him in the very mystery of God's love.

When the believer finally stands before the mystery of vocation in this light, something becomes unmistakably clear: the Christian life is not a project we construct. It is a gift we receive. It is not primarily about tasks to accomplish or roles to perform. It is about entering the life of God, a life that reveals itself through love poured out. The believer discovers that every joy, every trial, every sacrifice offered in fidelity is gathered by God into a story far larger than the sum of its parts. The vocation becomes not a burden, but a participation—a sharing in the very love that created and redeemed the world.

This is why the Church insists that the Cross belongs at the centre of Christian identity. The Cross is not simply an instrument of suffering. It is the fullest revelation of love the world has ever seen. And because it is the fullest revelation of love, it becomes the clearest revelation of vocation. Christ does not call His people to a life He Himself refused to live. He calls them into the very life He lived: a life of giving, a life of fidelity, a life marked by sacrificial love. To carry the Cross is to walk the path He walked. It is to allow His love to shape our lives from within.

And this shaping is not confined to extraordinary moments. It is woven into the daily fabric of ordinary life. Every act of patience, every moment of listening, every sacrifice made in hiddenness becomes a stroke of the divine chisel. God uses these small fidelities to carve the soul into the likeness of His Son. The believer begins to see that the greatest transformations occur not in dramatic gestures, but in the sustained faithfulness of ordinary love. A marriage held together through forgiveness. A parent who perseveres through exhaustion. A priest who continues to offer his life. A Christian who keeps praying, serving, loving. These are the places where vocation becomes cruciform, and where cruciform love becomes radiant.

From the outside, such sacrifices may appear small. From the inside, they often feel costly. But in the mystery of the Kingdom, nothing offered in love is ever lost. Nothing is wasted. Nothing disappears into silence. The God who sees in secret receives every sacrifice, sanctifies every offering, and uses every act of love to advance His purposes. The believer who gives himself discovers that he is not giving alone. He is giving with Christ. And Christ is giving Himself through him.

This is why the Christian vocation cannot be understood apart from the Cross. The Cross reveals not only who God is, but who we are meant to become. We were created for love, and love draws us into sacrifice, not as a punishment, but as a participation. Through sacrifice, the heart becomes capable of communion. Through sacrifice, love becomes steadfast. Through sacrifice, vocation becomes the place where God's grace takes root and grows.

A life that refuses sacrifice becomes small. It contracts. It protects itself. It looks inward. But a life that embraces sacrificial love expands. It reaches outward. It welcomes others. It becomes a vessel for God's mercy. The human heart was not made to protect itself from love's cost; it was made to bear it, because in bearing it, the heart learns to give as God gives.

The saints understood this with a clarity that is both challenging and liberating. They knew that vocation is not measured by what we accomplish, but by what we give. They knew that the sacrifices that stretch us are the very sacrifices that sanctify us. They knew that suffering embraced in love becomes the place where Christ is most present. And because they knew this, they could live their vocations with a joy the world could not explain.

In the end, the mystery of vocation brings us back to the very beginning: we were created in the image of a God who gives Himself. To be faithful to our vocation is to allow that image to unfold within us. It is to embrace love that bears a cost, not because suffering is desirable, but because love is priceless. It is to discover that the Cross is not simply the instrument of our salvation, but the pattern of our lives.

When the believer accepts this pattern—when he lets love shape his sacrifices and lets sacrifice shape his love—he begins to live not only *for* God, but *with* God. His vocation becomes the place where the divine life enters the human story. And it becomes the place where the human story is taken up into the divine.

13

When Love Meets A Wounded Age

Every journey through Scripture eventually returns us to the world we inhabit. It is one thing to contemplate the beauty of divine love revealed in Christ, to see how suffering becomes fruitful in the saints, and to trace the cruciform pattern that shapes every Christian vocation. It is another thing entirely to carry that vision into the world as it stands today—a world that has forgotten what love is and therefore forgotten what suffering means. The Gospel gives us a way of understanding the human heart, the human story, and the human vocation. But the culture around us tells a very different story.

The contrast is impossible to ignore. Everything we have explored so far—the dignity of sacrifice, the fruitfulness of suffering offered in love, the communion of the Body of Christ—is built on a worldview in which God is present and love is costly. But the modern world has embraced a different creed, one that treats suffering not as a place of encounter but as a problem to eliminate. It is a worldview that understands neither suffering nor love because it refuses to accept the reality of the Cross. And when the Cross disappears, so does meaning.

We stand now at a turning point in this book. Up to this moment, we have looked at suffering from within the life of faith. We have listened to the cries of the human heart, traced the story God tells from Genesis to the Resurrection, and walked alongside the saints who embraced the Cross not out of masochism, but out of love. We have seen how suffering becomes redemptive when united with Christ. We have seen how every vocation—marriage, parenthood, priesthood, discipleship—takes on the shape of His self-giving. These truths form the bedrock of a Christian understanding of suffering.

Now we must turn our eyes outward.

We must confront a world that no longer shares the grammar of Scripture, the vision of covenant, or the hope of the Resurrection. A world that fears weakness, rejects limits, and flees from dependency. A world that searches for escape rather than meaning. A world that has tried to build human life on the assumption that suffering is not only undesirable, but intolerable. And in doing so, it has created a culture in which suffering no longer deepens the heart, but fractures it.

The great crisis of our age is not merely that people suffer. Every age has suffered. The crisis is that our age does not know what suffering is for. It has no horizon beyond the self. No transcendence beyond the moment. No place to set its pain except in the hands of technology, medication, or despair. When suffering arrives—and it always arrives—it finds a society unprepared, unequipped, and unearthed. A society that does not know how to hope because it no longer knows how to love.

The erosion did not happen all at once. It began when we severed suffering from purpose. It continued when we severed love from sacrifice. And it reached a breaking point when we severed the human person from God. Once God disappears from the human story, suffering becomes nothing more than a flaw in the system. A malfunction. A defect. Something to be removed, escaped, or ended. And when suffering becomes meaningless, so does life—especially life marked by dependence, limitation, or weakness.

This is the soil in which new and troubling realities have taken root. A culture that fears suffering more than death begins to redefine mercy. A culture that idolises autonomy begins to see dependency as indignity. A culture that has lost the inner life begins to drown in anxiety, depression, and isolation. And a culture that refuses transcendence is left speechless before innocent suffering—the death of a child, the destruction of a community, the tragedies that defy every earthly explanation.

These are not abstract problems. They are the defining wounds of our generation.

A culture that once asked, "How should we live?" now asks, "How can we escape?"

A culture that once sought meaning now seeks oblivion.

A culture that once honoured weakness now hides it.

A culture that once turned to God now turns inward and finds nothing there but fear.

Yet the Gospel is not silent in the face of these wounds. The Church does not respond with denial, avoidance, or platitudes. The Church responds with a paradox: the dignity of weakness, the sanctity of dependence, the hope that rises from suffering, and the love that accompanies every sorrow. The Church proclaims a truth the modern world has forgotten—that suffering need not destroy meaning, because God has entered suffering Himself.

As we step into Part IV, we enter the valley where cultural fears meet the Cross. We confront a world that wants to eliminate suffering but cannot face what it becomes when suffering is stripped of meaning. We face the rise of assisted dying, not as a political issue, but as a spiritual one—a symptom of a world terrified of dependence. We face the epidemic of mental suffering, not with simplistic answers, but with the depth of the Church's wisdom. And we face the most haunting question of all: the suffering of the innocent, the places where the heart cries out for justice and meets a mystery instead.

We will not approach these questions with sentimentality or with cold abstraction. We will approach them as Christians—people shaped by the Cross, strengthened by the Resurrection, and called to carry light into places where hope has grown thin. The crisis of the modern world is not merely that it suffers. It is that it suffers without hope. The task before us is to show that hope is not the denial of suffering, but its transformation.

We have seen what suffering becomes in the hands of God.

Now we must see what suffering becomes in the hands of a culture that has forgotten Him.

IV

The Modern Crisis

14

The World That Cannot Suffer

Modern people have inherited a world that has forgotten how to suffer. The loss is so profound, so quiet, so unquestioned, that most never notice it until they stand face to face with pain themselves. Then the illusion breaks. Then the soul falters. For the first time in history, entire cultures treat discomfort not simply as unpleasant but as unjust. A setback at work becomes a crisis of identity. Loneliness becomes an emergency. Illness becomes an outrage. Even the ordinary burdens that shaped every previous generation—fatigue, financial strain, family conflict, aging, disappointment—feel somehow wrong, as though life has violated an unspoken promise.

This is the first symptom of a deeper sickness: modernity believes that suffering is not merely undesirable, but senseless. If pain has no transcendent meaning, then pain must be a mistake. If sorrow has no purpose, then sorrow must be a failure. A generation that has lost the meaning of suffering will soon lose the capacity to endure it. That is where we now stand—not because human beings are weaker by nature, but because the story we live inside has changed.

Every human being interprets suffering through a story, whether they realize it or not. Israel understood suffering through the story of covenant: creation, fall, promise, exodus, exile, restoration. The early Christians understood suffering through the story of Christ: incarnation, passion, death, resurrection, glory. But modern man has no such story. He has technology, comfort, and self-expression—but no narrative large enough to hold the weight of sorrow. He knows how to distract himself, but he does not know how to carry a cross.

This is why suffering upends the modern soul so violently. Without a story, suffering is meaningless. Without a horizon, suffering is endless. Without a covenant, suffering is lonely. Modernity did not simply lose God; it lost the plot. And without a plot, every pain becomes a threat, every inconvenience an injustice, every sorrow a personal violation. The human heart cannot bear pain in isolation. It must be woven into a story. When that story is erased, fragility follows.

To understand how we arrived here, we must look not first at suffering itself, but at the worldview that surrounds it—a worldview shaped not by Scripture but by secularism, individualism, and the myth of self-creation. These forces have not merely changed what we believe. They have changed who we believe ourselves to be. They have formed a new kind of self, a new kind of society, a new understanding of meaning, and therefore a new understanding of suffering. The change has been subtle, but its effects are devastating.

It begins with the disappearance of transcendence. For most of human history, suffering was understood in relation to something beyond the visible world. The ancient Israelites saw suffering through the promises of God. The prophets saw suffering through divine justice and mercy. The apostles saw suffering through the Cross. The martyrs saw suffering through the hope of resurrection. Even pagan cultures, for all their error, believed suffering was woven into some cosmic order—fate, virtue, destiny, honor.

But modernity broke the link between earth and heaven. In the secular imagination, the world is flat. There is no divine horizon, no eternal meaning, no sacred story. There is only the present moment, the autonomous self, and the fragile pursuit of personal fulfillment. Without transcendence, suffering shrinks in meaning and grows in intensity. A broken heart is not simply painful; it is existential. A chronic illness is not simply a trial; it becomes the collapse of identity. A loss is not simply sorrow; it becomes a crisis of self.

Ecclesiastes knew this feeling well. "Under the sun," the preacher said, the world becomes vanity—breath, vapor, fleeting wind. Without God, suffering is absurd. Without eternity, justice is impossible. Without transcendence, every tear is wasted. Modernity has embraced Ecclesiastes without ever hearing his voice. It lives under the sun and wonders why the darkness feels so near.

This loss of transcendence paved the way for something even more fragile: the rise of the autonomous self. Modern identity is built not on covenant but on self-expression. We define ourselves not by the God who created us, not by the family who bore us, not by the community that formed us, not by the vocation that claims us, but by the self we construct. "I must be true to myself" has replaced "I belong to Someone." We are taught to look inward for meaning rather than upward or outward.

But a self built on personal preference cannot withstand suffering. When meaning comes only from within, suffering becomes a thief—it steals my freedom, my dreams, my plans, my sense of control. The self collapses because it was never meant to carry the weight of its own identity. In Scripture, identity is received, not invented. It comes from the God who calls, the covenant that binds, the story that claims us. When identity is self-created, anything that disrupts the self becomes intolerable.

This is why modern souls shatter under pressures that previous generations endured with resilience. Our ancestors lived inside stories larger than themselves. They bore suffering not because they were inherently stronger, but because they belonged—to God, to kin, to community, to tradition, to destiny. They saw sorrow as a chapter, not a conclusion; as a trial, not a betrayal. Modern man, having severed himself from transcendence, now bears suffering alone. Isolation magnifies pain. Narcissism inflates it. Autonomy collapses beneath it.

Into this fragile self stepped a new cultural force: the therapeutic age. The shift was subtle but seismic. For centuries, virtue was the measure of maturity. Patience, courage, temperance, perseverance—these were the pillars of a resilient soul. But in the last century, the moral center shifted. Feeling good became the goal. Emotional comfort became the standard of well-being. Happiness became a psychological state rather than a theological virtue.

The result? A culture where discomfort feels like failure and suffering feels like injustice. The therapeutic worldview teaches that the primary purpose of life is to avoid pain, manage emotion, and preserve personal comfort. Virtue becomes optional. Sacrifice becomes suspicious. Endurance becomes pathological. The soul that lives by feelings will die by them. When suffering arrives—and it always arrives—this fragile self cannot stand. It buckles because it has never been trained to kneel.

This is where many modern believers stumble. They approach God through the lens of the therapeutic age. God becomes a divine counselor whose purpose is to soothe, uplift, and remove discomfort. Prayer becomes a way of managing feelings. Faith becomes a form of psychological support. When suffering disrupts this arrangement, faith collapses. The believer is shocked not only by the pain but by the apparent failure of God to prevent it.

But the God of Scripture does not promise a painless story. He promises a meaningful one. He does not remove every suffering; He redeems them. He does not shield us from every sorrow; He enters them. The therapeutic age cannot understand this because it has no place for sacrifice—yet sacrifice is the very heartbeat of the biblical world.

When a culture rejects sacrifice, it rejects the very structure of love, for love always costs. In the next movement of this chapter, we must look at how the disappearance of sacrifice reshaped modern relationships, vocations, and communities—and why avoiding suffering has destroyed the capacity for courage, fidelity, maturity, and hope.

The disappearance of sacrifice did not happen overnight. It eroded slowly, almost invisibly, as the modern world exchanged the biblical vision of love for the consumer vision of comfort. In Scripture, sacrifice is woven into the fabric of covenant life. Noah builds an altar after the flood. Abraham ascends Mount Moriah. Israel stands before Sinai and learns that worship is not entertainment but offering. The entire Temple system is built upon sacrifice—not because God delights in loss, but because love always gives. Love is measured not by sentiment but by self-gift. That is why St. Paul sums up the Christian life in one extraordinary phrase: "Present your bodies as a living sacrifice" (Rom 12:1).

But modernity replaced the altar with the mirror. The logic shifted from "What is God asking of me?" to "What do I feel drawn to?" From "What must I give?" to "What must I avoid?" From "How do I remain faithful?" to "How do I maximize my emotional comfort?" In this new vision, sacrifice no longer makes sense. It feels threatening, even unjust. If suffering has no transcendent meaning, then anything that causes suffering becomes an enemy—commitment, discipline, responsibility, endurance, covenant, vocation. Modern people flee these not because they are evil, but because they cost something.

Here is the great paradox: the more we flee the cost of love, the more fragile we become. A culture built on avoiding suffering is a culture incapable of love, because love is cruciform. It stretches the heart. It wounds the heart. It matures the heart. Love requires dying to oneself, whether in marriage, parenthood, friendship, or even ordinary acts of charity. When a generation grows convinced that suffering is always harmful, it grows incapable of love—which means it grows incapable of meaning.

This fragility becomes visible everywhere. The rise of "ghosting" in relationships; the epidemic of breakups caused not by betrayal but by discomfort; the avoidance of marriage because it requires sacrifice; the rejection of children because they demand endurance; the collapse of long-term commitments across society—all reveal a soul untrained in suffering. When the slightest discomfort feels catastrophic, the heart can no longer remain steadfast. It retreats, protects itself, and narrows its world until nothing costly can enter.

The therapeutic culture enabled this collapse by redefining happiness. In Scripture, happiness (makarios in Greek) refers to the blessedness of those who walk with God, even amid hardship. In the Beatitudes, Jesus proclaims blessed those who mourn, those who hunger, those who are persecuted. Modernity flipped this upside down. Happiness became emotional satisfaction, and emotional satisfaction became the ultimate goal. Suffering, once understood as a teacher, became the ultimate threat.

Yet Scripture refuses this vision. From Genesis to Revelation, God shapes His people through trials, not despite them. Israel learns trust in the desert, not in prosperity. Joseph discovers God's providence in prison, not in privilege. David learns dependence in exile, not in victory. Daniel encounters God's faithfulness in the lions' den, not in the palace. The apostles learn courage through persecution, not applause. The pattern is unmistakable: suffering is not an interruption of the Christian life; it is the arena in which the Christian life becomes real.

Modernity rejects this not because it is unreasonable, but because it is unthinkable. When transcendence disappears, when the self becomes fragile, when comfort becomes a god, suffering must be avoided at all costs. This is how a culture begins to treat pain as an injustice and inconvenience as an assault. Even mild discomfort becomes intolerable. Every generation before ours knew what we have forgotten: virtues grow only through struggle. You cannot learn patience without delay, courage without fear, forgiveness without injury, faith without darkness, hope without trial, or love without sacrifice.

Remove suffering, and you remove the soil where virtues grow.

This lies at the heart of the modern crisis of fragility. Our ancestors endured famine, war, death, hardship, persecution, and loss—yet they also built civilizations, founded families, raised saints, and forged communities. They did not do this because they were superhuman. They did this because they expected life to cost something. They lived inside a story that taught them how to interpret suffering, not run from it.

In contrast, modern people increasingly expect life to be smooth, predictable, and comfortable. Any deviation feels like betrayal. When the standard is comfort, the soul becomes weak. When life becomes easy, the heart becomes brittle. When every minor trial is treated like trauma, resilience collapses.

This is why modern people often lose faith at the first touch of suffering. Their worldview has not prepared them for the cost of discipleship. They have been taught that God exists to ensure well-being, not to sanctify the heart. They have absorbed a therapeutic gospel, not the biblical one. When suffering arrives—and it always arrives—they feel deceived. They feel abandoned. They feel shocked that the world does not obey their expectations.

But the true crisis is deeper: suffering exposes the hollowness of the modern self. It reveals that a worldview built entirely on comfort cannot withstand reality. Suffering does not create fragility. It exposes it.

At the same time, suffering exposes something even more painful: the modern loss of meaning. Human beings can endure almost anything if they believe their suffering has purpose. Soldiers endure hardship for the sake of comrades. Parents endure sleepless nights for the sake of children. Athletes endure training for the sake of victory. Christians endure trials for the sake of Christ. But modernity has stripped suffering of purpose. Pain becomes pointless. Loss becomes absurd. Tragedy becomes proof that the world is unjust.

When the meaning is stripped away, suffering becomes unbearable. The solution is not to eliminate suffering—that is impossible—but to restore meaning. And meaning cannot be restored without rediscovering the story in which suffering belongs.

Scripture does not minimise suffering. It locates it. It names it. It reveals it. It places it inside a story larger than human sorrow. Without that story, suffering crushes the soul. Inside that story, suffering becomes the place where the soul is strengthened, purified, awakened, humbled, and transformed.

Here we must address an uncomfortable truth: modern people are not simply afraid of suffering. They are unprepared for it. They have been formed by a culture that treats every pain as a problem to be solved rather than a mystery to be lived. This is why the slightest suffering often destabilises identity itself. The modern self depends entirely on circumstances, feelings, and personal success. Remove one of these pillars and the entire structure collapses.

Scripture presents a different vision. Identity is not built on circumstance but on covenant. You are not who you feel you are; you are who God declares you to be. You are not defined by your suffering; you are defined by the One who bears your suffering. Modernity says, "I am what I feel." Christianity says, "I am what God has done."

This difference is everything.

Because when suffering arrives, feelings collapse. God does not.

This is why rediscovering the biblical meaning of suffering is not merely comforting—it is liberating. It restores the soul to a story where suffering is neither absurd nor accidental but part of a divine economy of love. Yet the modern world rejects this vision not because it is untrue, but because it is uncomfortable. If suffering can be meaningful, then life cannot be reduced to pleasure. If suffering can be formative, then the goal of life cannot be comfort. If suffering can be redeemed, then we must learn endurance, not escape. And this is precisely what modernity refuses to learn.

To see the difference clearly, consider how Scripture frames suffering. The very first command given to Adam—"till and keep" the garden—comes with effort. After the fall, this effort becomes toil; and yet even then, God clothes the fallen couple with garments of skin. Judgment mingles with mercy. Pain carries promise. And in the memorable words spoken to Eve, pain in childbearing is tied to life itself. Suffering becomes the pathway to the future. In Scripture, pain is not a dead end. It is often a doorway.

Modernity, however, treats every doorway of suffering as a wall. It sees no purpose in sorrow, no beauty in endurance, no redemption in loss. It responds to suffering not with reverence but with revolt. This revolt appears in the rhetoric of rights—"I deserve to be happy, I deserve a life free of struggle"—as though God or society owes us exemption from the human condition. But suffering is not a glitch in the system. It is part of the story that shapes the soul. When we treat it as a violation, we turn against reality itself.

This revolt against reality has consequences far beyond personal psychology. It corrodes communities. When people fear suffering, they fear commitment. Marriage becomes fragile. Parenting becomes optional. Vocation becomes negotiable. Friendship becomes transactional. Any relationship that demands endurance becomes too costly.

But societies built on escape rather than endurance cannot sustain themselves. They unravel because they have lost the virtues that hold them together.

The biblical worldview forms resilience because it forms realism. Scripture teaches that suffering will come. Jesus Himself promises it: "In this world you will have tribulation." But He does not stop there. He adds, "Be of good cheer; I have overcome the world." Notice the order. Tribulation first, triumph second. Modernity tries to reverse this: triumph first, tribulation never. That reversal is not only spiritually disastrous—it is psychologically devastating. A soul unprepared for suffering will be undone by it.

This is one reason mental suffering has exploded in our time. Modern people do not simply experience suffering; they *interpret* it as evidence that something is fundamentally wrong with their life, or with God, or with themselves. Scripture never promises a painless life. It promises a meaningful one. The therapeutic age promises a painless life. It cannot deliver it. Modern people find themselves trapped between their expectations and reality, and the gap between the two becomes unbearable.

Add to this the technological illusion of control. For the first time in history, people live with the sense that almost everything can be managed, optimized, medicated, predicted, or solved. Entire industries exist to ensure we never have to wait, never have to struggle, never have to endure discomfort. In such a world, suffering feels like an intrusion into a carefully maintained illusion. Rather than being woven into the rhythm of life, it feels like a failure of the system—and therefore a failure of the self.

But technology cannot change the nature of the human soul. It can only distract it. And distraction does not strengthen character; it erodes it. The more we surround ourselves with artificial comfort, the less capable we are of facing reality when comfort collapses. That is why the smallest trials often feel overwhelming to modern hearts. It is not because the trials are greater. It is because the hearts are unformed.

When transcendence disappears, suffering becomes claustrophobic. Without a horizon beyond the self, pain has nowhere to go except inward. It collapses the soul into itself. Augustine once wrote that sin curves the soul inward. Modernity has done something even stranger: it has curved the soul inward by convincing people that the self is all there is, all there ever was, and all there ever will be. In such a vision, suffering has no direction—no offering to make, no sacrifice to join, no story to inhabit.

Christianity contradicts this at every point. It teaches that suffering gains meaning not within the self but beyond it—within the covenant, within Christ, within a story where God Himself enters suffering and fills it with His presence. The modern world sees suffering as the end of meaning. Christianity sees suffering as the meeting place of divine love and human frailty. Scripture does not romanticize suffering; it redeems it.

This is why avoiding suffering at all costs destroys freedom. A person cannot be free if he must flee anything painful. Freedom requires discipline, courage, sacrifice, and the ability to choose the good even when it hurts. When suffering becomes the greatest evil, virtue becomes impossible. Courage collapses. Sacrifice disappears. Fidelity feels like slavery. Love becomes sentimental instead of self-giving. Commitment becomes optional. Freedom itself becomes distorted into self-protection rather than self-gift.

True freedom requires the ability to endure what is difficult for the sake of what is good. This is why Christ tells His disciples to take up their cross. He is not placing a burden upon them; He is giving them back their freedom. Only a person who can carry a cross can carry love. Only a person who can endure hardship can persevere in joy. Only a person who knows how to suffer can know how to love, because love without sacrifice is a contradiction.

This brings us to one of the most painful realities of our age: *why many modern people lose faith when suffering enters their lives.* It is not because suffering disproves God. It is because suffering disproves the god modernity has invented—the god of comfort, convenience, and emotional well-being. When this false god fails, people feel betrayed. But the God of Scripture never promised a life free of suffering. He promised a life *transformed* by suffering. He promised a Cross—and a Resurrection.

Modern people often lose faith not because God is absent, but because their expectations were formed by a secular worldview, not a biblical one. They were told that faith would eliminate suffering. Scripture says faith gives suffering meaning. They were told that God exists to prevent pain. Scripture says God enters pain to redeem us. They were told that feeling good is the goal of life. Scripture says holiness is the goal of life. These two visions cannot coexist.

When suffering arrives, one of them must collapse.

And the one built on comfort always collapses first.

If the modern world cannot endure suffering, it is because it has forgotten the story it was made to live in. Human beings do not interpret suffering instinctively. We interpret it through lenses handed to us—through culture, ritual, memory, worship, and family. When those lenses fracture, suffering becomes intolerable. When those lenses are grounded in eternity, suffering becomes endurable. Everything depends on the story we inhabit.

This is why Israel's memory matters so profoundly. When suffering struck, Israel did not look inward for answers. She looked backward and upward. She remembered the God who delivered her from Egypt. She remembered the covenant sealed in blood. She remembered the God who fed her in the wilderness, who raised up judges, who restored her from exile, who spoke through prophets. Israel's memory became Israel's strength. Her history anchored her identity.

This stands in stark contrast with the modern soul, whose history has been erased. Secular culture teaches us to define ourselves not by covenant but by preference; not by memory but by emotion; not by God but by the self. In such a vision, identity floats, unmoored and untethered. When suffering strikes, the soul has nothing stable to hold. It collapses because it stands on nothing.

This collapse is visible in the rise of what psychologists call "intolerance of distress." Modern people increasingly interpret normal hardship as crisis-level trauma. Grief becomes pathology. Loneliness becomes catastrophe. Disappointment becomes devastation. This is not because people are weaker than previous generations; it is because the cultural scaffolding that once supported endurance has been dismantled.

Generations before ours understood suffering as a normal part of life. They lived with it daily—illness, scarcity, death, warfare, famine, and hardship were woven into existence. They were not stronger by temperament; they were stronger by formation. They were trained by a world that expected suffering. They were formed by a faith that interpreted suffering. They were raised in a story that made suffering meaningful.

We have lost that formation. We have kept the language of resilience while stripping away the structures that create resilience: religious practice, stable families, communal bonds, moral clarity, sacrificial love, covenant fidelity. A culture without these cannot produce souls capable of suffering well. It produces souls that feel betrayed by suffering because nothing in their world has prepared them for it.

This fragility becomes particularly dangerous when it meets secularism. Secularism removes transcendence—God, heaven, eternity, judgment, grace, providence—and leaves us with a world closed in on itself. A world without heaven is a world without horizon. In such a world, suffering can only be absurd. It cannot be redemptive. It cannot be revelatory. It cannot be formative. It can only be cruel.

Without transcendence, the soul has nowhere to place its pain. There is no altar on which to lay it. There is no God to receive it. There is no eternity to redeem it. This is why secular culture grows increasingly desperate to eliminate suffering altogether. If suffering has no meaning, then suffering must have no place. And so modernity seeks to remove it through any means available—technology, medication, distraction, entertainment, autonomy, and even death.

But the attempt to eliminate suffering eliminates humanity along with it. A world without suffering would be a world without courage, without sacrifice, without endurance, without compassion. It would be a world without saints. Above all, it would be a world without Christ. The refusal of suffering is the refusal of love incarnate. When the culture rejects the Cross, it rejects the story that gives suffering meaning.

Here the Christian imagination stands as a prophetic contradiction. Christianity is the only religion in which God enters human suffering, not to explain it away but to transfigure it from within. The Cross does not answer the philosophical problem of suffering—it overthrows it. It turns suffering from a threat into a place of meeting. The world sees suffering as the destruction of meaning; Christianity sees suffering as the revelation of love.

But to live with this vision requires formation, not feeling. It requires catechesis, not comfort. The early Christians understood this. Their world was harsh, often violent, frequently unjust. Yet they possessed a strength that astonished their pagan neighbors. They cared for the sick during plagues. They rescued abandoned infants. They endured persecution with courage. They faced death with serenity. This was not because they lacked fear. It was because they lived inside a story in which suffering was not the end of life but the beginning of glory.

This story remains available, but it must be chosen. Modern Christians cannot assume that the culture will support their understanding of suffering. The culture will oppose it at every turn. That is why Catholics today must recover the biblical imagination. We must reclaim the story that makes suffering intelligible. And this begins by refusing the modern lie that suffering is meaningless. It is not. It is mysterious, painful, and often overwhelming—but never meaningless.

To recover the meaning of suffering is to recover the meaning of love. The two cannot be separated. Everywhere Scripture speaks of love, it speaks of sacrifice. Everywhere it speaks of covenant, it speaks of endurance. Everywhere it speaks of holiness, it speaks of purification. Suffering is not the opposite of love; it is the cost of love. And when modernity eliminates the cost, it eliminates the love.

This is why the rise of entitlement is so spiritually dangerous. Entitlement convinces the soul that nothing difficult should be required. It confuses blessing with ease. But Scripture teaches the opposite. Blessing is not ease; blessing is presence. Blessing is not the absence of suffering but the assurance of God in suffering. Entitlement blinds the soul to this. It trains the heart to expect comfort and to resent sacrifice. And where resentment grows, love dies.

The collapse of sacrifice leads inevitably to the collapse of identity. A person cannot know who he is if he does not know what he is willing to suffer for. This is why the saints have such clarity. They know exactly who they are, because they know exactly who they love. Their identity is anchored in the Cross. Their purpose is sealed in covenant. Their lives are shaped by sacrifice freely embraced. They reveal what modernity hides: identity is forged in the fires of fidelity.

The modern world speaks endlessly about authenticity but refuses the sacrifices required to attain it. True authenticity—the kind Scripture speaks of—comes not from expressing oneself but from offering oneself. The modern world tells us to "find ourselves." Christ tells us to "lose ourselves" for His sake and thus be found. The one who avoids suffering loses himself. The one who offers suffering gains himself. This is the paradox at the heart of the Gospel.

And so the Christian who rediscovers the biblical meaning of suffering rediscovers himself. He learns who he is by learning what Christ has endured for him. He learns why he exists by learning what he is called to endure for love. He learns that suffering is not the destruction of identity but the door into deeper identity. The world says, "Avoid pain and become yourself." Christ says, "Take up your cross and become Mine."

One of these leads to collapse.

The other leads to resurrection.

If modern souls cannot endure suffering, it is because they cannot *locate* themselves within a story large enough to carry it. The Christian does not stand alone before sorrow. He stands inside a narrative stretching from Abraham to Christ, from Cross to Resurrection, from Pentecost to the New Creation. The modern person stands alone before suffering because he has forgotten the Author. Without that Author, the plot collapses. Without the plot, suffering becomes chaos. And when chaos touches the heart, the heart breaks.

But when the Author is remembered, suffering becomes something else entirely. It becomes revelation: not the revelation of why evil exists, but the revelation of who God is. The God of Scripture does not stand distant from human pain. He binds Himself to a suffering people. He enters their affliction. He bears their grief. He takes their wounds into His own flesh. This is not the God of the philosophers, who governs by distance. This is the God of covenant, who rescues by drawing near.

The prophets proclaim this with astonishing clarity. Isaiah calls the Messiah a "Man of Sorrows." Jeremiah weeps with the wounds of Israel. Ezekiel learns that God Himself shepherds the broken. Hosea discovers that divine love remains faithful even when the beloved is faithless. The Old Testament does not simply describe suffering—it teaches us how to suffer. It gives voice to lament. It demands honesty. It calls the soul to trust in the God who remembers His covenant even when His people forget.

Modernity silenced this vocabulary. Lament disappeared from the cultural imagination. Grief became something to medicate. Sorrow became something to hide. Loss became something to rush past. But Scripture invites the believer to bring every wound into the presence of God. It allows the heart to cry, "How long, O Lord?" It gives permission to protest and permission to trust, without forcing the soul to choose between the two. This balance is foreign to the modern world, which sees suffering as failure rather than formation.

This disappearance of lament has consequences. When people do not know how to lament, they do not know how to endure. When they do not know how to endure, they do not know how to hope. And so suffering, instead of deepening the soul, fractures it. It becomes a weight too heavy for a heart trained only for ease. The result is a society that crumbles under pressures that previous generations absorbed with resilience. This is not because we lack strength, but because we lack the story that gives strength.

The story we have inherited from Scripture is not sentimental. It does not promise that God will remove every thorn. It promises that God will redeem every wound. It does not promise that the believer will be spared darkness. It promises that the darkness cannot overcome the Light. It does not promise that suffering will make sense immediately. It promises that suffering will not be wasted eternally.

This promise changes everything. When suffering arrives—

unwanted, unexpected, unchosen—the Christian does not ask, "How do I escape this?" but "How do I meet God here?" Because God is always here. This is the truth modernity has forgotten. The world imagines God as absent from suffering. Christianity reveals God as most present in suffering. "The LORD is near to the brokenhearted," the psalmist says, "and saves those crushed in spirit." Modernity hears this and calls it naïve. But only because modernity has lost the capacity for wonder.

This loss of wonder is perhaps the greatest tragedy of all. Wonder is the ability to perceive that the world is charged with God's presence. It is the ability to see grace hidden beneath the surface of things. When wonder disappears, only what is visible feels real. Only what is comfortable feels good. Only what is pleasurable feels meaningful. Suffering, therefore, becomes intolerable not because it is worse, but because the soul can no longer recognize the God who draws near within it.

To restore wonder is to restore the ability to endure. It is to recover the spiritual sight that allows us to see what modernity cannot: that God does some of His most profound work in the places where we feel weakest, most vulnerable, most afraid. The saints knew this. They knew that suffering was not an obstacle to God's action but a channel. They believed that Christ draws closest to those who draw closest to Him in their wounds. They trusted the Cross, not because they enjoyed pain, but because they knew who was crucified upon it.

This, ultimately, is how rediscovering biblical suffering restores identity. It reconnects the soul to the God who shapes His people through trial. It reconnects the heart to the Christ who redeems through wounds. It reconnects the believer to the Church that suffers and rejoices with him. Suffering becomes the place where identity is purified, deepened, clarified. The modern self collapses under pain because it has no foundation. The biblical self endures pain because its foundation is Christ.

Identity is not found in comfort. Identity is forged in communion. The believer learns who he is not by avoiding suffering, but by encountering God in suffering. He learns that he is a son, not an orphan. He learns that he is part of a body, not a solitary soul. He learns that he belongs to a people whose entire story—from Abraham to Mary to the martyrs—is a story shaped by sacrifice and crowned in glory.

The world tells us to ask, "How do I escape suffering?"

Scripture tells us to ask, "Who is with me in suffering?"

The world says, "Avoid pain at all costs."

Christ says, "Take up your cross and follow Me."

The world says, "You are alone in this."

The Cross says, "You are never alone."

This is the truth modernity has lost—but it is the truth the Church must proclaim again with courage, clarity, and compassion. A world allergic to pain needs Christians who are unafraid of it. A world shaped by comfort needs believers shaped by the Cross. A world drowning in meaninglessness needs disciples who reveal that suffering, when united to Christ, becomes the door through which meaning enters.

Suffering will always be mysterious. It will always be difficult. It will always wound. But it does not have to destroy. When we rediscover the biblical story, when we reclaim the sacramental worldview, when we embrace the Cross rather than flee it—then suffering ceases to collapse the soul. It becomes the place where the soul encounters the God who bears our sorrows.

And once you have met Him there, you discover something modernity cannot imagine:

suffering does not diminish life.

It enlarges it.

THE GOD WHO BEARS OUR SORROWS

It sanctifies it.
It prepares it for glory.

15

The Rise Of Assisted Dying And The Culture Of Escape

Suffering has always raised hard questions, but only in our generation has the question grown so sharp that people have begun asking whether life is still worth living once suffering enters the room. Earlier ages feared death; our age fears suffering more than death itself. The shift reveals something profound about the modern heart. It tells us that our crisis is not simply medical or political. It is spiritual. We no longer know what life is for, so we no longer know what suffering means.

To understand why assisted dying has risen so quickly—and why it speaks so persuasively to so many—we have to understand the imagination behind it. Not the legal structures, the clinical terminology, or the policy debates, but the deeper story modern culture tells about what it means to live and what it means to be human. Every society, whether it acknowledges it or not, rests upon a vision of the human person. And assisted dying reveals that the modern world now sees the human person primarily through the lens of autonomy. Freedom, once rooted in truth and oriented toward communion, has been remade into the power to choose without reference to God, nature, or community. When autonomy becomes the measure of dignity, anything that threatens autonomy begins to feel like a threat to dignity itself.

This is why suffering has become so frightening. Suffering strips away the illusion of control. It confronts us with weakness, dependence, and vulnerability—realities modern culture works hard to hide. We surround ourselves with technologies designed to insulate us from limitation. We build medical systems that promise to manage every discomfort. We develop therapies to alleviate every inner restlessness. Yet the more we attempt to conquer weakness, the more intolerable weakness becomes. A culture that prides itself on mastery will eventually come to see suffering not as a human experience to endure, but as a failure to prevent.

Scripture tells a very different story. From Genesis onward, humanity is defined not by autonomy but by relationship—relationship with God, with creation, and with one another. Adam's first breath is a gift, not an achievement. His identity is received, not earned. Even before the Fall, he is a creature dependent on the One who formed him from the dust. Dependency is not a consequence of sin; it is part of the order of creation. But when the modern world rejects dependence, it rejects the very structure through which God communicates His love.

This is the soil in which assisted dying has flourished. It offers an escape from dependence. It promises dignity through control. It interprets human weakness as something beneath human dignity rather than as the place where God draws close. It answers not the question of suffering, but the fear of suffering. And because the fear is real, the answer appears compassionate. But compassion severed from truth can wound more deeply than cruelty. The very word compassion means "to suffer with," yet assisted dying offers a compassion that refuses to accompany. Instead of walking with the sufferer, it removes the sufferer. Instead of presence, it offers elimination. Instead of communion, it offers a clean exit.

The pastoral danger is subtle because the emotional appeal is strong. We all know people who have endured terrible suffering. We all know families that have watched loved ones weaken slowly, painfully, helplessly. The desire to spare them is real, and it comes from love. But Christian love does not measure mercy by the removal of pain. Christian love measures mercy by fidelity—by remaining beside the one who suffers, bearing the weight with them, carrying the burden that cannot be lifted. The world defines dignity as control; the Gospel defines dignity as communion. The difference could not be greater, and the consequences could not be more profound.

When the Cross is removed from the horizon of meaning, suffering becomes unintelligible. But when the Cross stands at the centre, suffering becomes the place where love is revealed most clearly. This is why the rise of assisted dying is not merely a social shift. It is a theological crisis. It reveals what happens when a culture loses its transcendent reference point. Without God, suffering does not lead anywhere. It does not purify. It does not unite. It does not reveal. It simply hurts. And when pain loses its meaning, life touched by pain loses its meaning as well.

Our age avoids transcendence not because it is too complex, but because transcendence demands trust. Trust in a God who remains Lord even when He seems silent. Trust in a love that is deeper than fear. Trust in a meaning that is larger than the visible moment. When transcendence disappears, suffering becomes a wall rather than a doorway. It closes the heart instead of opening it. It isolates rather than binds. And in that isolation, the temptation to end suffering by ending life becomes understandable, even rational—precisely because the larger story has been forgotten.

But the Gospel insists that suffering can never be interpreted in isolation. It belongs to a covenant, a communion, a relationship. It belongs to a God who does not stand far off, but who enters human frailty and embraces it from within. Christ did not come to eliminate suffering by eliminating the sufferer. He came to transfigure suffering by transforming the one who suffers. The Incarnation is the ultimate refutation of assisted dying because it reveals that dignity is not destroyed by weakness. It is revealed through weakness. God Himself becomes weak so that human weakness might become a place where divine love can dwell.

In the next movement of this chapter, we will trace how the modern idea of "dignity" has been reshaped into something Christ never taught and the Church has never believed. But first we must understand this: the crisis of assisted dying is not fundamentally about medicine. It is about meaning. It emerges from a world that has forgotten the God who entered suffering, the God who made weakness holy, the God who transforms dying into a passage rather than an escape.

The modern redefinition of dignity did not happen overnight. It unfolded slowly, almost quietly, as the spiritual foundations of the West shifted. For centuries, Christians understood dignity as something rooted in God's love rather than in human control. It was a dignity revealed above all in the Incarnation—God choosing to become small, vulnerable, dependent. The Child in the manger, the Son carried from place to place in His mother's arms, the condemned man hanging helplessly on the Cross—these were not failures of dignity, but revelations of it. They showed that dignity is not an achievement but a gift. It is not the expression of power but the expression of love.

Modernity slowly replaced this vision with a different measuring stick: efficiency, autonomy, productivity. The human person began to be viewed less as a mystery to be received and more as a project to be managed. When life goes well, this worldview seems plausible. But when suffering enters the picture, the foundation cracks. If dignity depends on autonomy, what happens when autonomy disappears? If meaning depends on productivity, what happens when a person can no longer produce? If identity depends on self-expression, what happens when the self can no longer express anything at all?

These questions haunt modern culture, even if they are rarely spoken aloud. They haunt families watching loved ones fade. They haunt hospital rooms where machines sustain failing bodies. They haunt nursing homes where the elderly feel forgotten. They haunt individuals who fear that illness or disability will change the way they are seen by others. Beneath the push for assisted dying lies not a thirst for death but a terror of losing worth. The fear is not of suffering itself but of becoming "a burden."

The tragedy is that this fear has been shaped by a society that no longer understands dependence as belonging. In Scripture, dependence is woven into the fabric of covenant life. Israel depends on God for manna in the desert. The apostles depend on Christ for courage, strength, and purpose. The early Church depends on one another as members of one Body. St. Paul goes so far as to say that the "weaker" members are indispensable—not despite their weakness, but because of it. Weakness creates space for love. It draws forth compassion, patience, and sacrificial generosity. A society that hides the weak robs the strong of the chance to become holy.

But if dependence becomes a source of shame, then suffering becomes unbearable, and death begins to look like dignity. This is the heart of the cultural crisis. Assisted dying presents itself as a solution to the problem of pain, but the problem it claims to solve is deeper than pain. It is the problem of a culture that has lost the ability to see beauty in the dependent and sacredness in the weak. Once weakness is emptied of meaning, the logic of assisted dying becomes disturbingly persuasive. The most fragile lives appear to be the least dignified, the least valuable, and therefore the least worth preserving.

The Church sees things differently because the Church sees with the eyes of the Cross. The Cross was not efficient. It was not productive. It was not autonomous. It was, in every worldly sense, a failure. Yet it revealed the deepest truth about God and the deepest truth about us. It showed that love is strongest when it refuses to abandon the one who suffers. It showed that weakness is not something God avoids but something He embraces. It showed that the measure of a life is not its power but its capacity to give and receive love.

This is why the Church cannot accept the logic of assisted dying. Not because she glorifies pain. Not because she demands endurance at all costs. But because she refuses to surrender the truth that the vulnerable, the dependent, the frail, and the dying still bear the image of God. Their dignity does not diminish as their strength diminishes. If anything, their dignity becomes more transparent, because their dependence reveals the truth about every human soul: we are not self-sustaining. We live by grace. We live by love.

Assisted dying imagines that death can preserve dignity. The Gospel insists that only love can preserve dignity. The dignity of the dying person does not come from the ability to care for himself but from the fact that he is cared for by others. The dignity of the weak is revealed not in self-sufficiency but in being embraced by a community that refuses to let them face their suffering alone. True compassion does not eliminate the sufferer; it eliminates isolation. True mercy does not rush to end life; it rushes to fill the final season of life with presence, reverence, and love.

Yet to say these things is to confront a deeper wound in the modern psyche: the fear of being forgotten. Many who request assisted dying do so not because they want to die, but because they fear dying abandoned. They fear the loneliness of hospitals. They fear the emotional and financial strain their suffering might create for others. They fear losing the sense of self that has been shaped by a culture obsessed with autonomy. These fears are real, and they deserve honest compassion. They reveal how badly the modern world has failed to create communities of love.

The Church's answer to assisted dying is not a lecture about ethics but a way of life shaped by communion. It is a community that cares for the dying as Christ commands—with tenderness, patience, and reverence. It is a sacramental presence that brings grace to the bedside and hope to the heart. It is a witness to the truth that no life outgrows the reach of God's love and that no human being loses value by becoming dependent. Dependency is not the loss of dignity; it is the place where dignity is tested and revealed.

Once we recognise how deeply the modern fear of weakness runs, we begin to understand why assisted dying presents itself not as a rejection of life, but as a defence of dignity. Its advocates speak of compassion, autonomy, choice. The language is gentle, reassuring, humane. It appeals to something good within us—the desire to protect those we love. Yet the promise it makes is one the Gospel cannot affirm, because the Gospel reveals a truth that modern culture has forgotten: there is no dignity without communion. When communion is broken, dignity collapses, not because it has vanished, but because no one is present to witness it.

This is why the Church insists that the final stage of life is not a medical problem to be solved but a spiritual season to be lived. Scripture gives us countless examples of men and women who faced their last moments not with control, but with surrender. Jacob blessed his children from the weakness of his deathbed. David offered prayer and repentance in his final days. Simeon held the Child Jesus and declared that his life was complete. The early martyrs embraced their deaths not with despair but with trust. In every case, what made their dying holy was not their strength, but their dependence. The saints teach us that the last chapter of life is meant to be a chapter of grace.

The modern imagination struggles to accept this because it has lost the sense that dying itself can be meaningful. When transcendence disappears, the horizon shrinks. Death becomes a full stop rather than a passage. Suffering becomes a wall rather than a doorway. Life becomes a possession rather than a pilgrimage. And so the fear of suffering becomes the fear of losing the only story a person believes he has. This fear is not new—Scripture speaks of those "who through fear of death were subject to lifelong bondage"—but it has gained new intensity in a culture that no longer knows how to hope.

Hope is not optimism. Hope is not the conviction that suffering will be brief or bearable. Hope is the theological certainty that God is present and that His faithfulness endures even when strength fails. Hope does not deny the reality of pain; it denies the finality of pain. This is why assisted dying and Christian hope cannot coexist. One sees suffering as an interruption of life; the other sees it as a moment in the story of God's faithfulness. One sees dependence as indignity; the other sees it as communion. One seeks control; the other seeks surrender.

At the heart of assisted dying is the claim that suffering destroys dignity. At the heart of the Gospel is the claim that love reveals dignity, especially when suffering strips everything else away. Christ does not say, "Blessed are the autonomous." He says, "Blessed are the poor in spirit." He does not say, "This is My commandment, that you never burden one another." He says, "Bear one another's burdens." He does not say, "Greater love has no man than to preserve his independence." He says, "Greater love has no man than this, that he lay down his life for his friends."

The difference is not subtle. It is absolute. Assisted dying arises from a worldview in which burden-bearing is seen as a violation of dignity. The Gospel arises from a worldview in which burden-bearing is the very essence of love. The Christian life is cruciform, not because suffering is good in itself, but because love always descends into the places where another person's weakness is greatest. The Cross is not merely the place where Christ suffered; it is the place where He revealed what love looks like when it refuses to flee.

One of the most striking features of the push for assisted dying is the way it redefines the role of community. Throughout Scripture, community is the place where the weak are strengthened and the suffering are supported. Israel cared for its widows, orphans, and strangers because covenant demanded it. The early Christians cared for the sick and the dying because they saw Christ in them. But modern culture has inverted this logic. Weakness is no longer seen as an invitation to communion but as an interruption of convenience. Dependency becomes a threat to the smooth functioning of life. And so, without intending to, society pressures the weak into believing that their continued existence is a burden rather than a gift.

This is not merely a cultural failing; it is a theological one. If the weak are burdens, then Christ was a burden. If dependence undermines dignity, then the Incarnation undermines dignity. If receiving care from others makes life unworthy, then the entire Gospel collapses, because the Gospel begins with a God who became helpless. But the Gospel does not collapse. It stands firm against every false measure of dignity because dignity is rooted not in what we can do, but in the love God lavishes upon us.

And yet, the modern world does not see this. It sees a person who can no longer function independently and concludes that life has lost its meaning. It sees suffering and concludes that life has lost its quality. It sees the dying and concludes that life has lost its purpose. These conclusions arise not from cruelty but from confusion. A worldview that worships autonomy cannot help but fear dependence. A worldview that mistrusts transcendence cannot help but fear death. And a worldview that avoids suffering cannot help but propose escape as compassion.

What the Gospel reveals is the opposite: the dying are entrusted to us so that we might love them with the love that loved us to the end. Their suffering is not a burden we must erase but a call we must answer. Their weakness is not a threat to dignity but a doorway into communion. Their final days are not a meaningless decline but a profound spiritual season—one in which grace often works with a clarity unavailable in any other time of life.

If we are truly honest, the appeal of assisted dying reveals something uncomfortable about the modern soul. Beneath the language of compassion lies a worldview that has forgotten how to accompany. We have become skilled at relieving discomfort, but we have forgotten how to bear discomfort with others. We have developed sophisticated systems to manage illness, but we have forgotten how to be present to the ill. We can monitor vital signs with extraordinary precision, but we have forgotten how to recognise the signs of a soul longing for communion, reassurance, and love.

The crisis, in other words, is not primarily in the hospital. It is in the home, in the community, in the culture. It is the crisis of a people who have forgotten that love does not run from weakness—it leans toward it. In the ancient world, the poor, the sick, and the dying were often left to fend for themselves. Christians scandalised the empire by doing the opposite. They cared for their dead with tenderness. They washed the wounds of strangers. They visited the dying who had no family. They risked contagion to offer consolation. They did these things not because it was efficient, but because it was Christian. Their love revealed a truth the world had not seen: the dying are not a burden to be removed but a revelation of Christ to be encountered.

That witness changed the world once. It can change the world again.

The Church still believes what she has always believed: that the final stage of life is one of the holiest stages of life. It is the season in which a person is prepared to meet God. It is the time in which reconciliation, forgiveness, confession, and peace become the soul's deepest desires. This is why the sacraments are never more luminous than when they are celebrated at a bedside. In the Anointing of the Sick, Christ touches the wounded body with healing grace. In the Eucharist, Christ feeds the dying with His own life. In the prayers of commendation, He receives the soul into His mercy. These are not rituals of resignation. They are rituals of hope.

But a culture that has lost the sense of transcendence can no longer see this. It views dying as a medical event, nothing more. It limits its vision to heart rates and blood pressure. It measures life by biological functioning and measures meaning by personal autonomy. When transcendence collapses, so does the ability to see the soul—to recognise the dignity that remains even when the body weakens, the mind falters, and the strength ebbs away.

This collapse of transcendence is why assisted dying appears compassionate to so many. If physical suffering is the only suffering that matters, then ending physical suffering appears merciful. But Christianity has always known that suffering runs deeper than the body. The greatest suffering is not pain but isolation. It is the sense that one's life no longer matters, that one's weakness is a burden, that one is alone. When assisted dying offers relief, it is not primarily offering relief from pain. It is offering relief from loneliness, from fear, from the sense of being forgotten. But these fears are not solved by death. They are solved by love.

There is a profound sadness at the heart of assisted dying: not that people seek death, but that they believe no one will stand with them if they do not. It is a confession of loneliness disguised as autonomy. A declaration that life has become too heavy to carry and no one is near enough to help bear the weight. Many who request assisted dying do not want their lives to end; they want to know that their lives still matter. They want to be seen. They want to be held. They want to be loved to the end.

This is precisely the promise Christ makes: *"I am with you always."* He does not abandon. He does not withdraw. He does not deem anyone a burden. If we lose this truth, we lose the heart of the Gospel. And if the Church ceases to embody this truth for the dying, then we cease to be the Church.

This is why the Catholic response to assisted dying must go deeper than argument. We must become a people whose presence contradicts the lie that weakness diminishes worth. We must become a people who reveal Christ's tenderness at the bedside, Christ's patience in the long hours of decline, Christ's fidelity when strength fades. We must become communities where the dying are not exiled from daily life but drawn into the heart of it. Where elders are honoured. Where disability is not hidden. Where weakness is not treated as failure. Where dependence is not shameful but sacred.

The witness of the Church in these moments becomes a theology in action—a lived proclamation that human dignity does not expire, diminish, or decay. It shines most clearly when everything else is stripped away. The person who can no longer speak still communicates worth. The person who can no longer control their body still manifests God's image. The person who can no longer care for himself still calls forth the love that gives life its deepest meaning.

Assisted dying claims that a life touched by weakness is a life not worth living. The Gospel claims that weakness is the very place where God reveals His strength. Assisted dying claims that dignity ends when autonomy ends. The Gospel claims that dignity is the permanent mark of being created in God's image. Assisted dying claims that the burden is too heavy to bear. The Gospel claims that "love bears all things." The two visions cannot be reconciled. Only one can form a culture of life. Only one can form a community of hope.

The rise of assisted dying reveals a truth about our age that is as painful as it is urgent: we have forgotten how to suffer together. Not suffer in isolation, not suffer silently, but suffer *with*. This is the heart of Christian compassion. Christ did not redeem us from a distance. He entered our condition. He took on our weakness. He embraced our frailty. And He showed that love is proven not by avoiding suffering but by remaining present in it. A Church that forgets this loses not only its mission but its identity.

Yet this is precisely what the modern world longs for without realising it. Behind the demand for assisted dying lies a deeper demand: a plea for companionship in a moment when the soul feels most exposed. The person facing terminal illness does not fear pain alone. He fears abandonment. He fears being unseen, unheard, unremembered. He fears dying in a room where the machines speak louder than human voices. He fears that his life no longer holds a place in the story of others. These fears are not solved by offering death. They are healed by offering love.

This is why the Gospel stands as the only enduring answer to the crisis of assisted dying. The Gospel restores the meaning of weakness because it reveals that God Himself chose weakness. The Gospel restores the meaning of suffering because it reveals that God draws near in suffering. The Gospel restores the meaning of dying because it reveals that death is not a collapse into nothingness, but a passage into the presence of the One who has walked before us. When the dying are accompanied with faith, hope, and love, the final chapter of life becomes a chapter of grace.

Christian hope does not promise that suffering will disappear. It promises that suffering will be transformed. It promises that no pain is wasted, no tear unseen, no moment isolated from the love of God. Assisted dying cannot offer this. It offers escape, not transformation. It offers silence, not communion. It offers an end, not a fulfilment.

The choice between these two visions is not merely moral. It is theological. It is a choice between a world that believes God enters human weakness and a world that believes weakness has no meaning at all.

The Church's response to assisted dying, therefore, must be more than a defence of doctrine. It must be a renewal of presence. It must be a recovery of the ancient Christian art of accompanying the dying. It must take flesh in families who refuse to turn away, in parishes that pray at the bedside, in communities that surround the weak with reverence rather than embarrassment. It must take flesh in priests who bring the sacraments with tenderness and patience. It must take flesh in friendships that do not evaporate when suffering begins.

The renewal must also take place in the interior life. The Christian must learn again the sacredness of dependence. We must learn to see in our own weakness an invitation to trust God more deeply. We must learn to accept help without shame, to ask for prayer without fear, to rest our hearts in the knowledge that God is closest when our strength fails. When Christians live this way, they testify to something the world has forgotten: that the measure of life is not capability but communion, not independence but love.

The modern world claims that assisted dying is a mercy. But mercy, according to Scripture, is not the act of removing the one who suffers; it is the act of remaining with the one who suffers. Mercy does not rush toward elimination. Mercy enters into the suffering and redeems it with presence. True mercy can sit at the bedside through long nights, can offer consolation when words fail, can hold a trembling hand and whisper prayers when the soul grows weary. True mercy endures. True mercy accompanies. True mercy loves to the end.

The crisis of assisted dying is the crisis of a culture that has forgotten how to love the weak. The answer is not a louder argument but a clearer witness. When Christians accompany the dying with the tenderness of Christ, assisted dying is exposed for what it is: not a path to dignity, but a concession to despair. When Christians reveal the beauty of dependence and the holiness of frailty, the world begins to remember what it has lost. And when Christians live the mystery of the Cross in the presence of the dying, the fear that drives assisted dying loses its power.

For the Cross reveals a truth deeper than death: no life is meaningless, no suffering is wasted, and no soul is ever abandoned. Christ has gone before us. He has sanctified dependence. He has made weakness a place of encounter. He has filled dying with hope. In Him, the final season of life is never an exit from dignity but an entrance into grace.

16

Mental Suffering And The Age Of Fragile Souls

There are sufferings that strike the body, and there are sufferings that strike the heart. The first can be seen, measured, named, and treated. The second often remain hidden, even from those who carry them. Yet the hidden wounds may be the deepest. In every age, human beings have endured physical pain. Wars, diseases, famines, and accidents have been constant companions of human history. But our age faces something different, something that does not show itself in broken bones or fever charts. Our age suffers in the interior of the soul.

Anxiety, depression, loneliness—these have become the new afflictions of modern life. They may not leave visible scars, but they leave the person disoriented, restless, and afraid. The irony is that we have more comfort, more convenience, and more technological power than any generation before us, yet our inner lives are more fragile than ever. The human heart, created for communion with God, finds itself surrounded by noise but starving for meaning. Surrounded by connection but starving for belonging. Surrounded by stimulation but starving for peace.

This interior suffering is not a minor subplot in the drama of human life. It is one of the central crises of our age. People who can endure physical hardship with remarkable courage can be undone by a loneliness they cannot name or a fear they cannot silence. A person may carry out his daily responsibilities with apparent strength while internally feeling as though he walks through shadowed valleys without a guide. The external world may see competence; the interior world feels like a wilderness.

Scripture does not ignore this kind of suffering. In fact, it might speak of it more than any other. The Psalms are filled with cries from hearts pierced not by swords but by sorrow. "My tears have been my food day and night," writes the psalmist, describing an anguish that no physician can diagnose. Elijah, after defeating the prophets of Baal in one of the most dramatic moments of the Old Testament, collapses under a broom tree and begs God to take his life. Jeremiah speaks of a fire in his bones when he tries to hold back his grief. Even the apostles, filled with the Holy Spirit, faced fears that drove them to prayer with trembling hands. The Bible is not embarrassed by spiritual suffering; it gives it words.

But modern culture does not give it words. It gives categories, labels, and diagnoses, but it does not give meaning. It treats the interior life as a psychological phenomenon rather than a spiritual mystery. It speaks of mood, energy, trauma, imbalance, dysfunction. These are not false descriptions, but they are incomplete. They describe important dimensions of the human experience, but they do not reach the depth of the human person. The soul is not satisfied with analysis; it longs for purpose. It longs for belonging. It longs for God.

When the horizon of transcendence disappears, the interior life collapses under its own weight. Suffering that once drove people to prayer now drives them to distraction. Suffering that once opened hearts to God now leaves them closed, numb, or terrified. Without a story larger than the self, the self becomes too small to bear its own sorrows. When a person no longer knows who he is before God, he no longer knows what to do with the pain that rises within him.

This is why spiritual suffering often hurts more than bodily pain. Bodily pain has an obvious cause and an obvious limit. The body signals what is wrong, and medical wisdom attempts to restore order. But spiritual suffering attacks identity. It raises questions that strike at the very centre of the person: *Who am I? What is my life for? Does anyone see me? Does God hear me? Does my suffering matter?* These are not questions that can be answered by clinical charts. They are questions of covenant, questions of communion, questions of hope.

The heart becomes fragile when it no longer knows where it belongs. Loneliness intensifies when a person no longer trusts that God sees. Anxiety multiplies when the future is no longer held by a Father. Depression deepens when the soul feels cut off from meaning. These afflictions are not signs of spiritual failure; they are signs of spiritual starvation. They reveal what happens when a person built for covenant finds himself in a culture that has forgotten covenant altogether.

Our technological age has given us countless ways to communicate, yet communication has become thinner, more fleeting, more fragmented. We can contact one another instantly, but we struggle to encounter one another deeply. We can scroll through the lives of thousands, yet feel unknown by even a few. A generation raised on screens has learned to express emotions without ever learning how to endure them. We have words for everything except the ones that matter most.

This is not simply a cultural problem; it is a theological one. The human person was not made to live enclosed within his own mind. He was made to live in relationship—with God, with family, with community, with the Church. When these relationships fracture, the soul begins to wither. The interior suffering that follows is not the result of weakness, but of isolation. And isolation, Scripture tells us, was the one thing God declared "not good" before sin ever entered the world.

The age of fragile souls is the age of forgotten communion. A heart that is not anchored in God becomes vulnerable to every fear. A mind that is not lifted by hope becomes burdened by every sorrow. A soul that is not supported by community becomes overwhelmed by every trial. The Psalmist understood this when he cried, "Why are you cast down, O my soul?" It is the cry of a person who knows that the interior life is capable of sinking, but also capable of being lifted.

To understand this crisis deeply, we must not look first to statistics or studies, but to Scripture and the Church. Modern psychology can describe the landscape, but only the Gospel can reveal the path through it. The fragility of the modern soul is not simply a mental state; it is a spiritual wound that requires spiritual healing. And the Church, with her sacraments, her Scriptures, her saints, and her communal life, holds treasures of grace that the world has forgotten it needs.

When we look honestly at the modern landscape, it becomes clear that interior suffering has become the dominant form of affliction in our time. People are not collapsing under the weight of persecution or famine; they are collapsing under the weight of meaninglessness. We have created a world in which a person may live comfortably, yet feel deeply unsafe within his own thoughts. The heart becomes restless not because life is dangerous, but because life feels directionless. The soul becomes weary not because burdens are heavy, but because purpose feels light.

This is why anxiety has become so pervasive. Anxiety is not simply fear; it is fear without an anchor. Fear becomes anxiety when there is nothing to hold onto. In Scripture, fear is not condemned when it drives a person toward God. The Psalms are full of such fear—fear that brings the heart to prayer, fear that awakens trust, fear that becomes the doorway into a deeper surrender. But anxiety is fear that has lost its horizon. It is fear turned inward, circling itself without finding rest. It is fear separated from faith.

The rise of anxiety is, at its deepest level, a theological crisis. A person who tries to carry the weight of his own existence without reference to God will inevitably feel crushed. The human heart was never meant to be its own foundation. When a person becomes the centre of his own universe, every uncertainty becomes a threat, every decision becomes a burden, every weakness becomes a danger, and every future becomes a source of dread. The soul trembles because it has been asked to do something it cannot do: sustain itself.

Depression, too, reveals this inward collapse. Depression is the sense that life has lost its colour, its direction, its pulse. Scripture is not silent here. The psalmist cries, "My soul clings to the dust," describing a despair that drains the heart of desire. Jeremiah speaks of sitting alone in darkness. Job laments the day of his birth. These are not expressions of unbelief, but of souls wrestling with the experience of abandonment. Depression often arises when hope has been obscured—when the eyes of the heart can no longer see God's promise in the midst of present sorrow.

In older cultures, suffering drove people into the arms of community. Today, suffering drives people into isolation. The modern world has perfected the art of living alone, even while surrounded by others. We have more ways to communicate than any generation before us, yet we are more alone than any generation before us. Loneliness is no longer a rare experience; it has become the default condition of modern life. People long to be known, yet fear being seen. They long to belong, yet fear rejection. They long for communion, yet settle for connection that does not touch the soul.

This loneliness becomes spiritual suffering because it contradicts the deepest truth about the human person: we are made in the image of a God who is communion. The Father, the Son, and the Holy Spirit exist not in isolation but in eternal relationship. When a person lives without communion—without real relationships, without shared life, without spiritual family—he begins to feel a kind of hunger that no amount of entertainment or distraction can satisfy. The soul begins to ache because it is being deprived of the very thing it was made for.

The Church has always known this. This is why the first crisis the early believers faced was not persecution but division. Paul's letters are filled with exhortations not to abandon one another, not to fracture the Body, not to neglect meeting together. The apostles understood that spiritual life withers when community withers. A person cannot carry the weight of his own interior suffering alone—not because he is weak, but because he is human.

Yet modern culture encourages precisely this: a life lived inwardly, privately, self-referentially. It teaches people to create their own identity, their own truth, their own meaning. But meaning is not invented. Meaning is received. Identity is not constructed. Identity is revealed. When a person tries to build his life without God, he discovers quickly that the foundation is sand. When he tries to shape his identity without communion, he discovers quickly that the self collapses under its own contradictions. The result is fragility—not moral fragility, but spiritual fragility. The soul cracks under pressures it was never meant to face alone.

Even the modern vocabulary for interior suffering reveals this loss of transcendence. People speak of feeling "empty," "numb," "adrift," "lost." These are not merely emotional states; they are spiritual realities. They describe what happens when the soul becomes disconnected from its source. The human heart cannot live long without a horizon. It cannot thrive without a sense of belonging. It cannot endure without hope. When these spiritual anchors disappear, suffering deepens—even when life, externally, seems to be going well.

This is why spiritual suffering is often more feared than bodily pain. Bodily pain hurts, but it does not shake the foundations of the self. Spiritual suffering threatens identity. It makes a person question his worth, his purpose, his place in the world. It makes him feel unseen, unheard, and unanchored. This is why so many people who appear strong on the outside struggle silently within. Their suffering cannot be measured in medical terms because it is not the body that is wounded—it is the heart.

The Church understands this kind of suffering because Christ entered it. He knew what it meant to feel abandoned: "My God, My God, why hast Thou forsaken Me?" He knew what it meant to weep, to tremble, to feel the weight of sorrow in His soul. He knew what it meant to watch His friends fall asleep when He needed them the most. Christ's suffering was not only physical; it was spiritual. And because He entered this darkness, He can enter ours.

If Christ entered spiritual suffering, then no Christian can consider it a sign of divine absence. Yet this is precisely the temptation that haunts the modern heart. When the interior world darkens, people assume God has withdrawn. When anxiety grows heavy, they assume faith has failed. When depression settles in like a long, uninvited night, they assume their prayers have been ignored. These assumptions are understandable, but they are wrong. Scripture teaches us that God is often nearest when the soul feels most alone. The absence we feel is not His absence but our inability to see through the fog of our own fears.

This is why the saints speak so openly about interior desolation. They do not hide it or pretend that faith exempts them from it. St. Thérèse experienced seasons when she felt as though heaven were closed to her. St. John of the Cross wrote entire treatises on the "dark night of the soul," that mysterious time when God withdraws sensible consolation in order to deepen the soul's trust. Mother Teresa, in letters revealed only after her death, described years of profound interior darkness even as she radiated charity to the world. These saints were not losing faith. They were being drawn deeper into faith.

The dark night does not come to destroy the soul but to purify it. When God removes the supports we rely on—comfort, feeling, certainty—He is not abandoning us. He is teaching us to stand on the only foundation that will never shift: His love. He strips away the false securities that keep us from surrender. He removes the emotional assurances that can become idols masquerading as faith. He leads the soul into a deeper knowledge of Him—a knowledge rooted not in feeling, but in trust.

The modern world has little patience for this purification because it has forgotten the meaning of endurance. It treats every discomfort as a crisis and every sadness as a malfunction. It offers distraction in place of devotion and stimulation in place of contemplation. When the soul feels restless, the world encourages more noise, more movement, more activity. But interior suffering cannot be outrun. It must be faced, understood, and carried—preferably not alone, and never without God.

This is where the wisdom of the Church becomes essential. The Church understands the interior life far better than any modern discipline. She has accompanied saints, mystics, sinners, and ordinary believers for two thousand years. She knows the patterns of the heart, the movements of grace, the seasons of darkness and illumination. She knows that the soul does not grow in a straight line, that periods of dryness can be preparation for deeper union, and that trials of the mind can refine faith as fire refines gold.

One of the great tragedies of the modern age is that people face interior suffering without the guidance that previous generations received as a matter of course. They no longer have the prayers that once shaped the rhythms of the day. They no longer have the sacramental worldview that interpreted sorrow through the lens of Christ's Passion. They no longer have spiritual fathers or mothers to help them recognise God's work beneath the surface of their emotions. Deprived of these foundations, the soul becomes fragile. It is not sin that weakens it—it is starvation.

Loneliness reinforces this fragility. A person may have hundreds of contacts and no companions. He may be surrounded by voices and still feel unheard. He may participate in endless conversations yet never speak of what he truly carries. The human heart, created for communion, begins to curl inward, not because it wants isolation, but because it fears vulnerability. This creates a spiritual paradox: the more a person fears being alone, the more he withdraws from relationships. The more he withdraws, the more alone he becomes. The wound deepens because the heart has lost the courage to be seen.

This loneliness becomes even heavier when the conscience carries burdens that have not been confessed. Unspoken guilt becomes a weight that presses inward, darkening the heart. Shame isolates. Regret suffocates. Spiritual wounds left untreated become spiritual infections, spreading through the interior life until even joy feels fragile. The world cannot heal this kind of suffering. It can distract, but it cannot absolve. It can soothe, but it cannot reconcile. Only God can speak the word that the soul longs to hear: "Your sins are forgiven." Only the Church can make that word present through the sacrament Christ entrusted to her.

This is why confession has such power over interior suffering. It is not merely a ritual; it is a liberation. It releases the soul from the burden of secrecy. It restores the person to communion. It pulls the heart out of isolation and places it once again within the life of grace. Many modern Christians underestimate the sacrament of reconciliation because they have forgotten what it does. It does not simply cleanse; it heals. It does not merely forgive; it restores. A heart that has been carrying unspoken guilt often discovers, after confession, that the anxiety it could not explain begins to lift. Grace touches the very place where fear had taken root.

But confession is not the only sacrament that speaks to interior suffering. The Eucharist sustains the weary soul with the presence of Christ Himself. Baptism gave us the identity we could never create. Confirmation strengthened us with the Spirit who prays within us when we do not know how to pray. Anointing of the Sick brings healing to souls weighed down by fear. Marriage and Holy Orders provide vocations in which communion becomes the form of daily life. The sacraments are not symbols of comfort; they are encounters with the One who holds the interior life together.

The Church also offers something the modern world cannot imitate: a community that carries suffering together. When Christians pray for one another, visit one another, console one another, they become the living antidote to loneliness. They make visible the communion Christ created. They teach the fragile soul that it is not forgotten, not invisible, not alone. Even the simplest gestures—a shared meal, a quiet prayer, a faithful friendship—can become a lifeline for someone standing on the edge of spiritual exhaustion.

The renewal of Christian community is essential, because interior suffering cannot be healed in the abstract. It must be met by persons who reveal the faithfulness of God through their presence. The early Christians did not simply preach communion—they lived it. They carried one another's burdens. They prayed in one another's homes. They shared resources, meals, and time. Their communion was so visible, so tangible, that the world took notice. "See how they love one another," the pagans said. They saw Christians carry suffering together, and they recognised something divine at work among them.

Our age needs this witness again. People do not simply need advice for their anxiety; they need belonging. They do not simply need explanations for their depression; they need communion. They do not simply need reassurance that God is near; they need the nearness of His people. When the Body of Christ lives as a body—each member caring for the rest—the lonely discover hope. The fearful discover courage. The fragile discover strength. This is not idealism; it is the ordinary work of grace.

But Christian community does more than accompany suffering; it forms the soul so that it can endure suffering with faith. A heart shaped by prayer learns to speak to God even when it does not feel His presence. A heart shaped by Scripture learns to interpret its emotions through the lens of God's promises. A heart shaped by sacramental life learns to recognise grace even in dryness. Without these foundations, the soul becomes fragile when interior suffering arrives. With them, it becomes resilient—not because suffering becomes easy, but because suffering becomes meaningful.

This formation is especially important in an age that has lost the art of contemplation. The modern mind is overstimulated but undernourished. It rushes from one thought to the next, one notification to the next, one distraction to the next. Silence feels foreign. Rest feels uncomfortable. Stillness feels dangerous, because stillness reveals what is happening in the interior life. Many people discover only in silence the fears they have been carrying, the wounds they have been avoiding, and the longings they have been ignoring. Silence becomes unbearable because the heart has forgotten how to meet God there.

Yet contemplation is not an optional luxury for the spiritual elite; it is the normal posture of a soul that remembers it belongs to God. It is in contemplation that the anxious heart learns to breathe again. It is in contemplation that the depressed heart discovers what it cannot see in the darkness. It is in contemplation that the lonely heart hears the One who never abandons it. The saints teach us that interior suffering becomes transformative only when it is brought into the presence of God. Left alone, it becomes a weight. Brought into prayer, it becomes a path.

A Church that revives contemplation revives hope. Not a vague optimism, but a hope born of encounter—a hope that rests not on emotion, but on the faithfulness of God. When a person quiets his heart before the Lord, he begins to perceive the truth that his suffering does not have the last word. He begins to sense that grace is already at work, even if he cannot see how. He begins to rediscover the difference between silence and abandonment, between darkness and despair. The soul learns that God is present in ways too subtle for emotion to measure.

The saints show us that spiritual suffering is often the place where God prepares the soul for deeper communion. But this is difficult to see when the interior trial is at its height. The dark night feels like rejection, not preparation. The weight of sorrow feels like failure, not grace. The silence of God feels like distance, not invitation. This is why the witness of the saints is so necessary—because they speak from the other side of the darkness. They teach us that what feels like abandonment is often the work of God drawing the soul into a more mature faith.

Spiritual maturity does not require the absence of interior suffering; it requires the presence of trust. A person who suffers interiorly and continues to pray is already living the mystery of faith. A person who feels abandoned and continues to seek God is already imitating Christ in Gethsemane. A person who wakes each day carrying invisible burdens and entrusts them to the Lord is living a hidden martyrdom of hope. The world cannot understand this kind of endurance because it sees suffering only as a problem; the Christian sees suffering as a place where love is tested and purified.

This purification is not something the soul accomplishes on its own. It is the work of grace. But grace requires cooperation, and cooperation requires freedom. The person who turns to God in interior suffering, even with trembling hands and weary words, gives God permission to work in the places that hurt most. He opens a space in the heart for healing to begin. He discovers, slowly and often imperceptibly, that the suffering does not have to disappear for God to be present within it.

And when God is present, suffering becomes bearable—not because it is less painful, but because it is no longer empty. The soul begins to see its suffering through a different lens—not as a threat, but as a place where God draws near. The fragility that once seemed unbearable becomes, in the hands of grace, the very place where the soul learns humility, dependence, and compassion. It becomes a path to communion rather than a descent into isolation.

When interior suffering begins to take on meaning, something remarkable happens. The fragile soul does not suddenly become invulnerable—this is not the illusion the world offers—but it becomes rooted. The winds that once threatened to uproot now deepen the roots. The wounds that once seemed senseless now become places of encounter. The restlessness that once scattered the heart now becomes a longing that draws the heart toward God. Spiritual suffering, illumined by grace, becomes a teacher.

It teaches humility, because the person learns that he cannot save himself. It teaches dependence, because he discovers that he must lean on God and others if he is to endure. It teaches compassion, because those who have suffered interiorly are able to recognise the hidden wounds in others. They do not judge quickly. They do not dismiss fear. They do not speak lightly of sorrow. They accompany with patience, because they know what loneliness feels like, and they know how much a single act of love can matter.

This is why the Church's answer to interior suffering is never isolation. It is always communion. A suffering person needs not only prayer but people. Not only theology but tenderness. Not only truth but presence. The Church, when she is faithful to her Lord, becomes the place where no one suffers alone. The parish becomes the home where wandering hearts rediscover belonging. The sacraments become the anchors that keep the soul steady when emotions shift like waves. The community becomes the net that catches those who fall through the cracks of modern life.

But the Church also offers something deeper: she offers purpose. One of the great sources of interior suffering in our age is the loss of purpose—the sense that life has no direction, no mission, no sacred task. A heart without purpose becomes a heart without strength. Yet God never creates anyone without calling them. Every life carries a vocation. Every soul is summoned into the work of love. When a person discovers that he has a mission—however small, however hidden—his suffering takes on new meaning. He no longer suffers as a solitary individual; he suffers as a disciple following the cruciform path of Christ.

Purpose does not eliminate interior suffering, but it transforms it. A person who knows *why* he is suffering can endure sorrow that would otherwise crush him. This is the mystery revealed in the lives of the saints: their interior trials were not dead ends but doorways. They discovered that God uses even desolation to prepare the soul for deeper love. They learned to interpret their suffering through the eyes of faith, not through the fog of emotion. And they became, through this purification, witnesses to a hope that cannot be shaken.

This hope is the final gift the Church offers to fragile souls—not optimism, not positivity, but the theological virtue that anchors the heart in the faithfulness of God. Hope does not deny the darkness. It declares that the darkness is not final. Hope does not erase sorrow. It reveals the presence of God within sorrow. Hope does not silence the cry of the heart. It teaches the heart to cry out to the One who hears.

The modern world cannot offer this hope. It can distract the heart but cannot heal it. It can medicate anxiety but cannot quiet the soul. It can stimulate the mind but cannot give meaning. Only Christ can say, "Come to Me, all who labour and are heavy laden, and I will give you rest." Only Christ can take the fragile soul and make it strong—not by removing its wounds, but by inhabiting them.

Interior suffering may be the defining affliction of our age, but it is also the place where grace can work most deeply. The fragile soul is not a sign of cultural failure; it is a sign that human hearts still long for God. The anxiety, the loneliness, the depression that weigh down so many are not obstacles to faith—they are invitations. They are the places where the human person discovers, perhaps for the first time, that he cannot live without the One who made him. They are the places where the cry of the Psalmist becomes our own: "Out of the depths I cry to Thee, O Lord."

And the Lord who hears that cry does not remain silent. He enters the depths. He draws near. He gathers the fragile soul into His own wounded heart. And He teaches us, through those wounds, that our suffering is never wasted, never unseen, and never endured alone.

17

The Problem Of Innocent Suffering

In every age, one question has shaken the foundations of faith more than any other. It is not the question of why we suffer — every human being knows suffering is part of life in a fallen world. It is the question of why the innocent suffer. Why children die. Why families are torn apart by tragedies they did not cause. Why natural disasters strike without warning, collapsing homes and futures in a single night. Why sorrow falls not only on the guilty — or even primarily on the guilty — but on those who have done nothing to deserve it.

No question pierces the heart more deeply. No question brings more tears. No question has driven more souls to cry out like Job, "Let the Almighty answer me!" This is not a merely intellectual puzzle. It is a wound. It is a lament. It is the earthquake beneath the human heart.

And what is striking — what is almost scandalous — is that Scripture does not silence this question. It gives it a voice. It does not hide from it; it sings it, prays it, and places it on the lips of the faithful.

From the opening chapters of Genesis, innocent suffering stands in the centre of the human story. Abel dies, not because he sinned, but because his righteousness stirred Cain's envy. Rachel weeps for her children as they are carried into exile. The prophets cry over a people crushed by forces they cannot comprehend. The Book of Lamentations stands as a monument to grief that refuses to be explained away. Even the Psalms — the prayerbook of the Church — give us language for pain that is undeserved, unexpected, and unanswerable in purely human terms. "Why do the wicked prosper?" "Why have You forgotten me?" "Why do You hide Your face?"

The Bible is not embarrassed by these cries. It sanctifies them.

Innocent suffering is not an objection to faith — it is the stage on which faith becomes real. It is the very place where covenant is tested. It is where the human heart discovers whether it knows God or only the comforts God provides.

In our own time, this question has taken on a new weight. Modernity promised us safety, predictability, control. It promised that science, medicine, and technology could tame the world and protect us from the randomness of tragedy. And when those promises fail — as they inevitably must — the heartbreak is sharper, the disorientation deeper. We feel betrayed not only by circumstances but by the illusion that we ever held control to begin with.

Yet the grief itself is ancient. When a child dies, the heart refuses symmetry. This suffering does not "fit" into any moral equation the world tries to write. It resists the logic of cause and effect. It exposes the inadequacy of every simplistic notion of divine justice. And because it resists easy answers, it reveals a truth most of us would prefer to avoid: the world is not the way God made it. It is the way sin has scarred it.

This is where many people instinctively recoil. They imagine divine justice as symmetry — a one-to-one correspondence between good behaviour and blessing, between sin and suffering. But Scripture rejects that idea again and again. Jesus Himself rejects it when asked whether a man's blindness or the collapse of the tower in Siloam were punishments. "Do you think they were worse sinners?" He asks. "No, I tell you."

The Bible is clear: suffering is not a scorecard. Innocent suffering does not mean divine punishment. And divine justice does not mean mechanical fairness.

Justice, in biblical terms, means fidelity — God keeping His covenant, even when the world breaks apart. It means God refusing to abandon the ones who suffer, even when the suffering makes no earthly sense. Justice means presence, not symmetry. It means love stronger than chaos. It means a Father who holds His children even when the earth shakes beneath them.

But no truth is harder to see when tragedy strikes. In the moment of heartbreak, what the soul sees most clearly is what has been lost. A child who will not grow. A home that will not be rebuilt. A future that will not unfold. The heart trembles, and the question rises: "Where was God?"

And here the Gospel answers not with a theory, but with a Person.

God does not explain innocent suffering from afar — He enters it. He does not respond with an argument — He responds with a Cross. He does not remain distant from the darkest places — He descends into them.

Christ is the most innocent sufferer who ever lived. And He suffers not to erase our questions but to stand inside them. On Calvary, He takes up every cry ever raised from the lips of the grieving, the anguished, and the innocent. His death is not simply a ransom; it is revelation. It reveals that God is not the author of suffering but the companion of the sufferer. It reveals that divine justice is not the avoidance of pain but the redemption of pain. It reveals that God does not flee the darkest places — He fills them with Himself.

And because He enters innocent suffering, no innocent suffering is ever wasted.

When Jesus enters the world, He does not come as a philosopher offering explanations from a safe distance. He comes as a child — vulnerable, threatened, hunted by Herod before He has even spoken His first words. The Gospel begins with a massacre of innocents, and the Son of God placed in a manger not because it is picturesque, but because no place of safety could be found.

The story is not accidental. It foreshadows something essential:
God's answer to innocent suffering is not avoidance, but solidarity.
When the innocent suffer, God does not stand apart.
He draws near.

This nearness is not symbolic. It is literal. It is embodied. It is flesh and blood, tears and prayer, silence and agony. The Cross is the revelation of a God who steps inside the darkest mystery of human existence — not to erase the darkness, but to fill it with Himself.

Many people imagine divine love as protection from suffering. Scripture reveals something deeper. Divine love is presence in suffering. Divine love is fidelity through suffering. Divine love is the refusal to let suffering have the final word.

This is why the Cross cannot be understood as one more tragedy in a tragic world. The Cross is the moment in which God takes the consequences of a fallen world into Himself. Jesus does not simply endure innocent suffering — He makes it the place where redemption begins.

And that changes everything.

If the Cross were nothing more than an example, it would not touch the mystery we face when a child dies or when disaster strikes a family without warning. But the Cross is not an example. It is the centre of cosmic restoration. It is the place where God absorbs into His own life the full weight of the world's sorrow. Every moment of innocent suffering finds its echo — and its answer — in that moment.

This is why the New Testament speaks of Christ as the "Lamb slain from the foundation of the world." This is why the Apostles proclaim that His suffering is not only His, but ours: "He bore our griefs, and carried our sorrows." The language is not metaphor. It is covenantal reality. Christ does not merely sympathise with the innocent — He mystically unites Himself to them.

And because He unites Himself to them, their suffering is not swallowed by meaninglessness. It becomes part of the story He redeems.

Yet even this truth does not erase the anguish. The Christian faith does not pretend that mystery dissolves pain. It does not claim that faith removes tears. It insists only that tears are not shed alone. It insists only that suffering does not fall into a void. It insists that the Father who did not abandon His Son will not abandon His children.

Which brings us to a deeper truth that modern ears struggle to hear.

In Scripture, God's justice is not the balancing of scales. It is not the elimination of disparity. It is His unwavering faithfulness to His covenant — His refusal to let evil have the final word. Divine justice is revealed not when suffering is removed, but when suffering is redeemed.

We see this in the resurrection.

Christ does not rise without wounds. He rises with them. He presents them to His disciples. He sanctifies them. The wounds are no longer signs of defeat but signs of victory — the very marks through which grace is poured.

This is the pattern of redemption.

What evil inflicts, God transforms.

What grief shatters, God restores.

What death steals, God returns in glory.

But between the Cross and the resurrection lies the silence of Holy Saturday — the day when God seems absent, when no answer seems to come. Every parent who has buried a child knows something of that silence. Every person who has watched a loved one die suddenly knows something of that darkness. Every innocent life cut short enters that day of waiting.

The Church never rushes past that silence. It holds it. It honours it. It prays it. Because this silence is not abandonment — it is the threshold of resurrection.

Still, the mind wrestles.

Why does God not intervene?

Why does He not prevent the tragedy?

Why must the innocent walk this path at all?

These are not questions to be silenced. They are questions to be brought, trembling and unfiltered, to the foot of the Cross. For the Cross, more than any philosophical system, reveals that God's way of conquering evil is not by shielding us from the world, but by entering the world so completely that evil cannot have the final word over any life united to Him.

If God had chosen to eliminate suffering by eliminating human freedom, He could have done so. But He would have destroyed the very dignity we were created to bear. Love cannot be forced; it must be chosen. And in a world where freedom exists, the possibility of tragedy exists with it — not because God delights in loss, but because God refuses to create a world in which love is impossible.

The finest biblical example of this is Joseph. Sold into slavery. Falsely accused. Imprisoned. Forgotten. A young man whose suffering was innocent from the start. Yet at the end of his story, Joseph speaks the words that define the mystery of providence: "You meant it for evil, but God meant it for good."

Joseph is not claiming that evil is good. He is claiming that God can bring good out of what evil intends. That is divine justice. That is divine sovereignty. That is divine love.

Joseph's words don't remove the sting of what happened. They don't justify the betrayal of his brothers. They don't diminish the years of confinement or the loneliness of innocence misunderstood. What they do is reveal the deepest truth of the biblical imagination: evil never has the last word in God's story. Even when God does not cause suffering, He refuses to let suffering be the final author of a person's life.

This conviction becomes the foundation for facing innocent suffering without collapsing under its weight. It is not optimism. Optimism is fragile. It depends on circumstances going well. Hope is stronger. Hope survives even when circumstances turn to ash. Hope is anchored not in what the eyes see but in what God has promised.

This difference becomes clear when we look at the way Scripture describes the presence of God in moments of tragedy. The Psalms, for example, do not imagine God watching from afar. They imagine Him hearing, remembering, drawing near. "The Lord is close to the broken hearted." "He hears the cry of the afflicted." "He keeps every tear in His bottle." These are not sentimental lines. They are covenant assertions. They declare that God binds Himself to His people even when His presence is not immediately felt.

The prophets echo this truth. When Israel suffers exile — the supreme example of national tragedy — God does not deny their anguish. He names it. He enters it. He promises to restore what was lost. But He also reveals a mystery: suffering, even innocent suffering, can become the place where the heart turns again to Him. "In their affliction," Hosea says, "they will seek Me earnestly." This is not to say suffering is good. It is to say suffering is not godless. God is not absent from it. He is at work within it, even when His work is hidden.

This hiddenness is often the stumbling block. The heart can endure only so much before it begins to cry out not only for relief but for explanation. Yet Scripture almost never answers the question of "why" in the way we expect. It gives reasons occasionally —

discipline, purification, preparation — but these reasons never attempt to encompass the mystery. They are glimpses, not full interpretations.

The fullest answer Scripture gives is not a reason but a revelation: the Cross.

The Cross is the moment in which the question of innocent suffering becomes inseparable from the person of Jesus Christ. The God who commands justice allows Himself to be condemned unjustly. The God who gives breath allows Himself to breathe His last. The God who holds all things together allows His own body to be torn apart.

And this is what changes the landscape of suffering forever.

God does not answer the cry of the innocent by sparing His Son from suffering. He answers by allowing His Son to suffer with us and for us. He answers by transforming suffering from the inside out.

This means something profound. In every innocent life that suffers, Christ is present — not merely in sympathy, but in solidarity. When a child suffers, Christ does not stand apart. He is the One who cried in a manger, fled from a tyrant, and hung on a Cross. When a family is devastated by tragedy, Christ is the One who wept for Lazarus and who felt the absence of the Father in the depths of His Passion. When a life is cut short, Christ is the One who entered death so that death could not remain a realm without God.

This truth does not eliminate grief. It dignifies it. It does not explain tragedy. It redeems it. The Christian response to innocent suffering is not an argument but an embrace — the embrace of a God who has descended into the darkest chambers of human history and declared that even there, we are not alone.

Still, the question lingers: If God is present, why does He not intervene? Why does He not stop the accident, prevent the illness, stay the hand of violence, calm the storm?

Here, too, Scripture urges us toward a deeper horizon. God's providence is not the manipulation of events to prevent all harm.

If it were, freedom would be an illusion, and love would be impossible. Providence is God's unwavering work to bring His people to Himself, even when the path is carved through sorrow. Providence is not God sparing us from all earthly tragedy; it is God ensuring that no tragedy has the power to sever us from Him.

This is why St. Paul can say, with breathtaking certainty, "Nothing can separate us from the love of God in Christ Jesus our Lord." Not tribulation, not distress, not persecution, not the sword. Not even death itself.

The logic of providence is covenantal. It does not promise worldly fairness. It promises divine fidelity. It promises that God will write the final chapter, even when evil appears to take the pen.

The clearest sign of this is the resurrection of Jesus. The resurrection is not merely the reversal of death. It is the revelation that justice in God's kingdom goes beyond this world's arithmetic. The resurrection vindicates the Innocent One, not by erasing the fact of the Cross but by transforming it into glory. Christ's wounds remain — not as reminders of defeat, but as trophies of victory.

And this is the Christian hope for every innocent sufferer.

What is lost will be restored.

What is broken will be healed.

What is unfinished will be completed in God.

What dies unjustly will rise in justice.

The resurrection does not trivialise pain. It promises that pain does not define the end.

This hope is not abstract. It is not a vague assurance that "things will work out." It is grounded in the most concrete event in history: a crucified body rising from the dead. Because of that event, the Christian can look at the deepest injustices of life without surrendering to despair. The Christian can grieve fully, honestly, without suppressing the sorrow or denying the magnitude of the loss. Yet grief is not the final horizon. The story moves toward restoration.

But this restoration is not always visible in this life. And this is precisely what makes innocent suffering so agonising. We are creatures who long for completion. We are made for justice, for harmony, for peace. When a child dies, that longing is torn open. When tragedy strikes without reason, the heart cries out for an ending we cannot yet see. Faith does not silence that longing. Faith enlarges it.

Faith tells us that what we desire is not wrong. Faith tells us we are right to expect justice, right to expect restoration, right to expect life rather than death. Faith insists that this longing is placed in us by God Himself — because He intends to fulfill it.

This is why Christian hope is not escapism. It is not a coping mechanism. It is not a comforting idea invented to soften the blow of tragedy. Hope is rooted in the very nature of God. He is faithful. He is just. He is merciful. And because He is faithful, His plan cannot be undone by the cruelty of a fallen world. Because He is just, no innocent suffering will be forgotten. Because He is merciful, even the wounds that sin and death inflict can be taken up into His healing hands.

We see glimpses of this healing even now. We see it in the way communities gather around grieving families. We see it in the way compassion springs up spontaneously when tragedy strikes. We see it in the quiet strength that emerges in people who never imagined they could endure what they now bear. We see it in the way love deepens in the presence of sorrow.

None of this diminishes the magnitude of the loss. But it does reveal something striking: suffering, even innocent suffering, awakens capacities of the human heart that comfort alone never touches. It draws forth tenderness, courage, sacrifice, solidarity — virtues that mark the image of God in us. These glimpses are not the full answer.

But they are the beginnings of what God will bring to completion.

Still, the hardest question remains: Why does God permit a world in which the innocent can be harmed? If God is sovereign, why does He not prevent every tragedy? Why does a God who delights in life allow death to strike those who have barely begun to live?

Here, humility becomes essential. Scripture reveals glimpses of the mystery, but it does not offer a formula. It teaches that suffering entered the world through sin — not necessarily the personal sin of the sufferer, but the cosmic rupture that fractured creation itself. Nature groans, Paul says, and groans in labour pains. This world is not as it was meant to be. It is not fully renewed. It is not yet whole.

To demand that God eliminate all suffering here and now would be to demand the end of history — the end of freedom — the end of the story God is telling. It would require God to bring the final judgment before the appointed time. And that judgment will come. Scripture promises it. But judgment is not the end of the story. Restoration is. Resurrection is. The new creation is. The justice we long for will not be partial, temporary, or fragile. It will be eternal.

Until that day, we live in the tension between promise and fulfillment. We weep, but we do not weep without hope. We grieve, but we do not grieve as those who think death has the final word. We ask questions, but we do not ask them into a void. We ask them at the foot of the Cross, where the Innocent One has already answered with His life.

If there is one truth that faith teaches most clearly in the face of innocent suffering, it is this: God does not look away. When tragedy strikes, God is not watching from a distance. He is not indifferent, not passive, not silent in the sense of absence. His silence is the silence of a Father holding His breath beside a child's bed. His silence is the silence of a God who has chosen to suffer with us rather than shield us from suffering in ways that would strip us of our freedom, our dignity, and our destiny.

This is why the saints can speak with such confidence about suffering, even when they faced tragedies that would crush the rest of us. They were not blind to the horror of innocent suffering. They simply saw the Cross behind it. They saw the resurrection ahead of it. They saw the God who walks in the furnace with His people, the God who stands in the storm, the God who enters the tomb in order to break it from the inside.

To stand before the mystery of innocent suffering is to stand before the deepest paradox of the Gospel. We face a God who does not cause suffering, but who allows it; a God who hates death, yet permits death; a God who is omnipotent, yet chooses to redeem the world through weakness. This paradox cannot be neatly resolved. It must be contemplated. It must be carried in prayer. It must be lived.

But it can be lived — because Christ has lived it first.

To live this mystery is not to pretend that suffering is good. It is not to claim that God wills tragedy in order to teach lessons. Scripture never speaks that way. Scripture never attributes evil to God. James puts it plainly: "God is not the author of evil." Jesus confirms this when He rebukes the idea that misfortune corresponds to guilt. The Christian must hold this truth with unwavering conviction: evil is evil. Death is an enemy. Loss is a wound. Injustice is real. Suffering is not divine craftsmanship; it is the cost of a creation that has not yet reached its completion.

But Scripture also teaches that God meets His people precisely where the wound is deepest. This is why the Cross stands at the centre of our faith. The Cross does not trivialise innocent suffering — it transfigures it. The Cross does not explain evil — it defeats it. The Cross does not remove grief — it ensures grief is never the end.

And in this light, even the most painful questions begin to shift.

The question is no longer: *Why does God allow suffering?*

The question becomes: *Where is God when the innocent suffer?*
And the Gospel answers:

He is there.

He is always there.

He is closer than breath, closer than grief, closer than the tear that falls.

He is in the arms of the mother who holds her dying child.

He is in the man who keeps vigil at a loved one's hospital bed.

He is in the friend who refuses to let sorrow isolate the grieving.

He is in the priest who carries the sacraments into places of unbearable pain.

He is in the cries of those who feel forsaken — because He Himself cried those words once, not so that we would never speak them, but so that when we do, we speak them *with Him*.

This companionship does not remove the tragedy. But it transforms the space in which the tragedy is lived. The Christian who suffers innocently is not abandoned to absurdity. He is united to a God who has made the path of sorrow the very place where redemption unfolds. This does not justify the tragedy. It consecrates the one who suffers.

Innocent suffering, perhaps more than anything else, reveals the profound dignity of the human person. It reveals that every life — no matter how brief, no matter how fragile — bears the weight of eternity. It reveals that there is no such thing as a meaningless life, no such thing as an insignificant death. The world may forget. God does not. In His eyes, no tear is wasted. No cry goes unheard. No injustice escapes His final and perfect restoration.

This is why Christians cling to the hope of the resurrection — not as an ideal, but as a certainty. The resurrection is God's answer not only to death, but to every question that innocent suffering raises. It does not erase the past; it restores it. It does not undo the story; it completes it. It does not deny the wound; it glorifies it. In the pierced hands of Christ, every unjust wound finds its vindication.

Until that day, we walk by faith. We grieve. We pray. We hold one another through the darkness. And we refuse to believe that suffering — even the suffering of the most innocent — is stronger than the God who has conquered death.

Innocent suffering remains a mystery. But it is no longer a godless mystery. It is a mystery illuminated from within by the Cross — a mystery carried by the One who bore the world's injustice so that no innocent suffering would ever be endured alone.

And so we stand, not with answers that silence grief, but with a hope that refuses to die, a hope grounded in the wounds of Christ Himself. In His wounds, the innocent find their defender. In His wounds, the grieving find their companion. In His wounds, every tragedy awaits its resurrection.

The God who bears our sorrows does not explain suffering.

He transforms it.

He does not eliminate the wound.

He keeps His own.

And in His keeping, the innocent are never lost.

18

When Revelation Becomes the Road

Suffering reveals its sharpest edges not only in the world's rebellion, but in the believer's own life. After tracing the story of suffering through Israel, through Christ, through the saints, and through the wounds of our modern age, we arrive at a threshold where contemplation is no longer enough. The truths we have uncovered press upon the heart with a question that can no longer be deferred: *What now?* For suffering is never simply a mystery to behold. It becomes a summons. It becomes a road. It becomes the place where the disciple must walk.

Throughout Scripture, this pattern is constant. God reveals Himself not so His people may admire the revelation, but so that they may live within it. Israel did not gaze at the Red Sea as spectators; they walked through its parted waters. They did not treat the Law as an ornament; they shaped their lives by its commands. The apostles did not witness the Transfiguration as a moment to freeze in time; they followed Jesus down the mountain toward Jerusalem, where the Cross awaited. The Resurrection itself did not end the story; it inaugurated the mission. Christ appears to His disciples not to dazzle them, but to commission them. He breathes the Spirit upon them, not for private consolation, but for public witness. Once the truth is revealed, the life of faith begins. Revelation always moves toward vocation.

So too here.

We have stood before the greatest mysteries: the goodness of creation, the fracture of sin, the fidelity of God, the suffering of the innocent, the victory of Christ, the witness of the saints, and the crisis of a world that denies what it cannot escape. We have seen suffering from every angle Scripture offers. But now we must turn toward the life that these revelations demand. For the Cross is not only an event to contemplate; it is a pattern to inhabit. The Resurrection is not only a proclamation; it is a power poured into human weakness. Pentecost is not only the birth of the Church; it is the moment when ordinary men and women begin to live the mystery they once only beheld.

Part V is where this book crosses that threshold.

For all the beauty contained in theology, suffering eventually brings the soul to a place where theory cannot stand on its own. There comes a moment when the believer must pray within the wound, trust within the silence, persevere within the darkness, and love within the ache. There comes a moment when suffering is no longer something explained, but something offered. Not offered in stoic resignation, but offered in union with the One whose wounds have become fountains of grace. This is the moment Scripture prepares us for. This is the moment the Church accompanies us through. This is the moment where suffering is no longer merely seen; it is sanctified.

And here, the witness of the saints becomes indispensable. For they show us what revelation looks like when it becomes endurance. They show us what hope looks like when it breathes under pressure. They show us what love becomes when it refuses to retreat before pain. The saints do not live alongside suffering; they live through it, with Christ, for the sake of the world. Their lives are not commentaries on theology; they are theology incarnate. They reveal that suffering, when carried in grace, does not diminish the human heart — it expands it. It purifies it. It prepares it for a love stronger than death itself.

But the saints also teach us something else: no one carries suffering alone. The Church bears it with them. She does this through prayer, through sacrament, through community, through intercession, through the simple, abiding presence that refuses to abandon the wounded. The Church is not a refuge from suffering; she is the place where suffering is taken up into the life of Christ. She is the home where tears are gathered, where lament becomes liturgy, where wounds become openings for grace, where even the heaviest burdens find companions along the way.

This is where Part V leads us.

Not to a set of techniques, not to strategies of coping, not to psychological reductionism, but to the heart of Christian discipleship under the Cross — a discipleship that prays honestly, suffers faithfully, accompanies generously, and hopes fiercely. The world around us knows how to fear suffering; the Christian must learn how to face it. The world knows how to escape suffering; the Christian must learn how to offer it. The world knows how to hide suffering; the Christian must learn how to carry it with Christ and for others. This is not stoicism. It is not spiritual heroism. It is the ordinary vocation of every believer whose life flows from the Paschal Mystery.

We have seen what suffering becomes in the hands of a world without God.

Now we must see what suffering becomes in the hands of grace.

Part V begins the movement from revelation to transformation — from what suffering *means* to what suffering *asks*; from what Christ has done to what Christ now does in His people; from beholding the mystery to becoming participants in it. The chapters ahead will not offer a different Gospel; they will show how the Gospel takes flesh in prayer, in presence, in perseverance, and in hope.

This is where the journey turns.
This is where theology becomes life.
This is where the God who bears our sorrows teaches us how to bear them with Him.

V

Living the Mystery

19

How To Face Suffering Without Losing Faith

Suffering exposes the truth of a person. It does not ask permission; it does not arrive on schedule; it does not stay within the limits we set for it. When it comes, it cuts deep into the hidden places of the soul, uncovering fears, doubts, attachments, and desires we did not even know were there. It is in this place—the interior chamber where joy feels distant and God seems silent—that faith either withers or grows roots. Every disciple eventually finds himself here, not at the edge of theology but at the heart of it. For the question of suffering is not a philosophical puzzle—it is the question that touches the very nerve of trust.

Scripture does not pretend otherwise. From the earliest chapters of Genesis to the final visions of Revelation, the Bible speaks to people whose lives have been interrupted by fear, grief, illness, betrayal, loss, confusion, and death. The sacred text is astonishingly honest about what it feels like when God seems distant. When we open the pages of Scripture, we are not stepping into a world immune from sorrow; we are entering a world in which God reveals Himself precisely in the places where human beings are most wounded.

The Book of Job stands as the great monument of this truth. Job is introduced to us as "blameless and upright" (Job 1:1), a man who walks with God in integrity. Yet in a sudden storm of events, his entire life collapses. His children die. His wealth disappears. His body becomes afflicted with sores. His reputation is shattered. And perhaps most painfully of all, he finds himself surrounded by companions who offer explanations instead of compassion. Their theology is neat, tidy, and wrong. They assume that Job's suffering must reflect divine punishment. But the reader knows something far deeper is at work: God Himself has declared Job righteous. His suffering is not a sign that he has been rejected. It is the place where his faith will be purified.

In the ashes, Job does not pretend. He refuses to speak lies about God, and he refuses to speak lies to God. He cries out. He questions. He pleads. He laments. He confronts the silence that meets him. The astonishing thing about the Book of Job is that God does not condemn this honesty. Instead, at the end of the drama, He says to Job's friends, "You have not spoken of Me what is right, as My servant Job has" (Job 42:7). Job's anguished prayer is called "right," not because it is comfortable, but because it is real. Real faith does not consist in polite phrases recited from a distance. Real faith is the courage to bring the whole heart—even the bruised, confused, trembling heart—into the presence of God.

This is what separates lament from despair. Despair turns away from God. Lament turns toward Him. Despair collapses in on itself and stops speaking. Lament continues to speak, even when the soul trembles. The psalms are full of such cries. "How long, O LORD?" (Ps 13:1). "Why have You forgotten me?" (Ps 42:9). "Why do You hide Your face?" (Ps 44:24). The psalmists are not ashamed to say what they feel. They bring their terror, their loneliness, their bitterness, their confusion—all of it—into prayer. And because they do, the prayer becomes a lifeline of faith. The lament psalms do not remove suffering, but they prevent suffering from becoming isolation. They prevent the soul from closing in on itself.

One of the most misunderstood truths of the spiritual life is that lament is not the opposite of trust. Lament is the expression of trust under pressure. The only reason Israel dares to cry "How long?" is because she believes God is the One who hears. The only reason she says, "Why have You forgotten me?" is because she remembers that God once delivered her. The lament psalms are the proof that faith does not mean the absence of anguish. Faith means bringing anguish into relationship.

This truth reaches its climax in Christ. If anyone could have bypassed suffering, it was the Son of God. Yet He does not bypass it. He embraces it, enters it, and redeems it from within. In Gethsemane, we see the Lord trembling. The eternal Word made flesh falls to the ground, praying, "Father, if it be possible, let this cup pass from Me" (Mt 26:39). This prayer is not play-acting. It is the agony of a real human soul. Jesus is not pretending to fear death; He is allowing Himself to feel the full weight of human sorrow. And in that place, He obeys. His "not My will, but Yours be done" is not spoken from emotional ease—it is spoken from a heart that is breaking. And so, He sanctifies the breaking.

On the Cross, Jesus goes still further. He takes into His mouth the first line of Psalm 22: "My God, My God, why have You forsaken Me?" (Mt 27:46). These words do not mean the Trinity has been fractured. They mean that the Son, in His human soul, enters the experience of abandonment down to its deepest depth. He prays as Israel prayed. He prays as Job prayed. He prays as every believer has prayed in their own darkness. Jesus enters the darkest corner of human experience so that no believer's darkness can be a place where He is absent.

This divine solidarity transforms the meaning of suffering. Christ does not merely sympathise with our wounds—He shares them. He transforms the question "Where is God?" into a revelation: God is right here, in the heart of human anguish. He is Emmanuel—God with us—not only in Bethlehem, but in Gethsemane and Golgotha.

This is why the saint who suffers is not imitating Christ from afar—he is participating in Christ's own prayer. It is why St Paul can say, "I rejoice in my sufferings for your sake… for in my flesh I complete what is lacking in Christ's afflictions" (Col 1:24). He does not mean Christ's sacrifice is insufficient. He means that Christ has drawn the Church into His sufferings, not for redemption but for communion. Every cross borne in faith becomes a place of union with Him who bore the Cross in love.

Yet none of this denies the real danger of suffering. There is no sentimentalism in the Gospel. Pain can distort the heart. It can generate resentment, bitterness, cynicism, self-pity, or despair. Suffering does not simply happen to us; it acts upon us. And unless grace takes hold of that interior action, suffering will deform rather than transform the soul. This is why Scripture gives such serious attention to the interior battle that suffering provokes.

The interior battle is almost always subtle at first. Few believers wake up one morning and consciously decide, "I no longer trust God." Rather, pain begins to whisper interpretations of God's character that differ from what Scripture proclaims. When Israel suffers in the wilderness, the first temptation is not idolatry—it is reinterpretation. They begin to say that God led them into the desert to destroy them (Ex 14:11). This is not simply an emotional outburst; it is a theological crisis. Pain has begun to reshape their understanding of God.

This is why resentment is more dangerous than suffering itself. Pain wounds the body; resentment wounds the soul. Pain can coexist with love; resentment corrodes love. Pain can drive a person to prayer; resentment drives a person away from prayer. Pain can lead to humility; resentment leads to accusation. If the believer allows resentment to take root, suffering becomes unbearable—not because the suffering itself increases, but because the heart interprets it in a way that disconnects it from the God who alone can carry it.

The Israelites' murmuring reveals a core spiritual truth: suffering exposes the contents of the heart. When comfort is abundant, trust often lies untested. In the desert, trust is revealed for what it actually is. The desert shows whether the heart follows God because He is useful, or because He is God. This distinction appears again and again throughout salvation history. Hannah's sorrow over her barrenness leads her to pour out her soul before the Lord (1 Sam 1:15), and in her lament she discovers the faithfulness of God. David, hunted by Saul, learns to pray psalms that express both terror and trust. Jeremiah, thrown into a cistern, cries out, "O LORD, You deceived me..." (Jer 20:7), yet still surrenders to his prophetic mission. Habakkuk stands before God demanding answers for injustice, yet ends his book with a hymn of praise (Hab 3:17–19). These figures are not models of stoicism. They are models of fidelity forged through sorrow.

Such fidelity is impossible without truth. To endure suffering with faith, the believer must cling—not to interpretations shaped by pain, but to the truth revealed by God. This is why Scripture places so much emphasis on memory. "Remember the LORD your God" (Deut 8:18) is not a mild suggestion; it is a command. God commands remembrance because He knows the human heart is forgetful. Under pressure, memories of grace fade faster than memories of wounds. The Israelites remember the onions and cucumbers of Egypt but forget the slavery, the lashes, the infanticide. Pain distorts the past; Scripture restores it.

When suffering strikes, the believer must wage a deliberate battle to remember God's works. The psalmist shows us how: "I will remember the deeds of the LORD... I will meditate on all Your works" (Ps 77:11–12). This remembering is active. It is not waiting passively for comfort to return; it is the intentional act of interpreting the present in light of God's past. Without this, suffering becomes a closed world in which the only voice heard is the one that says, "God has forgotten you." With this, the voice of faith cuts through the darkness: "He has been faithful before; He will be faithful again."

But even this discipline does not remove the ache of God's apparent silence. The spiritual masters have always been honest: divine silence is one of the most painful trials a believer will ever face. The silence of God in the Book of Job stretches through thirty-seven chapters before the Lord finally speaks out of the whirlwind. The psalmists cry repeatedly, "Do not be silent, O God" (Ps 109:1). The prophets ask, "Why do You remain silent when the wicked swallow up those more righteous than they?" (Hab 1:13). And even the saints stand beneath the weight of God's quiet. St Teresa of Calcutta endured decades in which she could not feel the presence of God, yet she continued her mission with unwavering fidelity.

The silence of God is not indifference. If God were indifferent, Scripture would never urge us to pray. Christ would not have promised that the Father hears every cry. The silence of God is pedagogical. It forms the believer in a way that consolations cannot. When God speaks, He reveals Himself. When God is silent, He reveals the heart of the believer. Without silence, faith would remain shallow. Silence forces the soul to ask: Do I desire God, or do I desire the feelings God gives? Do I trust His character, or do I trust only His visible actions? Do I love Him, or do I merely enjoy His comforts?

This is what the Carmelite tradition calls the "purgation of the appetites." St John of the Cross explains that God sometimes withdraws the felt sweetness of prayer not to punish but to purify. The soul that once depended on spiritual emotion must now depend on God Himself. The believer who once prayed because it felt peaceful must now pray because God is worthy. The soul that once believed because it understood must now believe because God is trustworthy. In the dark night, the believer is stripped of all supports except God—and that is precisely the grace. God becomes the soul's only anchor, and therefore, the soul's true freedom.

To stand in this darkness without losing faith requires a shift in how we understand faith itself. Many imagine faith as emotional conviction or intellectual clarity. But Scripture teaches something much deeper. Faith is covenant fidelity. Faith is the act of placing one's life in the hands of God, regardless of what circumstances suggest. This is why Abraham becomes the father of faith—not because he felt certain, but because he obeyed in uncertainty. He leaves his land without knowing where he is going. He believes the promise even when he and Sarah are old. He ascends Mount Moriah with Isaac, carrying not understanding but trust. In Abraham, faith is revealed not as insight, but as surrender.

The deepest expression of faith in Scripture is the faith of Christ Himself. "Into Your hands, I commit My spirit" (Lk 23:46) is the cry of a man who feels forsaken yet refuses to withdraw His trust. Christ reveals what faith looks like when faith is most costly. Faith is not the avoidance of the cross. Faith is the willingness to stand with the Father *through* the cross. Faith is not certainty that pain will disappear. Faith is certainty that God will be faithful no matter what the pain contains. Faith is not the refusal to tremble. Faith is the refusal to let trembling silence prayer.

This is why the saints speak of suffering not as an obstacle to prayer but as the ground in which prayer grows stronger. St Thérèse of Lisieux believed that when she felt least capable of prayer, her prayer was most pleasing to God because it came from pure desire, not from consolation. St Augustine writes that God sometimes delays His response so that "He may enlarge our desire"—so that our longing for God grows deeper than our longing for relief. St Gregory the Great says that when God appears silent, He is sharpening the soul's hunger for Him. The saints understood that suffering, far from proving God's absence, is the place where the believer learns to cling to Him without conditions.

As this clinging deepens, suffering begins to reveal not only the fragility of the human heart but its capacity for communion. The soul discovers that its own wounds can become places where it touches the wounds of Christ. This is not poetic imagery. Scripture is clear: "He Himself bore our sorrows" (Isa 53:4). When the believer stands in his own sorrow, he stands mysteriously within the sorrow of Christ. The wounds of Christ become the shelter for human wounds. The love Christ revealed on the Cross becomes the strength by which the believer endures his own cross.

This reveals the central truth of Christian suffering: the presence of pain does not mean the absence of God.

The presence of God does not mean the absence of pain.

The two coexist on Calvary.

Therefore, they can coexist in us.

The moment the believer accepts this truth—that God's nearness and our suffering are not mutually exclusive—the spiritual landscape begins to shift. The cross no longer appears as a contradiction of God's love, but as its supreme revelation. Yet this shift does not happen automatically. The heart must learn this truth gradually, and often painfully. Scripture guides this learning through examples that illuminate how disciples before us discovered the faithfulness of God in the midst of crushing trial.

Consider Joseph, the beloved son betrayed by his brothers, sold into slavery, falsely accused, and left to rot in an Egyptian prison. Years pass before any hint of redemption appears. Yet when Joseph finally reveals himself to his brothers, he speaks a sentence that could only have come from a heart schooled in suffering: "You meant evil against me, but God meant it for good" (Gen 50:20). Joseph does not deny the evil. He does not pretend that betrayal, slavery, and imprisonment were pleasant. He does not attribute wicked actions to God. What he sees is something deeper: that God's providence is so masterful that even human malice cannot derail His purpose. God is not the author of evil, but He is the redeemer of all that evil touches. The believer who suffers is invited into this same vision—not to trivialize his pain, but to trust that no pain is beyond God's capacity to transform.

Consider David, hounded by Saul, surrounded by enemies, wrestling with fear and exhaustion. Many of David's psalms were written not from thrones but from caves—literal and spiritual. Psalm 22 begins with the very cry Christ would later utter on the Cross. Psalm 13 begins with the haunting "How long?" For David, suffering did not merely test his faith; it formed it. He learned how to speak truth to God, not by glossing over his fear but by bringing it into the covenant: "But I have trusted in Your steadfast love; my heart shall rejoice in Your salvation" (Ps 13:5). David does not rejoice because his circumstances changed; he rejoices because he remembers who God is. This memory becomes his anchor.

Consider Jeremiah, the "weeping prophet," whose entire ministry unfolded under rejection, ridicule, and political hostility. Jeremiah accused God of deceiving him (Jer 20:7), yet he could not stop proclaiming God's word. He was thrown into a cistern, left to die, yet he continued to pray. Jeremiah's faith was not a warm feeling; it was a fire "shut up in [his] bones" (Jer 20:9). He reveals that faith is not always triumphant confidence; sometimes faith is simply the inability to walk away from God despite the cost.

Consider Hannah, whose aching barrenness led her to pour out her soul in such raw prayer that Eli thought she was drunk (1 Sam 1). God answered her, but not because she mastered a technique—because she refused to hide her pain from Him. Her lament became the womb in which Samuel was conceived. Her sorrow became the soil in which Israel's greatest prophet was born. Suffering in the biblical world is not merely endured; it becomes the very place where God brings forth new beginnings.

Consider Habakkuk, who stands before God bewildered by injustice and violence. His book begins with complaint: "O LORD, how long shall I cry for help, and You will not hear?" (Hab 1:2). Yet by the end, Habakkuk has learned to wait with a hope that transcends circumstances: "Though the fig tree does not blossom... yet I will rejoice in the LORD" (Hab 3:17–18). Habakkuk does not rejoice because suffering disappears, but because he sees the God who remains.

These figures reveal a common pattern: suffering strips away illusions and creates space where grace can reshape the heart. No one grows in faith because life is easy. We grow because suffering forces us to discover what our faith is truly built upon. A faith built on feelings collapses when feelings fade. A faith built on circumstances crumbles when circumstances turn dark. But a faith built on the character of God—His fidelity, His covenant, His mercy—remains steady even in the storm.

This is where we must pause and examine the interior dynamics of suffering with theological precision. What exactly happens inside a person when they confront pain? The Church teaches that suffering touches every dimension of the human person: physical, emotional, intellectual, relational, and spiritual. Aquinas says that suffering wounds our "appetites"—meaning our desires, hopes, loves, and fears. Pain disrupts the harmony of the soul. The passions become turbulent. The intellect becomes clouded. The will feels weakened. In such moments, the believer stands in profound vulnerability.

Yet it is precisely in this vulnerability that grace does its deepest work. Thomas Aquinas insists that suffering can serve charity by removing "impediments." What does he mean? When life is comfortable, the heart often becomes attached to lesser goods—security, reputation, comfort, affirmation, predictability. These things are not evil, but they can occupy the place meant for God. Suffering loosens our grip on them. When those supports fall away, the heart is freed to cling more deeply to God Himself. The desert fathers knew this well. They spoke of suffering as the "furnace of purification"—not because pain is good, but because the attachments it burns away make room for holy desire.

Here lies one of the great paradoxes of the spiritual life: what feels like abandonment is often preparation. What feels like divine distance is often the deepening of divine intimacy. What feels like loss is often the removal of what cannot save. God does not cause all suffering; but God uses all suffering to purify, strengthen, and transform the heart—if the heart consents.

This consent does not mean liking suffering. It means refusing to let suffering sever communion. It means saying, "Lord, I do not understand, but I am Yours." It means repeating the words of Scripture when one's own words are gone. It means enduring the night with the conviction—borrowed from Christ Himself—that the Father remains faithful even when He feels hidden.

This brings us to what is perhaps the most difficult aspect of suffering: *the experience of divine silence.* The silence of God is not merely the absence of felt consolation; it is the experience of unanswered questions, unresolved tensions, and unfulfilled desires. It is the ache of prayers that seem to go nowhere. It is the weight of waiting with no end in sight. Even the greatest saints trembled beneath this silence.

St John of the Cross describes the "dark night of the spirit" as a purification so deep that it leaves the believer feeling stripped of every spiritual sense. His language is stark: the soul feels abandoned, emptied, bewildered. Yet he insists that God is closest when He feels most distant because the soul is being freed from all that is not God. In silence, God draws the soul into a purer faith—a faith that rests not on understanding but on union.

This union is the essence of Christian suffering. Christ has united Himself to every human sorrow. When we suffer, we do not suffer alongside Christ; we suffer *within* Him. This is why St Paul speaks of "sharing His sufferings" (Phil 3:10). Not because our suffering adds something lacking to His, but because His suffering has opened a path through which ours may become communion. The disciple stands beneath the Cross not to imitate a distant example but to enter the mystery of a love that redeems from the inside out.

This is also why Jesus invites His disciples to "take up their cross" (Mt 16:24). He is not romanticizing pain. He is revealing that discipleship cannot be separated from the pattern of His own life. Christ loves us enough not to spare us from suffering, but to accompany us through it. The Cross is not an interruption of God's plan; it is the revelation of God's heart. If the Son of God walked the path of sorrow, the disciple should not be surprised when he is called to walk the same. What matters is not the weight of the cross, but the presence of the One who carries it with us.

With this truth in place, we can finally say what the entire biblical tradition whispers: suffering can sanctify, not because suffering itself is holy, but because the God who meets us in suffering is holy.

If suffering can sanctify, the question becomes: *How?* What actually happens inside the soul when suffering is taken up in faith rather than resentment? The answer is not sentimental and not abstract. It unfolds through the theological realities the Church has always taught—realities that only suffering can illuminate with such clarity.

The first reality is humility. Not the false humility that pretends weakness, but the true humility that discovers it. Suffering forces the soul to confront the limits it has always carried but rarely acknowledged. The illusion of self-sufficiency, so natural in comfort, collapses the moment pain strikes. Illness reveals the fragility of the body. Fear reveals the fragility of the heart. Loss reveals the fragility of every earthly good. Yet within this revelation lies a gift. Only when a person discovers his dependency can he discover the God who sustains him. Augustine writes that "God is nearer to us than we are to ourselves," but it is often suffering that makes us aware of this nearness. The proud heart resists grace. The humbled heart receives it.

The second reality is patience. Scripture treats patience not as passivity, but as the endurance of love. St Paul lists it as the first characteristic of charity: "Love is patient" (1 Cor 13:4). Patience is the willingness to remain in relationship when relationship becomes costly. This is precisely the patience God shows Israel throughout salvation history. He remains faithful even when they are faithless. He waits for their return. He bears with their complaints, their rebellions, their doubts. When the believer suffers and continues to turn toward God—even slowly, even painfully—he learns to share in God's own long-suffering love. Patience in suffering is not inactivity. It is active fidelity.

The third reality is compassion. The Greek word for compassion, *splagchnizomai*, literally means "to be moved in the inward parts." It is the word used repeatedly of Jesus in the Gospels when He sees the crowds, the sick, the hungry, the lost. Compassion is born of suffering. The person who has wept learns how to comfort the weeping. The person who has been wounded learns how to care for the wounded. The heart that has felt the absence of consolation becomes a vessel through which consolation flows to others. Paul says that God "comforts us in all our affliction, so that we may be able to comfort those who are in any affliction" (2 Cor 1:4). Suffering, received with faith, forms the heart that resembles Christ's. It expands the soul so that it can hold the sorrows of others without collapsing.

The fourth reality is purity of love. When many attachments are stripped away, the soul learns to desire God for His own sake. This is the greatest fruit of suffering. Many love God for His gifts. Many love Him because He protects, guides, blesses, and comforts. But when the gifts seem withdrawn—when blessing feels distant, when prayer feels dry, when consolation is absent—the soul must decide whether it loves God or the emotions God once provided. In this crucible, love is purified. Bernard of Clairvaux speaks of this movement as rising from the "love of self for self's sake" to the "love of God for God's sake." Suffering accelerates this ascent. It burns away mixed motives. It reveals whether God is truly the centre.

If these interior realities shape the soul through suffering, what sustains the believer in this transformation? Scripture gives the answer with unwavering clarity: prayer. Not eloquent prayer, not emotional prayer, not successful prayer—simply prayer. The decision to keep speaking to God in the midst of sorrow is the beating heart of Christian endurance.

Prayer in suffering is often stripped of words. The psalmist says, "My soul refuses to be comforted… I am so troubled that I cannot speak" (Ps 77:2,4). St Paul speaks of the Spirit praying within us "with groanings too deep for words" (Rom 8:26). The believer who suffers may not feel capable of articulating anything coherent. But prayer is not measured by eloquence. Prayer is measured by direction. If the heart continues to turn toward God, even in silence, prayer survives.

This prayer is not only personal. It is also ecclesial. The suffering believer does not pray alone; the Church prays with and for him. The psalms he whispers in the night are the same psalms prayed by monks at vigils, by the sick in hospital beds, by mothers awake with fear for their children, by martyrs awaiting execution. The prayers of the

Church become a refuge for the soul whose own voice grows faint. When the believer cannot stand, the Church holds him. When he cannot pray, the Church prays in his stead. This is why Christ gives us His Body, not simply His teachings. The Body of Christ carries its members.

But prayer alone is not the only anchor. The sacraments are divine conduits of endurance. When words fail, gestures speak. When emotions falter, signs reveal truth. When the heart trembles, grace stands firm. The sacraments do not provide explanations; they provide presence. They make Christ present in ways deeper than emotion or intellect.

The Eucharist becomes the primary anchor in suffering. Here the believer receives the very Body that suffered, the very Blood poured out for love, the very Presence that endured abandonment and conquered death. To receive the Eucharist in suffering is to unite one's own pain to Christ's sacrifice. It is to place one's weakness upon the altar where Christ has placed His strength. It is to be fed with the Bread of endurance, the Bread that "gives life to the world" (Jn 6:33). Many saints testify that the Eucharist carried them through seasons of darkness when everything else failed.

Confession becomes the healing place where suffering is prevented from turning into bitterness. Sorrow often surfaces sins long dormant: resentment, anger, jealousy, despair, harsh speech, inward rage. Confession cleanses these poisons before they take root. It restores trust. It restores perspective. It releases the soul from the narratives pain tries to tell.

The Anointing of the Sick is not only for the dying. It is the sacrament in which Christ touches human weakness with His own strength. James writes, "Is anyone among you sick? Let him call the elders of the church" (Jas 5:14). The anointing grants grace to endure illness, to sanctify pain, to resist despair, and to unite suffering to Christ. No believer should face chronic pain, serious illness, or emotional collapse without this sacrament. It is Christ's own hand extended.

And then there is Baptism. The believer who suffers must remember his identity. Suffering tries to tell us we are abandoned, forgotten, insignificant, or cursed. But baptism tells another truth: "You are My beloved son; you are My beloved daughter." Suffering cannot rewrite that sentence. It cannot remove the mark of Christ. It cannot undo the adoption sealed by water and Spirit. The believer faces suffering not as a stranger but as a child who belongs to the Father.

Still, even with all these anchors, suffering brings the soul to a decisive threshold. The question arises: *What if suffering lasts? What if the healing does not come? What if the night does not lift?* Scripture does not hide this possibility. Moses dies outside the Promised Land. Jeremiah never lives to see the restoration. John the Baptist dies in a dungeon. Paul's "thorn" remains. Many saints carry interior agony for decades.

What sustains them? One truth: God does not waste suffering. Nothing offered to Him in faith is ever lost. Not one tear. Not one prayer. Not one act of endurance. God takes all of it and weaves it into the very mystery of redemption. This is why St Paul can call suffering a "weight of glory" (2 Cor 4:17). Glory is not the removal of suffering; it is the transformation of suffering into communion.

This mystery of glory within suffering is nowhere more brilliantly revealed than in the New Testament's theology of participation. Paul speaks of believers sharing "the fellowship of His sufferings" (Phil 3:10), being "conformed to His death" (Rom 6:5), and "filling up what is lacking in Christ's afflictions" (Col 1:24). These are not rhetorical flourishes. They express the astonishing truth that Christ has gathered all human suffering into Himself, and those who belong to Him share in that mystery not as spectators but as participants.

This participation is not additive, as though Christ's Passion were incomplete. Christ's sacrifice is perfect, complete, definitive. What Paul means is that the sufferings of the believer become extensions of Christ's own redemptive love—branches that grow from the same vine, flames ignited from the same fire. When the Christian suffers in union with Christ, that suffering becomes a conduit of grace in the Body. It becomes a prayer, a sacrifice, a hidden intercession. Through Christ, ordinary pain becomes supernatural charity. Through Christ, the wounds that wound us become wounds through which grace enters the world.

This truth is difficult for modern ears, shaped as they are by utilitarian standards. We instinctively ask, "What purpose could this possibly serve?" The cross answers: "A divine purpose beyond your calculation." Suffering united to Christ becomes fruitful even when invisible. It becomes prayer not because the sufferer feels prayerful, but because Christ prays within him. It becomes love not because the sufferer feels loving, but because Christ loves within him. The believer in the hospital bed, in the prison cell, in the depths of depression, in the quiet, unseen agony of chronic pain—when he unites his life to Christ, his suffering becomes part of the very heartbeat of the Church.

This is why the saints bear their sorrows with such deep reverence. They see in suffering not an obstacle to communion, but a doorway into it. St Thérèse saw her tuberculosis as an altar. St Maximilian Kolbe saw Auschwitz as his mission field. St John Paul II saw his Parkinson's as his final sermon. None of them enjoyed their pain. They felt every bit of it. But they discovered what only suffering can reveal: that when Christ takes up residence in the wound, the wound becomes a place of grace.

Still, none of this explains away the existential weight of long-term suffering. The believer must learn a second truth: God's silence is not His absence; it is His invitation to deeper faith. When God seems silent, He is often drawing the believer into a hidden participation in Christ's own interior life. This life is not always radiant. It is often marked by the same mystery Christ felt in Gethsemane and on Calvary—a mysterious sense of distance that is itself the place where perfect trust is born.

The saints testify to this. St Teresa of Calcutta lived nearly fifty years in interior spiritual darkness. Her journals reveal a soul who felt abandoned, unseen, unheard—yet she responded with daily fidelity, daily prayer, daily service. Her hidden darkness became the source of her radiant charity. Her suffering did not hinder her mission; it sanctified it. God was not absent. He was drawing her into Christ's own thirst for souls.

But what of those who do not feel sanctified by suffering? What of those who feel crushed, overwhelmed, spiritually paralysed? Scripture does not dismiss such experiences as failures. Instead, it names them: the pit, the valley, the shadow, the flood. Job speaks of the "darkness" that covers his path. The psalmist says, "Deep calls to deep." Paul speaks of being "so utterly burdened beyond strength" (2 Cor 1:8). The Bible does not spiritualize pain. It validates it. It names it. It brings it into the covenant.

This is crucial: God does not ask the believer to pretend. He asks the believer to remain. Remaining does not mean suppressing emotion. It means refusing to let emotion rewrite theology. Faith under trial is not a matter of feeling God; it is the stubborn decision to trust what God has revealed even when the heart feels nothing. Emotions are weather. Covenant is climate. Storms come and go, but God remains.

This is why Scripture commands remembrance so insistently. "Remember the LORD your God." "Remember His works." "Remember His covenant." When suffering overwhelms the heart, memory becomes the soul's anchor. The believer must recall what God has done—creation, deliverance, incarnation, crucifixion, resurrection, the sacraments, personal moments of grace. The God who has acted will act again. The God who was faithful will remain faithful. This remembrance does not remove pain; it gives pain a horizon. It allows the sufferer to see beyond the immediate wound.

And here we must confront one of the most dangerous temptations: the temptation to interpret God through the lens of present suffering. When the heart hurts, it is easy to rewrite God's character in the image of pain—distant, cold, uncaring, punitive. But the Cross forbids this. The Cross reveals that God is not the enemy of the sufferer; He is the companion of the sufferer. God does not stand above suffering; He goes beneath it, bearing its weight, entering its darkness, filling it with Himself.

The Cross is not only the answer to the problem of evil; it is the revelation of God's heart. The Crucified Christ does not explain suffering. He accompanies it. He transforms it. He refuses to spare Himself from it. This is why the Cross stands at the centre of Christianity—not as a theological symbol, but as the unshakeable proof that suffering cannot separate humanity from God's love.

Still, the believer must contend with a troubling question: *If God is good, why does He allow suffering at all?* The answer is not simplistic, and Scripture gives several interwoven truths rather than one tidy explanation.

First, suffering is permitted because we live in a fallen world. Disorder entered creation through sin, and suffering is part of that fracture. God does not will this disorder, but He permits it because He respects the freedom He has given creatures.

Second, suffering reveals the scarcity of earthly goods and redirects the heart toward the eternal. It prevents us from mistaking the temporal for the ultimate. Without suffering, the world becomes a false paradise. With suffering, the world becomes a place of pilgrimage.

Third, suffering forms virtue. Patience, humility, compassion, perseverance—all these virtues grow precisely where comfort cannot sustain them.

Fourth, suffering becomes a site of communion. When believers suffer with Christ, they are drawn into the mystery of His redemptive love.

And fifth—most mysteriously—suffering prepares the soul for glory. Paul calls suffering a "light momentary affliction" only because he compares it to the "eternal weight of glory" being prepared through it (2 Cor 4:17). Suffering, in this sense, becomes the shaping of the soul for a capacity of joy that surpasses earthly imagination.

Yet these truths do not diminish the rawness of pain. They illuminate it. They reveal that God's involvement in suffering is not the involvement of an observer but of a Father. A Father who allows what He will redeem. A Father who wounds only to heal deeper. A Father whose silence is never abandonment and whose presence is never withdrawn even when unfelt.

Here, the believer stands at the threshold of the deepest lesson suffering has to offer: to cling to God not because we understand Him, but because He is God. Because He is faithful. Because He is good. Because He has spoken His love from a Cross and sealed it in an empty tomb.

If the believer reaches this point—this place where faith is purified, memory awakened, trust re-anchored—the heart begins to discover what suffering was always meant to reveal: not the absence of God, but the depth of His companionship. Suffering does not become easier. But it becomes inhabited. It becomes shared. It becomes radiant with a Presence the world cannot see but the soul cannot deny.

This discovery leads to a final and essential truth: suffering must be lived not only before God, but with the Church.

One of the great tragedies of modern life is the isolation of the sufferer. People face illness behind closed doors, grief alone in bedrooms, depression hidden under polite smiles. The Body of Christ is replaced by individual coping strategies. Yet the Church was never meant to be a collection of isolated believers. She is the communion of saints—the living Body of Christ, entrusted with the mission of bearing one another's burdens.

Paul's command in Galatians is not optional: "Bear one another's burdens, and so fulfill the law of Christ" (Gal 6:2). The "law of Christ" here is not a rule but a revelation—love that carries, love that stays, love that kneels beside the wounded. When we sit beside someone who suffers, we do the very thing Christ did in Gethsemane: we watch, we remain, we refuse to let them endure the night alone.

This means that no believer must face suffering unaccompanied. The Church prays when the sufferer cannot pray. The Church hopes when the sufferer cannot hope. The Church believes when the sufferer's faith trembles. The Church remembers the promises of God when the sufferer forgets. In this way, the wounds of the suffering believer become the place where the Church herself becomes visibly Christlike.

But accompaniment requires more than presence; it requires listening. When Job's friends first arrive, they do the one wise thing in the entire book: they sit with him in silence for seven days. It is only when they open their mouths to give explanations that they go astray. This is a lesson for every Christian: suffering is not primarily a puzzle to be solved but a mystery to be reverenced. The sufferer does not need quick answers. He needs companionship. He needs someone who can hold the tension of the question without trying to erase it.

And yet, accompaniment also means gently reintroducing hope when the heart is ready. Hope, in Scripture, is never a mood or a vague optimism. It is a theological virtue, rooted in the resurrection of Christ and the fidelity of God. The believer does not hope for an escape from suffering but for the redemption of suffering. He hopes not that God will remove every cross, but that God will bring every cross to resurrection.

This is why Christian hope looks at death—our final and greatest suffering—and refuses despair. Christ has entered death. Christ has transformed death. Christ has risen from death. And Christ now walks with every believer through death. This is why the New Testament speaks of death as "sleep," "exodus," "homecoming," "gain," and "the crown of life." The believer's final suffering becomes the moment when faith becomes sight, hope becomes possession, and love becomes unending.

But hope is not only for the final moment. It is the daily sustenance of the believer who suffers. Hope is what allows a parent to continue loving a prodigal child. Hope is what allows a widow to rise each morning after devastating loss. Hope is what allows the chronically ill to pray, "Your will be done," even when healing is not granted. Hope is what allows the depressed soul to whisper the simplest prayer: "Lord, have mercy." Hope is what allows the frightened believer to entrust his future to God even when the horizon looks dark.

Christian hope is not the denial of suffering but the defiance of suffering. It refuses to let suffering dictate the final meaning of life. It refuses to let sorrow write the final chapter. It refuses to let the grave have the last word. Christ has spoken a better word—His risen life—and suffering must bow before it.

This leads to the final lesson: to face suffering without losing faith is to allow suffering to become the place of union, not separation. Union with Christ. Union with the Cross. Union with the Church. Union with hope. Union with love.

This union is not passive. It is the daily choice to entrust the heart to God even when the heart feels fragile. It is the daily choice to pray even when words fail. It is the daily choice to receive the sacraments even when consolation is absent. It is the daily choice to forgive others even when one's own wounds are deep. It is the daily choice to remain when everything in us wants to flee.

The believer who lives this way discovers something astonishing: suffering, which once threatened to destroy faith, becomes the place where faith becomes indestructible. Suffering, which once felt meaningless, becomes the place where meaning is forged. Suffering, which once seemed like divine abandonment, becomes the place where divine presence is revealed.

And then, almost imperceptibly, the believer begins to resemble Christ. His patience becomes Christ's patience. His endurance becomes Christ's endurance. His compassion becomes Christ's compassion. His prayer becomes Christ's prayer. His wounds become Christ's wounds—transformed, illumined, made fruitful. The more he clings to God in suffering, the more he discovers that God has already been clinging to him.

This is why the saints say that suffering is one of God's most severe mercies. Not because pain is good, but because God's love is so vast that it can turn even pain into communion. What once felt like punishment becomes participation. What once felt like chaos becomes calling. What once felt like loss becomes love.

The final image Scripture gives us—an image that completes this entire chapter—is the image of the risen Christ in the upper room. The first thing Christ shows His disciples is not His face, not His glory, not His power—He shows them His wounds. Glorified wounds. Transfigured wounds. Wounds that have become the sign of victory. Wounds that preach a sermon no words can express: nothing offered to God is wasted. Nothing surrendered in faith is forgotten. Nothing endured with Christ fails to bear fruit.

This is the truth the believer must carry into every season of suffering:

God does not merely understand sorrow.
God has entered sorrow.
God has redeemed sorrow.
God will complete that redemption in us.

The path through suffering is therefore the path toward deeper union with the God who bears our sorrows. A God who does not stand far off. A God who does not remain on the throne while His creatures weep. A God who has taken flesh, entered our wounds, carried our griefs, and risen with scars that now shine like stars.

To face suffering without losing faith is not heroic. It is relational. It is covenantal. It is trust learned beneath a cross and confirmed beside an empty tomb. It is the humble, steady, persevering decision to remain with the One who has remained with us.

And when the believer stands before God at last, healed and whole, he will discover that every tear was gathered, every wound was remembered, every sorrow was carried, and every suffering was woven—mysteriously, mercifully—into the glory he now beholds.

Thus, the Cross is not the end of faith. It is the place where faith becomes sight.

And the God who bears our sorrows becomes the God who dries every tear.

20

How to Accompany Someone Who Suffers

There is a sacred silence that surrounds every suffering soul, a silence that does not demand explanations but asks for presence. Scripture begins with a God who draws near, not a God who stands far off. From the opening pages of Genesis to the final vision of Revelation, the deepest truth about God is not that He observes human suffering, but that He enters it. This is the pattern that shapes all Christian accompaniment. We do not stand beside the suffering because we have wise answers; we stand with them because God has stood with us.

The whole biblical story can be read as the unfolding of that truth. God does not rescue Israel from Egypt by shouting encouragement from the heavens. He descends. He hears their groaning. He remembers His covenant. He enters the fire with Moses, the battle with Joshua, the exile with Ezekiel, the lament with Jeremiah. He is the God who dwells with His people even when their world collapses. The Incarnation is the climax of that nearness: the Word becomes flesh and dwells among us, not above us. Christ does not teach salvation from a distance; He heals with hands that touch lepers, bless children, wash feet, and break bread for the hungry. His entire ministry is one long act of accompaniment.

This is why Christians cannot treat suffering as a problem to solve. Suffering is a place to love. And love, in Scripture, always draws near. It is covenantal, not clinical. This is the difference between Job's friends at the start of the story and Job's friends at the end. When they first come, they sit in silence for seven days — and that silence is their finest moment. Their presence reveals compassion, humility, and reverence for a sorrow they do not understand. But when they begin to speak, they speak too much. They speak beyond what has been revealed. They try to interpret what only God can interpret. Their words become wounds. Their theology becomes accusation. Their attempts to explain become the very thing God rebukes.

There is wisdom in this. When we accompany someone who suffers, silence is not failure. It is fidelity. It is a recognition of the holiness of the moment — a holiness that comes from the fragility of the one who suffers and the presence of the God who enters that fragility. To sit with someone in their sorrow is to acknowledge that suffering is not solved by speech but carried by love. It is the ministry of presence, the first and greatest act of accompaniment.

Ruth embodies this ministry perfectly. Naomi has lost husband and sons. Her life has collapsed. She has no future in the land of Moab. She urges her daughters-in-law to return to their own families, to begin anew. Orpah weeps and kisses her goodbye. Ruth does something more. She binds her life to Naomi's with a vow so profound it echoes the language of covenant: "Where you go, I will go. Where you lodge, I will lodge. Your people shall be my people, and your God my God." Ruth does not promise solutions. She promises presence. She enters Naomi's poverty, her bitterness, her uncertainty. And in doing so, Ruth becomes the means by which God writes a new chapter in Naomi's life — one that leads to David, and eventually to Christ.

God often works through companionship that refuses to abandon.

People rarely remember the eloquent explanations they were given in suffering, but they remember who stayed. They remember who listened. They remember who prayed when they could not pray. They remember who bore the weight of silence with them. This is how Christ Himself loved. He did not remove Gethsemane from His disciples; He asked them to stay with Him. And at the Cross, He did not ask Mary or John to speak. He asked them to stand.

To accompany someone who suffers requires the courage to stand in a place we cannot fix. This is something the modern world struggles to accept because the modern world worships solutions. Yet most suffering is not a puzzle to be solved. It is a mystery to be lived in the light of faith. We do not accompany the suffering as experts; we accompany them as disciples who know the One who has entered suffering ahead of us.

This means learning the discipline of listening — listening with reverence, patience, and self-forgetfulness. Suffering unearths the deepest truths of the human heart, but those truths do not surface under pressure. They emerge when the sufferer feels safe enough to speak, and safety is created not by clever words but by humble presence. A suffering person does not need to be analysed. They need to be heard. They do not need their pain explained; they need it witnessed. They do not need the weight of theology dropped on their shoulders; they need the quiet conviction that God has not left them.

Words do have their place, but only after presence. And when words come, they must be few, true, and tender. Scripture never hurries speech in the face of sorrow. Jesus does not flood Mary Magdalene with assurances at the tomb. He speaks her name. Elijah does not hear God in wind or fire, but in a still small voice. St. Paul urges believers to "weep with those who weep," not "instruct those who weep." Accompaniment begins with tears, not teaching.

This does not mean we abandon truth. It means we reveal truth the way Christ reveals it — slowly, gently, personally. A single verse of Scripture read with love can comfort more than an entire lecture spoken without discernment. A heartfelt "I am with you," spoken with Christ's presence behind it, can do more than an hour of attempted explanations. A quiet prayer whispered in the company of the suffering can be a doorway through which grace enters the room.

Because accompaniment is not simply emotional support — it is sacramental in character. When a Christian sits beside someone in pain, Christ sits beside them. When a believer prays with a wounded friend, Christ intercedes. When we bear another's burden, Christ bears it with us. This is not sentiment; it is the theology of the Body of Christ. The Church is not merely an institution; she is Christ's presence on earth. And when one member suffers, every member shares that suffering because Christ Himself shares it.

Accompaniment, then, is participation in Christ's compassion. The word compassion literally means "to suffer with." This is what distinguishes Christian accompaniment from moral support or emotional solidarity. Christians do not simply feel for the suffering — they enter the suffering as Christ entered ours. Their presence becomes a sign of His presence. Their patience reflects His endurance. Their silence carries His peace. Their listening echoes His mercy. Their tears join the tears of the One who wept at the tomb of Lazarus.

The heart of accompaniment is not expertise but availability. It is the willingness to be present even when we feel inadequate, uncertain, or afraid of saying the wrong thing. Scripture shows again and again that God uses availability more than ability. Moses stuttered. Jeremiah trembled. The apostles were slow to understand. Yet God builds His kingdom through people who are willing to stand where love requires them to stand. When someone suffers, the greatest gift we offer is not our insight but our presence — because presence reveals love, and love reveals God.

Yet presence alone is not enough. It must be presence shaped by reverence for the mystery of the other person's suffering. Suffering is holy ground. When we enter the life of someone who is hurting, we enter a place where God is already at work in ways we cannot see. We walk softly because the soul before us is being shaped by grace in a way that is often invisible. The fathers and mothers of the Church understood this. They taught that the sufferer stands in a kind of sanctuary, where God often speaks in whispers too delicate for the untrained ear. Our task is not to speak over that whisper but to help the sufferer hear it.

This is why certain kinds of speech harm more than heal. There is a cruelty hidden inside many well-intentioned clichés. "It's God's will," spoken too quickly, reduces mystery to mechanism. "Everything happens for a reason," spoken without discernment, flattens providence into inevitability. "God won't give you more than you can handle," spoken to someone already drowning, places responsibility on the sufferer instead of on the God who carries us. These phrases come from a desire to comfort, but they often bypass the real ache of the heart. They skip the Cross and aim for the Resurrection without passing through the tomb.

Christ never speaks that way. When the widow of Nain weeps over her son, He does not offer an explanation. He is moved with compassion — with a suffering that enters her suffering. When Mary and Martha face the death of Lazarus, Christ does not begin with doctrine. He begins with tears. His words come only after His tears, and even then they are personal, not abstract: "I am the Resurrection and the Life." Christ's compassion is not theoretical. It is incarnate. It is embodied. It is expressed in nearness, silence, tears, and only then in truth.

The pattern for Christian accompaniment is found here. We do not begin with theology; we begin with love. Theology comes, but it must come in the right moment and in the right measure. The aim is not to explain away suffering but to reveal God's nearness within it. This is why the early Christians understood accompaniment as a form of diakonia — service born from love, not strategy. The deacons of the early Church did not simply distribute goods; they distributed Christ's compassion. They entered homes where sorrow lived and brought with them the presence of the Church, which is the presence of Christ.

To accompany someone well, we must cultivate the humility to let their suffering speak before our opinions do. Suffering often brings to the surface long-buried fears, regrets, or questions. These do not need to be corrected immediately. They need to be honoured. The human heart often reaches for meaning through lament, and lament is not unbelief. The psalms are filled with lament — cries of confusion, protest, and grief. "Why, O Lord, do You stand far off?" "How long, O Lord?" "Has Your mercy ceased?" These are not the words of apostasy. They are the words of covenant faith struggling toward clarity.

A person who is suffering may say things that sound theologically imprecise. They may express anger toward God, disappointment in life, or fear of the future. Our task is not to silence these cries. Our task is to receive them the way God receives the psalms — with patience, tenderness, and truth that arrives only when the heart is ready to receive it. The goal of accompaniment is not to control someone's emotions but to shepherd them toward Christ gently, without pressure or haste.

Listening in this way is an act of love. It is also an act of spiritual warfare. Suffering often isolates the soul, leading it to believe it must carry its pain alone. When we listen, truly listen, we break that isolation. We become a sacrament of communion — a sign that God has not abandoned His child. This is the deep truth Paul reveals when he tells the Galatians to "bear one another's burdens." He is not speaking of sentiment. He is speaking of sharing the weight of another's Cross. The Church is the place where no one suffers unsupported. To carry another's burden is to let Christ carry them through us.

There is also a second form of accompaniment that is often overlooked: the ministry of practical care. Scripture places extraordinary dignity on the simplest acts of mercy. Jesus says that giving a cup of cold water in His name does not go unnoticed. Feeding the hungry, visiting the sick, comforting the mourning — these are not merely moral duties; they are acts through which Christ reveals His love. The suffering person often carries burdens that extend beyond the spiritual. They need meals, rest, help with children, assistance with appointments, or simply someone to sit with them through the night. These acts of mercy do not merely lighten the load; they remind the sufferer that God's love has hands, and those hands have drawn near.

Practical care becomes a theology of the body. Just as Christ's compassion was expressed through physical touch, so our care becomes embodied love. We do not love souls in abstraction; we love persons. And persons have bodies that tire, hearts that ache, and burdens that weigh heavily. Accompaniment that remains spiritual but never becomes practical is incomplete. Christ fed the hungry before He preached to them. He healed bodies before He healed memories. He touched wounds before He interpreted them. Christian accompaniment must do the same.

Every act of accompaniment participates in the mystery of the Incarnation. God did not save us by shouting from heaven. He saved us by dwelling among us, sharing our condition, bearing our wounds. This is why Christian accompaniment cannot remain detached or analytical. It must be incarnational. It must draw near with the humility of Christ, who "emptied Himself, taking the form of a servant," and who continues to empty Himself in every act of love expressed through His Body, the Church. When we accompany the suffering, we are not performing a task. We are revealing a mystery.

One of the greatest obstacles to this revelation is the temptation to fix rather than to accompany. This temptation often arises from compassion, but it can obscure the deeper work God is doing. Fixing shifts the focus to solutions; accompaniment shifts the focus to communion. Fixing presumes that suffering is an enemy to be conquered; accompaniment recognises that suffering can be a place where grace enters. Fixing moves quickly; accompaniment moves reverently. Fixing aims for resolution; accompaniment aims for faithfulness. The desire to fix is understandable — witnessing pain is difficult. Yet the Cross teaches us that love does not always remove pain; it shares it.

Christ's ministry reveals this repeatedly. He does not rush to end every sorrow. In Bethany, He does not arrive in time to prevent Lazarus's death. In Gethsemane, He does not spare the disciples the agony of watching Him suffer. At the Cross, He does not call down angels to end His Passion. Christ is not indifferent to suffering — His heart burns with compassion — but He redeems suffering from within, not from afar. Accompaniment follows the same pattern. It does not aim to erase the experience of suffering but to ensure that the one who suffers does not walk alone.

This is the essence of compassion. The word itself means "to suffer with," and this is exactly what Christ does. He suffers with humanity in every sense — physically, emotionally, spiritually — and He does so freely. Christian compassion is not pity; it is participation. It is the willingness to allow another's sorrow to enter our heart and the willingness to let our presence be a channel of God's love. Compassion is costly because love is costly. But Christ shows us that the cost is what makes love real. A love that cannot bear suffering is not love at all.

In this light, accompaniment becomes a sacred vocation. It is a calling rooted in baptism, where the believer is united to Christ's death and resurrection. Through baptism, we become members of His Body, and this means our lives are now places where His compassion takes flesh. The sufferer stands before us not as a problem but as a brother or sister entrusted to us by God. Their sorrow is an invitation to reveal Christ's heart. Their weakness is an opportunity for grace to become visible. Their tears are the ground on which our faith must become action.

This vocation has a particular shape, and Scripture gives it a name: consolation. St. Paul speaks of "the God of all consolation, who consoles us in all our afflictions, so that we may be able to console those who are in any affliction." Notice the pattern. Consolation does not begin with us. It begins with God. We do not accompany because we are naturally compassionate; we accompany because God has accompanied us. He consoles us so that we might console others with the same consolation. This is the logic of grace: what God gives becomes what God asks us to give. What God pours into us becomes what God pours through us.

This truth gives accompaniment both its humility and its confidence. Its humility comes from the knowledge that we are not the saviour of the person who suffers. Its confidence comes from the knowledge that the true Saviour is present, working through our presence. We carry Christ's compassion, not our own. We offer Christ's hope, not our own optimism. We provide Christ's patience, not our natural tolerance. Accompaniment becomes an act of faith because it requires us to believe that Christ will work in ways we cannot see.

This belief is tested most deeply when suffering persists. Many people accompany others readily at first, but their presence fades as the suffering continues. True accompaniment endures. It remains faithful even when progress is slow, when old wounds reopen, when the sufferer grows weary, or when the path seems to circle without end. Fidelity in accompaniment mirrors God's fidelity. He does not abandon His people halfway through their trials. He remains with Israel in the wilderness, with David in exile, with Elijah in despair, with Mary at the Cross. Accompaniment is the imitation of that endurance.

When we accompany someone who suffers, we often discover that our presence speaks louder than anything we could say. The sufferer sees in us a living sign that they are not forsaken. This is why the Church has always valued the ministry of visitation — visiting the sick, the homebound, the sorrowful, the dying. These visits are not interruptions; they are incarnations of Christ's love. They bring the Church into the rooms where pain lives. They bring grace into the spaces where darkness threatens. They bring hope into the moments when the soul feels fragile.

All of this leads to a profound truth: when we accompany the suffering, the one who suffers is not the only one transformed. Accompaniment changes us. It enlarges the heart. It teaches dependence on grace. It purifies motives. It reveals our own vulnerability. It forces us to let Christ love through us in ways we did not expect. Many people fear entering the suffering of others because they fear what it will cost. But the real cost is discovered to be grace. The more we enter another's sorrow, the more deeply we discover the heart of Christ.

True accompaniment always leads us deeper into the mystery of the Church, because the Church is not simply the community that surrounds the suffering — she is the Body through which Christ Himself accompanies His people. This is why our presence matters so profoundly. When we accompany someone, we are not offering them merely human comfort. We are offering them the presence of Christ made tangible through His members. The grace at work in accompaniment does not originate in us; it flows through us. It is Christ who consoles, but He consoles through the hands that serve, the ears that listen, and the hearts that remain faithful.

This becomes especially clear when we look at the way the early Christians described themselves. They did not think of the Church as an organisation that helps the suffering; they thought of themselves as a body in which every wound was shared. St. Paul's words in 1 Corinthians 12 are not metaphorical. "If one member suffers, all suffer together." This is not a poetic exaggeration. It is a description of what it means to belong to Christ. In baptism, the believer is joined not only to Christ's life but to Christ's people. Their suffering becomes our suffering because Christ's suffering became ours.

This is why the Church insists on the works of mercy. They are not optional; they are essential. They are the visible, embodied ways in which the invisible grace of Christ's compassion is extended to the world. To feed the hungry, to visit the sick, to comfort the grieving — these are not simply moral obligations. They are sacramental acts of accompaniment. They are the places where the love of God becomes flesh again. When Jesus says, "Whatever you did for the least of these, you did for Me," He is revealing that accompaniment is the privileged place where we meet Him.

But accompaniment is not only active; it is contemplative. There is a depth to this ministry that cannot be reached through activity alone. To accompany well, we must cultivate the interior life — the habit of prayer that keeps the heart rooted in Christ even as it enters the sorrows of others. Without prayer, accompaniment becomes a burden too heavy to bear. With prayer, accompaniment becomes the place where the strength of Christ flows through our weakness. The one who accompanies must learn to return again and again to the Lord who accompanied us first — in His Incarnation, His Passion, and His abiding presence in the Eucharist.

This is why the saints who accompanied best were those who prayed most. Think of St. Francis embracing the leper not with natural courage but with supernatural love. Think of St. Damian caring for the outcasts of Molokai, strengthened daily by the Eucharist he celebrated. Think of St. Teresa of Calcutta holding the dying not because of moral duty but because she saw in each person "Jesus in His distressing disguise." These saints teach us that effective accompaniment flows from union with Christ. They did not merely help others; they carried Christ to them. And in doing so, they allowed Christ to be carried into their own hearts as well.

This union with Christ also guards us from one of the greatest dangers in accompaniment: exhaustion of the soul. When we rely on our own strength, we eventually run dry. When we rely on Christ's strength, we discover that suffering becomes a place where grace multiplies. The one who accompanies becomes a vessel, not a source. And vessels that are filled by God do not empty; they overflow. This is why Jesus says, "Whoever believes in Me… out of his heart will flow rivers of living water." The water does not originate in us, but it flows through us. Accompaniment becomes the streambed through which Christ's living water reaches those who thirst.

Another danger in accompaniment is the temptation to take control of another person's journey. This temptation often arises when we care deeply and want to protect someone from further harm. But accompaniment is not control. It is cooperation. It is walking beside, not walking ahead. The Holy Spirit is the guide of the suffering soul, not us. Our role is to witness, not to steer; to support, not to overpower; to encourage, not to dominate. When we accompany well, we learn the humility of John the Baptist: "He must increase, and I must decrease." We make room for Christ's work by refusing to place ourselves at the centre.

At the same time, accompaniment requires discernment. Not every suffering is the same, and not every person needs the same kind of presence. Some need silence; others need Scripture. Some need practical help; others need gentle correction when despair narrows their vision. Some need companionship; others need a space for solitude protected by trust. The one who accompanies must listen not only to the sufferer but to the Spirit. Christ knows what every soul needs, and He reveals His wisdom when we remain attentive to His promptings. Without discernment, accompaniment becomes clumsy. With discernment, it becomes a channel of grace.

The heart of accompaniment, therefore, is love — not sentimental love, not superficial comfort, but covenant love. The love that reflects the fidelity of God. The love that remains when answers fall short. The love that listens when words fail. The love that sees Christ in the broken and believes Christ is working in the darkness. The love that dares to stay at the foot of the Cross because Christ stayed there for us.

This love has a shape. It looks like Mary standing beneath the Crucified Christ. She does not flee. She does not faint. She does not demand explanations. She shares the suffering of her Son through a silent fidelity that becomes the model for all Christian accompaniment. Her presence does not remove Christ's suffering, but it surrounds Him with love. Her faith does not erase the Cross, but it fills the Cross with meaning. Her endurance does not prevent death, but it prepares the way for resurrection. Mary's accompaniment is the purest image of the Church accompanying her suffering children — steadfast, compassionate, unwavering.

Accompaniment reaches its fullest meaning not when we understand someone's suffering, but when we share it. This is the mystery of the Church's life: we bear one another's burdens because Christ has borne ours. And because He has borne ours, we are free to enter the sorrows of others without fear. We do not bring ourselves; we bring Him. Our weakness does not hinder this mission. In fact, our weakness becomes the very means by which Christ's strength is made visible. When St. Paul heard the Lord say, "My grace is sufficient for you, for My power is made perfect in weakness," he was not receiving a private consolation. He was receiving the secret of every Christian who has ever accompanied the suffering. Christ does His deepest work through those who know their dependence.

This is why the Church calls accompaniment a work of mercy. Mercy is not sentiment. Mercy is the movement of God toward misery. It is love bending down to lift the wounded. When we accompany someone who suffers, we participate in God's own movement. Mercy becomes the shape of our presence. It becomes the character of our silence, the tone of our words, the strength behind our patience. Mercy is the tenderness of God made tangible in human hands. To accompany is to be a vessel through which that tenderness flows.

And yet mercy does not deny truth. It holds truth within the embrace of compassion. The one who accompanies does not lie about the weight of suffering, nor does he pretend to possess answers that have not been revealed. He speaks truth, but he speaks it slowly, in season, and only when truth can be received as gift rather than burden. This is why accompaniment is as much an art as a discipline. It requires sensitivity, patience, and prayer. It requires constant return to Christ, whose compassion never contradicted His truth, and whose truth never diminished His compassion.

Accompaniment also demands hope, but not the thin optimism our world confuses with hope. Christian hope is rooted in the Resurrection — the truth that nothing given to Christ in love is ever lost. Hope allows us to enter another's suffering without despair because we know that Christ is already present there. Hope allows us to remain when the suffering stretches on, because we trust that grace is at work in ways unseen. Hope allows us to speak of God's faithfulness even when the present moment feels barren, because God has bound Himself to His people with a covenant that no affliction can break. Accompaniment becomes credible only when it is sustained by this hope.

But something else happens in accompaniment — something unexpected, something doctrinal and mystical. The one who suffers reveals Christ to the one who accompanies. In their weakness, we meet His weakness; in their tears, we meet His sorrow; in their endurance, we meet His fidelity. The sufferer becomes an icon of the Crucified, and those who accompany find themselves standing closer to the mystery of Christ than they ever anticipated. This is why the saints sought the company of the poor, the sick, the widowed, and the dying. They did not descend from spiritual strength into human frailty; they ascended into the presence of Christ hidden in the wounds of His people.

Every act of accompaniment is therefore twofold:

we carry Christ to the suffering, and the suffering reveal Christ to us.

This is the exchange at the heart of the Church. This is the communion of saints in its most concrete form. And this is why accompaniment is not simply a response to suffering; it is participation in redemption. Not a redemption we accomplish, but a redemption we enter. Christ saved the world by sharing suffering. We serve the world by sharing it with Him.

And so, when we accompany someone who suffers, we must remember that what we offer is far deeper than presence. We offer a place where Christ can be encountered. We offer a companionship that traces its roots to Calvary. We offer a love that does not flinch before sorrow because it has been shaped by the Cross. We offer a hope born not of sentiment, but of the empty tomb. Accompaniment becomes the living sign that suffering is not the final word — not because we can remove suffering, but because Christ has transformed it from within.

As this chapter comes to its close, one truth rises above the rest: to accompany another is to enter the very heart of Christ. It is to love as He loved, to remain as He remained, to carry as He carried. In every room where pain is present, Christ waits to be revealed. The one who accompanies becomes the veil He lifts, the hand He extends, the consolation He gives. And the one who suffers becomes the place where His love is received anew.

In this mystery, suffering is no longer solitary, and love is no longer passive. Accompaniment becomes communion. Communion becomes hope. And hope becomes the light that no darkness can overcome. For the God who bears our sorrows bears them still — through His Body, through His saints, and through every believer who dares to walk beside the wounded with the courage of Christ.

21

Hope: The Last Word

Hope has always entered the world the same way light enters a room—quietly at first, then with a force no darkness can resist. Scripture speaks of hope not as a mood or a feeling, but as a virtue woven into the very fabric of creation. It is the thread that binds the first promise of Genesis to the final consummation of Revelation. It is the melody that continues even when the notes of our own lives fall into dissonance. And it is the last word in the Christian story because it is the first word spoken by God to a fallen world: *"I will come."*

Every human being knows the longing that gives shape to hope. It is the ache that rises in hospital rooms, the whispered prayer over a grave, the fragile courage of a parent kneeling beside a child who does not understand why the world can hurt so much. Hope is not born in comfort. It is born precisely in the places where comfort fails. The heart learns to hope not when life is easy, but when life exposes its limits. Only then do we recognise that the human spirit cries out for something greater than anything this world can offer.

The Christian imagination begins here. It begins by listening to that cry and refusing to dismiss it. The world may reduce hope to wishful thinking or positive psychology. But Scripture presents it as something far sturdier. Hope is a horizon. Hope is an anchor. Hope is the soul leaning toward the One who made it, trusting that His promises are stronger than our sorrow. Hope is not the denial of suffering. It is the conviction that suffering is not the end.

Yet to understand hope, we must first understand the world in which it arises. The modern person lives in the tension between two deep instincts: a hunger for meaning, and a fear of suffering. We have explored that fear throughout this book—how it distorts our choices, narrows our imagination, and makes the trials of life feel unbearable. But hope enters precisely at this point of tension. It is the virtue that teaches the heart how to stand within suffering without collapsing under it. It shows us that the story of our lives is not measured by our wounds but by the One who carries them.

This is why Christian hope cannot be understood apart from the Cross. Hope is not a sentimental escape from reality. It is the fruit of a love that has passed through death and emerged victorious. When Jesus rises from the dead, He does not erase His wounds. He bears them glorified. And in doing so, He reveals the deepest truth about hope: nothing given to God is lost. Not suffering. Not sacrifice. Not tears. The Resurrection does not reject the Cross; it redeems it. It gathers every moment of suffering into the mystery of divine love and lifts it into a meaning far beyond anything human logic could imagine.

That is the horizon toward which this chapter now turns—the horizon that gives shape to every chapter that came before it. Everything we have explored—the cry of the human heart, the story of Israel, the Cross of Christ, the endurance of the saints, the trials of the modern world, the disciplines that sustain faith—finds its fulfillment here. Hope is the point where theology touches destiny. It is the point where suffering ceases to be an argument against God and becomes the road that leads to Him.

But to see hope clearly, we must first remove the illusions that cloud our vision. Hope is not optimism. Optimism is fragile. It depends on circumstances, probabilities, and outcomes. It changes when conditions change. It falters when disappointment strikes. It collapses under the weight of real suffering. Optimism is the bright sky that vanishes at the first sign of a storm.

Hope is different. Hope is forged in the storm. It is the virtue that emerges when everything else has been stripped away. It is not rooted in outcomes, but in God—His character, His promises, His faithfulness. Hope is covenantal. It rests on the certainty that the God who spoke creation into existence is the same God who entered history, endured our sorrow, and rose with a promise sealed in His own blood. Hope is the virtue that looks at the Cross and sees not tragedy but triumph. It is the virtue that looks at the empty tomb and hears the future calling.

This is why the Scriptures speak of hope with such confidence. St. Paul can say, without exaggeration, that "hope does not disappoint us." He does not mean that life will always turn out as we expect. He means that God will always accomplish what He has promised, even if the path to that promise passes through shadows. Hope does not protect us from suffering. It protects us from despair. It allows the believer to walk through darkness with the light of God burning within.

And yet, hope is not simply a future reality. It is a present strength. It is the grace by which the believer endures trials, perseveres in prayer, rejects resentment, embraces sacrifice, and continues to love when sorrow tempts the heart to close. Hope is what allows the Christian to forgive. It is what allows the parent to pray for a prodigal child, the sick to trust when healing does not come, the mourner to believe that death is not final. Hope is the steady breath of faith in a world that has forgotten how to breathe.

As we enter this chapter, we stand at the threshold of the Christian mystery. We stand in the space where suffering and glory meet, where tears become seed, where wounds become witness. This chapter will not ignore the weight of sorrow. But neither will it treat sorrow as the final truth. The final truth is hope—the hope promised by the prophets, fulfilled in Christ, lived by the saints, and entrusted to the Church. The hope that does not grow dim with time, but grows brighter as the world grows dark. The hope that turns the last word of every suffering into the first word of a new creation.

Hope is the Christian's inheritance because it is Christ's own life poured into the soul. But to understand how hope becomes strength, we must first understand the horizon toward which it leads. Scripture refuses to reduce hope to endurance alone. Hope is oriented toward glory—toward a future that is not imagined but revealed. A future described not in metaphors of escape, but in the language of transformation. A future where human sorrow does not merely end, but is rewritten.

This is why the New Testament speaks of hope with the language of creation. St. Peter tells us that through Christ we have been given "a living hope"—a hope that breathes, grows, and renews. St. Paul tells us that all creation groans as it awaits the redemption of our bodies. Hope is not the promise that God will lift us out of the created world; it is the promise that He will restore creation itself. The final word of the Christian story is not disembodiment, but resurrection. Not escape from the world, but the transfiguration of the world. Hope reaches toward this destiny with the confidence of a child reaching toward the hand that has never failed him.

The early Christians lived by this truth. They spoke of heaven not as a distant ideal but as a homeland. They described themselves as citizens of another Kingdom, not because they rejected the earth, but because they saw the earth through the eyes of Christ. This vision allowed them to endure persecution without despair, poverty without fear, and suffering without losing their identity. Hope gave them a view of reality that could not be shaken by anything the world could inflict.

But this hope was not naive. It did not deny the suffering they endured. It did something far greater—it placed their suffering within a story large enough to hold it. A story in which God never abandons His people. A story in which the Cross becomes the path to glory. A story in which the Resurrection is not merely the end of Christ's suffering, but the beginning of a new creation that will one day gather every tear into joy.

Hope, in other words, draws its strength from revelation. It is not invented; it is received. It is not the work of imagination; it is the fruit of covenant. God reveals Himself as the One who brings life out of death, order out of chaos, beauty out of brokenness. Hope is the virtue that takes Him at His word even when the evidence seems otherwise. It is the virtue that remembers the Red Sea when standing before a new impossibility. It is the virtue that remembers the empty tomb when standing before an open grave.

This is why hope must be learned. The human heart does not naturally turn toward the unseen. It prefers what it can measure, control, or predict. But hope draws us beyond those limits. It calls the heart to trust what it cannot yet see because it knows the One who has spoken. It asks the believer to root his confidence not in circumstances but in covenant. Not in probability but in promise. The cultivation of hope, therefore, is not simply a psychological exercise; it is a spiritual discipline. It is the ongoing conversion of the heart from self-reliance to God-reliance.

The saints understood this with clarity. Their lives reveal the depth of hope because their lives were shaped by the God who keeps His promises. When they faced suffering, they faced it with an eye fixed on the horizon of glory. They saw suffering not as a contradiction of God's love but as a place where His grace could enter more deeply. Their hope did not eliminate pain, but it transformed their relationship to it. Pain no longer had the power to define them. Only Christ did. Only His promise had the right to speak the last word.

The writings of the early Fathers are filled with this vision. They speak of heaven as the perfection of communion—the communion begun in baptism, nourished in the Eucharist, and fulfilled in the life of the world to come. They describe hope as the virtue that lifts the heart toward this destiny without severing it from the responsibilities of the present. Hope does not lure the believer into passivity. It strengthens him for fidelity. It strengthens him to love, to persevere, to forgive, to endure. Hope is the virtue that empowers the Christian to live today in the light of eternity.

And yet, hope is not merely something to contemplate. It is something to practice. It is expressed when the believer prays even when prayer feels fruitless. It is expressed when the believer serves even when his strength is weak. It is expressed when the believer forgives even when his heart resists. Hope is enacted every time the Christian chooses faithfulness over fear. Every act of fidelity becomes a declaration that the world's darkness does not have the final word.

This is why the Scriptures speak of hope as an anchor. An anchor does not remove the storm. It gives stability within the storm. It holds the vessel in place when the winds rise and the waves beat against it. When the human heart is anchored in God, suffering cannot carry it away. Fear cannot uproot it. Despair cannot drown it. Hope is the anchor that binds the believer to the One who has already conquered every darkness.

This truth becomes clearest when we turn to the final promise of Scripture: *"Behold, I make all things new."* This is the horizon toward which hope leans. Not the restoration of the past, but the fulfillment of all creation in Christ. Heaven is not an escape from the world. It is the completion of the world's story. It is the moment when every sorrow becomes seed, every sacrifice becomes fruit, every unanswered question becomes light. Heaven is the place where God transfigures every tear into meaning.

And that is the promise that sustains the believer. Hope is not wishful thinking about what might be. It is trust in what will be. It is the certainty that God does not waste suffering, does not forget His children, and does not abandon His work. Hope assures the believer that every moment lived in faith becomes part of the glory to come. Nothing is lost. Nothing is wasted. Nothing is overlooked by the eyes of God.

Hope becomes even more striking when placed in contrast with the fears that dominate the modern imagination. Our age speaks often about anxiety, uncertainty, and the fragility of the human spirit—and yet it speaks very little about hope. It speaks of coping, managing, surviving, but rarely of destiny. It speaks of resilience, but not of resurrection. It speaks of healing, but not of holiness. Without the horizon of glory, every sorrow feels heavier. Without the promise of God, every trial feels final.

Scripture answers this darkness not with optimism, but with revelation. Optimism assumes that circumstances will improve. Hope knows that even if circumstances worsen, God remains faithful. Optimism rises and falls with probability. Hope rises and falls with nothing at all. It stands on the character of God, not the condition of the world. This is why the darkest nights of the Christian's life often become the moments when hope grows strongest. When every visible support is removed, the soul learns to anchor itself in the invisible fidelity of God.

This is the lesson written into the very heart of Israel's story. When the people stood at the Red Sea with the Egyptian army closing in behind them, there was no earthly reason to hope. But hope is not based on earthly reason. It is based on God's promise. When Isaiah announced consolation to a people in exile, it was not because their political prospects had improved; it was because God had spoken. When Ezekiel prophesied life over dry bones, it was not because he saw signs of revival; it was because he heard the word of the Lord. The entire narrative of salvation rests on the truth that God keeps His promises, even when His people cannot imagine how.

The New Testament continues this pattern. Hope becomes the lens through which the early Church interprets everything—persecution, martyrdom, suffering, and even death. St. Paul does not disguise the trials of his ministry; he lists them with disarming frankness. But he frames them within the greater truth of the Resurrection: "So we do not lose heart." Not because he avoids suffering, but because he reads suffering through the light of eternity. Paul's hope does not deny pain; it transforms its meaning. It becomes the place where the life of Christ is revealed.

This same hope becomes the heartbeat of Christian prayer. The believer prays not because life is easy, but because God is faithful. Prayer is an act of hope precisely when it feels most difficult. When the heavens seem silent, when the heart feels numb, when words fail—these are the moments when prayer becomes a declaration of trust in the God who hears even when He seems hidden. To pray in the darkness is to say, "I know who You are," even when I cannot see what You are doing.

This is why Christian hope is inseparable from memory. The believer remembers what God has done—creation, covenant, Passover, Exodus, the Cross, the Resurrection—and places his present trials within that history. Memory is not nostalgia; it is the foundation of hope. If God has acted in the past, He will act again. If God has been faithful before, His faithfulness is not suddenly suspended. Every act of divine rescue becomes a promise that suffering is not the end of the story. The believer prays, remembers, and hopes because the God who spoke then still speaks now.

The Fathers of the Church understood this with remarkable clarity. They describe hope as the virtue that stretches the soul toward its true homeland. Augustine calls it the "longing for what is to come." Gregory of Nyssa describes the Christian as a pilgrim who moves from glory to glory, drawn forward by the beauty of the God who awaits him. Hope is not passive. It does not sit idle. It moves the soul toward the future promised by God, a future in which the human heart will be fully healed, fully restored, and fully united to Christ.

And yet, this forward movement of hope never detaches the believer from the responsibilities of the present. Hope strengthens fidelity. It deepens love. It teaches patience. It gives courage. The believer who lives by hope does not withdraw from the world; he engages it with renewed strength. He serves with deeper compassion because he knows suffering is not meaningless. He forgives with greater generosity because he knows God is the final judge. He sacrifices without fear because he knows love is not lost. Hope gives the Christian eyes to see every moment of life—every trial, every sorrow, every burden—as a chapter in a story God Himself is writing.

This is why the New Testament speaks of the Christian life with the language of pilgrimage. We are "strangers and sojourners," not because the world is rejected, but because it is incomplete. We walk through this life with hope because we know it is leading somewhere. Hope gives shape to the journey. It gives meaning to the detours. It gives purpose to the wilderness. Without hope, the journey becomes directionless. With hope, every step becomes an act of faithfulness.

Hope also reveals something essential about the nature of suffering. Suffering is not wasted. It is gathered. It is remembered. It is transformed. The God who raised Jesus from the dead does not discard the wounds of His children. He redeems them. He weaves every act of endurance, every moment of trust, every cry of faith into the tapestry of glory that awaits. Hope tells the believer that nothing is lost in God's economy. The smallest act of perseverance becomes part of the eternal story.

This truth is not sentimental. It is profoundly concrete. It is seen in the martyrs who faced death without fear because they saw beyond the horizon of this world. It is seen in the sick who offered their pain for the salvation of souls. It is seen in the lonely who entrusted their longing to God. It is seen in the parents who sacrifice daily out of love for their children. These are not heroic exceptions. They are the ordinary paths through which hope takes flesh in the lives of believers.

Christian hope is not an escape from suffering. It is the only way to walk through suffering without losing the self. It is the virtue that allows the believer to carry the Cross with Christ and to see beyond the Cross to the glory that awaits. Hope is the virtue that leads the Christian through the valley of the shadow of death with the confidence that the Shepherd walks beside him. It is the certainty that the darkness cannot extinguish the light because the light has already conquered the grave.

Hope also reshapes the way a Christian understands time. The modern world experiences time as pressure—deadlines, aging, uncertainty, the fear of loss. But Scripture teaches a different vision. Time is not the enemy of the human spirit; it is the arena of God's faithfulness. Every moment becomes a place where grace can enter. Every season, even the most painful, becomes a place where God draws the believer toward maturity. Hope does not rush time, nor does it resist it. Hope receives time as gift because it trusts the Giver.

This is why hopelessness always collapses the horizon. It traps a person in the immediacy of pain. It makes the present absolute. When suffering arrives, the soul begins to believe that what is now is what will always be. Hope refuses this lie. Hope remembers that God has already changed the world once—at the Resurrection—and that He will change it again. Hope sees the present in light of the future. It stretches the heart toward the fulfillment that God has promised. It tells us that the present pain is not the final page of the story, even when the present feels overwhelming.

Christian hope is therefore deeply realistic. It does not sugarcoat suffering or pretend it does not hurt. It does not disguise the truth that life in a fallen world is marked by loss, disappointment, and sorrow. But it anchors that realism in the larger truth that suffering is not the final reality. God is. The Kingdom is. The Resurrection is. The promises of God are. Hope reads suffering through the light of what endures forever. Hope does not deny tears; it gathers them for the day when God Himself will wipe them away.

This is what gives Christian hope its distinctive strength. It is not rooted in human optimism, which rises and falls with emotional weather. It is rooted in divine fidelity, which does not change. The God who made the covenant with Abraham, led Israel through the desert, raised His Son from the dead, and poured out His Spirit upon the Church is the same God who holds the life of every believer. Hope is simply the virtue that takes Him at His word.

The saints lived this truth with remarkable confidence. Their hope was not born from comfort but from clarity. They saw reality as it truly is: a world sustained by the love of God, directed toward the glory of God, and redeemed by the sacrifice of God. They endured trials not because they were strong, but because they knew the One who was stronger. When persecution threatened the early Church, hope became their shield. When illness struck the saints, hope became their anchor. When martyrdom drew near, hope became their victory. Their lives reveal that hope is not the absence of sorrow; it is the presence of Christ within sorrow.

Even the saints who never faced persecution give witness to this truth. St. Thérèse endured sickness with a simplicity that astonished her sisters. St. Francis embraced poverty because he saw it as a participation in Christ's own life. St. Teresa of Calcutta faced spiritual darkness for decades, yet her hope remained unwavering because it was grounded not in her feelings, but in Christ's fidelity. These saints show that hope is not restricted to dramatic moments. It becomes visible in the ordinary fidelity of those who trust God day after day.

Hope also transforms the way the Christian interprets death. Without hope, death is simply the end—the moment when all meaning collapses. But with hope, death becomes a passage. It becomes the moment when faith becomes sight. The Christian does not deny the sorrow of death; the Gospels themselves weep at the tomb of Lazarus. But the Christian faces death with a confidence that no other worldview can provide: the confidence that Christ has already passed through death and transformed it from the inside. Hope transforms death from a wall into a door. From a final defeat into a final deliverance.

This is why the Church insists on speaking of death with the language of liturgy. Funeral rites are not acts of despair; they are acts of hope. They proclaim that the dead are entrusted into the hands of the God who defeated death. They announce that those who have died in Christ will rise with Christ. They remind the living that death does not have the last word. Christ does. Hope allows the Christian to stand before the grave with the same quiet confidence that marked the early disciples: "Christ is risen, and life reigns."

This hope becomes especially powerful when the believer endures long trials—chronic illness, aging, disability, loneliness, ongoing sorrow. These are the places where hope becomes more than a virtue; it becomes a discipline. It becomes the daily decision to see life in the light of the Resurrection. It becomes the daily surrender of fear into God's hands. It becomes the daily act of trusting that the God who has carried the believer this far will not abandon him now. Hope becomes the endurance of love.

This endurance is not cold stoicism. It is warm fidelity. It is the endurance that flows from a heart held by God. Hope teaches the believer to remain steadfast not because he is strong, but because Christ is. Hope teaches him to love not because he feels capable, but because grace sustains him. Hope teaches him to persevere not because he understands every trial, but because he knows that every trial is held within the hands of the One who loves him.

And yet, hope is not satisfied with endurance alone. It reaches toward transformation. It looks toward the glory that God has promised. It looks toward the healing of all wounds, the restoration of all things, the reunion of all who have died in Christ. Hope does not cling merely to the possibility of consolation. It clings to the certainty of communion. Heaven is not a compensation given after a long trial. Heaven is the fulfillment of everything the human heart was created for. Hope longs for this fulfillment with the confidence of faith.

Hope also reveals the true identity of the Christian. In a world that measures worth by achievement, beauty, productivity, or power, hope announces a different truth: the believer's identity is rooted in belonging to God. Hope teaches the soul to say, "I am His," even when everything else is shaken. Suffering cannot rob the Christian of this identity. Failure cannot undo it. Death cannot threaten it. Identity rooted in God becomes unassailable because it is grounded in the One who does not change.

This is why hope produces joy even in sorrow. Not the thin, fragile joy of distraction, but the deep joy that comes from knowing that one's life is hidden in Christ. Hope does not eliminate grief; it gives grief a horizon. It does not erase tears; it tells the believer that tears are gathered by the hands of God. Hope does not suppress lament; it sanctifies it. Hope gives the believer a way to stand before God with honesty, to cry out with the psalmist, "How long, O Lord?" while still trusting that the answer is already on its way.

Christian hope is woven deeply into the life of prayer. Every "Our Father" is an act of hope, a confession that God's will is good, His kingdom is coming, and His providence is enough. Every "Hail Mary" is an act of hope, a request for the intercession of the Mother who stood at the Cross and believed in the promise even when she held her dead Son in her arms. Every Mass is an act of hope, the sacramental proclamation that Christ has died, Christ is risen, and Christ will come again. Hope is not an idea; it is a posture of the heart. It is the posture of a child trusting his Father.

This posture becomes especially clear in the Eucharist. The Eucharist is the pledge of future glory. It is the downpayment of the Kingdom. It is the moment in which the believer receives, under the veil of bread and wine, the very Body of the risen Christ. In this sacrament, heaven bends low. The future touches the present. The glory that awaits the Church becomes present on the altar. Hope finds its nourishment in this mystery. The believer who receives the Eucharist receives not only grace for the moment, but promise for eternity. He receives the One who will raise his body on the last day. He receives the seed of immortality.

This is why the Church has always described the Christian life as a movement from glory to glory. Not because life becomes easier, but because hope becomes stronger. The believer is drawn deeper into the mystery of Christ through every trial, every joy, every season. The sufferings of this present life become the sculptor's tools, shaping the soul into the likeness of Christ. The joys become foretastes of the kingdom. Hope gathers both into the story of redemption.

Yet hope does more than interpret suffering and strengthen endurance. Hope prepares the Christian for the final encounter with God. Hope teaches the soul to live with an eye fixed on eternity.

Not to escape the world, but to see the world through the lens of its fulfillment. Hope makes a person more alive, not less. It teaches him to cherish what is good, to sacrifice for what is holy, to work for what is just. Hope gives meaning to mission because it reveals the destiny of all things in Christ.

This is why the Scriptures describe heaven not with images of escape, but with images of fulfillment—wedding feast, new Jerusalem, home. Heaven is the perfection of communion. It is the restoration of everything lost. It is the healing of every wound. It is the fulfillment of every longing. It is the place where the human heart finally rests, not in isolation, but in union—with God, with others, with creation transfigured in glory. Hope strains toward this communion because the human person was created for nothing less.

Even in the face of mysteries we cannot fully understand, hope remains firm. The believer may not know how God will bring good from a particular sorrow, but he knows that God will. He may not understand why a certain trial endures, but he knows the trial is held within the hands of a Father who wastes nothing. Hope does not require comprehension; it requires trust. It requires the confidence that God's wisdom exceeds the believer's vision, and that His plans are always toward salvation.

This trust allows the believer to approach the end of life with peace. Death becomes not the collapse of meaning, but the completion of the journey. In death, the Christian hands his life back to the One who gave it, confident that the Giver is faithful. Hope allows the believer to approach death not with terror, but with the same expectation that filled the early Church: "Come, Lord Jesus." Hope transforms the fear of death into the desire for communion. It teaches the heart to long for the day when faith becomes sight.

In this way, hope becomes the final word of the Christian life because hope is the first word of eternal life. The believer who dies in hope does not fall into darkness. He falls into God. He falls into the arms of the One who has pursued him from the beginning. Hope is the virtue that guides the believer through the final door, not with resignation, but with trust.

Hope is the virtue that allows a person to die as a Christian.

And for this reason, hope must also become the virtue that allows a person to live as a Christian. It must shape every day, every choice, every trial, every act of love. The believer who lives in hope becomes a sign of the world to come. He becomes a living testimony that suffering does not have the last word, that death is not the end, that God's promises remain true. The Christian marked by hope becomes, in his own quiet way, an icon of the Resurrection in a world that has forgotten that such a thing is possible.

Hope, then, is not simply the virtue that sustains the Christian in this life. It is the virtue that opens the door to the next. It is the virtue that allows the believer to stand before God not as a stranger, but as a son. When a Christian dies in hope, he dies the way Scripture teaches us to live: with trust in the Father, union with the Son, and the breath of the Spirit drawing him toward the glory that has awaited him from the beginning.

This is why the Church speaks of the *"Christian death"* with language woven from promise rather than fear. The prayers for the dying are filled with hope—hope in the mercy of Christ, hope in the prayers of the saints, hope in the resurrection of the body, hope in the life of the world to come. Even the final commendation—the moment when the Church places the soul of the departed into the hands of God—is an act of hope. It echoes the words of Christ on the Cross: *"Father, into Your hands I commend My spirit."* In that moment, the pattern of Christ's surrender becomes the pattern of the Christian's surrender. Hope becomes the final breath.

And yet, for the ones left behind—those who mourn, those who wait, those who carry grief as a silent companion—hope continues to do its quiet work. The bereaved learn that grief and hope are not opposites. Christian grief is grief illuminated. It is grief that knows death is not the end because Christ has already conquered it. Hope allows the mourner to weep without despair. It allows him to remember without collapse. It allows him to long for reunion without idolising the past. The tears of the Christian are not signs of unbelief; they are signs of love waiting for fulfillment.

Hope speaks into the wound of loss with a confidence the world cannot offer. It says, "The separation is real, but it is not ultimate." It says, "The grave is deep, but the promise of God is deeper." It says, "The one you love is not gone; he is held." Hope does not silence grief; it sanctifies it. It gives grief a place within the story God is writing—a story that ends not in separation, but in communion.

This is why the Scriptures imagine the end of all things not as annihilation or escape, but as wedding. The final vision of the Bible is a feast, a bride, a city descending from heaven, radiant with the glory of God. It is a vision of homecoming. It is a vision of fulfillment. It is a vision in which heaven and earth are united, creation is restored, and the children of God stand before Him with hearts finally healed. Hope leans into this vision because it is the destiny for which humanity was made. Hope tells the believer that every longing for justice, every thirst for beauty, every ache for communion finds its answer here.

The Book of Revelation closes with the words, *"God will wipe away every tear from their eyes."* This is not a metaphor. It is a promise. The same God who shaped Adam from the earth will one day gather the tears of His children and turn them into glory. The wounds that marked the journey will not be forgotten; they will be transfigured. The sorrows that weighed on the heart will not be erased; they will be fulfilled. Heaven will not obscure our stories; it will complete them. Hope assures us that every chapter of suffering becomes, in the hands of God, a chapter of redemption.

This is the last truth every believer must hold: hope is not merely the ending of the Christian story—it is the meaning of the Christian story. It is the virtue that ties Genesis to Revelation, the Fall to the Resurrection, the Cross to the empty tomb. It is the virtue that binds every human sorrow to the promise of divine love. Hope is what allows the believer to say, even in darkness, "God is faithful." Hope is what enables the heart to endure what it does not understand. Hope is what keeps the soul steady when the storm rises.

And hope is ultimately a Person.

The Christian does not hope in an idea or an abstraction. He hopes in Christ. He hopes in the One who entered suffering, embraced death, and rose again. He hopes in the One who carries his wounds in glory. He hopes in the One who has promised to make all things new. Hope clings to Christ not because life is easy, but because Christ is true.

And so, the final word is not suffering.

The final word is not sorrow.

The final word is not death.

The final word is Christ.

Christ who bears our sorrows.

Christ who enters our wounds.

Christ who transforms our tears.

Christ who raises our bodies.

Christ who restores our hearts.

Christ who makes all things new.

This is the hope that sustains the Church.

This is the hope that strengthens the saints.

This is the hope that carries every believer home.

And for this reason, hope must be the last word of this book.

It must be the last word of every Christian story.

It must be the last word whispered over every grave, every trial, every fear.

    Hope—because Christ has risen.

    Hope—because Christ reigns.

    Hope—because Christ will return.

    The God who bears our sorrows will also bear us to glory.

    And in His presence, every tear becomes meaning,

    every wound becomes wisdom,

    every sorrow becomes song.

    Hope is the last word—because Christ is the last Word.

Epilogue

The Wounded Hands Of God

The Gospels tell us that on the first day of the week, when the stone had been rolled away and the tomb stood empty, the disciples were not met with the kind of glory they expected. They had imagined vindication without memory, triumph without trace, resurrection without residue. They expected the victory of God to arrive with a kind of heavenly perfection that erased the scandal of Friday. But when the risen Christ stood before them, everything they thought they understood had to be re-examined.

Because the victory still bore wounds.

On the evening of that first day, when Jesus appeared in the Upper Room, He did not hide His hands. He did not conceal His side. He did not step forward in a perfection that ignored the Cross. He came exactly as the One who had suffered—glorified, yes, but still marked. His wounds shone with a beauty the world had never seen. They were no longer signs of violence. They were signs of love. They were no longer evidence of death. They were evidence that death had been defeated from the inside.

This is the surprise of Easter.

Christ does not erase His wounds; He reveals them.

He shows them to Thomas not as reminders of pain, but as invitations to faith. He speaks peace over the disciples while His hands still bear the prints of nails. The victory of God does not undo the

Passion; it unveils its purpose. The wounds are not an embarrassment to be hidden. They are a truth to be proclaimed. Every time Christ raises His hands in blessing, the marks of redemption shine.

From the beginning of Scripture, God has revealed Himself through covenant—through promises sealed in sacrifice, through commitments written in blood. But the new covenant, the covenant fulfilled in Christ, is not carved in stone or spoken from the cloud of Sinai. It is inscribed into the flesh of the Son of God. His wounds are the covenant made visible. They are the everlasting testimony that God has bound Himself to His people with a love that nothing—not even death—can sever.

The disciples do not immediately understand this. They stare at His hands because they cannot comprehend what they mean. These are the hands that lifted the poor, blessed the children, cleansed the lepers, broke the bread, calmed the sea. These are the hands that carried the weight of human suffering with gentleness. And now those same hands carry the marks of nails—and yet they radiate peace. The very place of Christ's agony has become the place of revelation.

This is no minor detail of the Resurrection. It is the key to understanding everything suffering has meant in God's plan. If Christ had risen without wounds, the Passion could be mistaken as a tragedy God simply corrected. But Christ rises with wounds, and so the Passion becomes something far greater: the place where divine love has done its deepest work. The wounds teach us that God does not rescue us from suffering by avoiding it. He rescues us by entering it. By filling it with Himself. By transforming it from within.

This is what the disciples carry into their preaching. This is what Thomas touches. This is what the early Church contemplates when it describes Christ in the Book of Revelation as "a Lamb standing as though slain." Standing—alive, victorious, radiant. Slain—bearing the marks of sacrifice. The paradox is the very heart of Christian hope:

the wounds remain, but they remain in glory.

The Fathers of the Church never tired of this truth. They saw in Christ's wounds the fulfillment of every promise spoken to Israel—the promise that God would draw near to the brokenhearted, that He would bind up the wounds of His people, that He would heal the world not through force, but through faithful love. When believers gazed upon Christ's glorified wounds, they were seeing the covenant completed. They were seeing the prophecy of Isaiah fulfilled: *"By His wounds we are healed."*

And this is where the Christian finds courage. The wounds of Christ tell us that suffering is never unseen, never forgotten, never left outside the story of salvation. God has taken suffering into Himself. He has woven it into the mystery of redemption. Every sorrow, every burden, every tear has a place because Christ has made room for it in His own flesh.

The God who bears our sorrows bears them still.

The hands that hold the Church are wounded hands.

And therefore, they are trustworthy.

The mystery of the risen wounds also reveals something essential about the heart of God. The world often imagines divinity as distant, immune, untouched by the fragility of human life. But the Gospel overturns that imagination. The God of Christianity is not the God of distance; He is the God who draws near. Near enough to hunger. Near enough to weep. Near enough to bleed. Near enough to carry, in His glorified body, the marks of love forever.

The wounds of Christ are the final refutation of the ancient lie that God stands far from human suffering. They are the permanent declaration that God has chosen solidarity rather than separation. When the believer prays, he prays to a God who knows suffering from the inside. When he weeps, he weeps before a God who has tasted sorrow with human lips. When he carries the weight of his own crosses, he carries them under the gaze of a God whose shoulders have already borne the wood of salvation.

This is why the saints have always found strength in contemplating the wounds of Christ. The wounds become a kind of sanctuary—a place where the heart discovers that its fears are not foreign to God, its grief is not unspoken, its pain is not without meaning. St. Bernard spoke of entering the "wound of Christ's side" as entering the heart of God Himself. The pierced Heart becomes the place where human wounds are brought for healing, where sorrows are met with mercy, where suffering is held in the tenderness of divine compassion.

And yet, Christ's wounds do something even more astonishing. They not only console; they transform. The believer who contemplates the wounded Christ learns that suffering does not have the authority to define him. The wounds of Christ define him. The Cross tells him who he is: redeemed, beloved, carried. The Resurrection tells him where he is going: into glory, into communion, into the presence of the God who bears him. Suffering becomes the place where this identity is tested, but never lost.

In this way, the wounds of Christ do not explain suffering—they transfigure it. They do not answer every question, but they answer the one question every suffering person eventually asks: *"Where is God in all of this?"* The answer, spoken not in theory but in flesh, is simple and unshakeable:

God is here.

In the wounds.

In the Cross.

In the sorrow carried into glory.

The risen Christ stands before the Church as the One who has carried suffering into the very life of God. He does not only heal wounds. He glorifies them. He folds them into His victory. The believer's hope rests on this truth: nothing surrendered to Christ remains a mark of defeat. Every wound placed in His hands becomes part of the story of redemption.

This is why the Christian can face his own wounds—physical, emotional, spiritual—not with stoic resignation, but with trust. The wounds Christ carries are not symbols of despair; they are the instruments of salvation. They remind the believer that his own suffering can be united to Christ and drawn into that same mystery. They remind him that love has already triumphed. They remind him that suffering is not the final horizon of his existence. The love of God is.

This love accompanies the believer through every valley. It sustains him when hope seems thin, when faith feels heavy, when the night grows long. The wounded Christ walks with him—quietly, faithfully, unceasingly. The Christian who contemplates the wounds of Christ discovers that nothing can separate him from the love of God, because that love has already passed through death and emerged victorious.

And this is why the final word of the Christian life is hope. Not a hope born of optimism or denial, but a hope rooted in the wounded hands that hold the Church. The believer's confidence rests not on his strength, but on the faithfulness of the One whose wounds proclaim: *"I have loved you to the end."*

Everything in this book has led to this place:
the cries of the human heart,
the story of Israel,
the Cross of Christ,
the endurance of the saints,
the promise of glory.
All of it converges here—
in the wounded hands lifted in blessing.

If you stand before any icon of the risen Christ—from the earliest centuries in the catacombs to the great mosaics of the East—you will notice something remarkable. Christ is always shown blessing with wounded hands. The Church has never imagined Him otherwise. The wounds are not edited out of glory. They are part of glory. The God who reigns is the God who suffered. The King enthroned is the King whose hands still bear the cost of His love.

And that is precisely why the believer can trust Him.

He does not reign with hands unfamiliar with human pain. He does not bless with hands untouched by human sorrow. He does not guide history with hands that have never trembled beneath the weight of suffering. The hands that uphold the universe are scarred by love. The hands that shepherd the Church bear the memory of nails. The hands that will one day wipe away every tear are the same hands that once bled for the salvation of the world.

This is the great consolation offered to every Christian heart:

God has not explained suffering from the outside; He has redeemed it from within.

He has taken suffering into His own body and transformed it into the means of salvation. He has entered every valley a believer will ever walk. And He has carried those valleys into glory.

Nothing is lost.

Nothing is wasted.

Nothing endured in faith disappears into darkness.

Because the risen Christ carries His wounds forever, our wounds can be carried into healing.

This truth becomes the final lens through which we read every page of Scripture.

When Adam and Eve hid among the trees, the wounded Christ was already promised.

When Israel cried out under Pharaoh, the wounded Christ was already foreshadowed.

When the prophets described the Servant pierced for our transgressions, the wounded Christ was already on His way.

When Christ stretched out His hands on Good Friday, He was revealing the love that would define His eternal life.

And when He rose, He did not put that love aside.

He enthroned it.

The Christian life ends where Christ's life has already gone—into the heart of the Father, through the wounds of the Son, in the fire of the Spirit. The believer's destiny is not to escape suffering, nor to pretend it does not exist, but to bring it into the wounded hands that make all things new. In those hands, sorrow finds its meaning. In those hands, weakness finds its dignity. In those hands, death itself becomes the doorway to life.

This is why the final act of the Christian is surrender. Not a surrender of despair, but a surrender of trust—placing one's life into the hands that have never failed. The hands that were opened in creation, extended in healing, pierced in sacrifice, raised in blessing, and lifted in ascension are the hands that receive every soul that dies in Christ.

And those hands are wounded.

This is the last meditation of the believer:

God does not hide His wounds because He does not hide His love.

He keeps His wounds because He keeps His promises.

He shows His wounds because He desires to show His heart.

And we, who bear our own wounds, can place them in His without fear.

For in His hands, every wound becomes a place of glory.

In His hands, every sorrow becomes seed.

In His hands, every tear becomes meaning.

In His hands, suffering itself becomes the path toward the embrace for which the human heart was made.

This is the last word.

EPILOGUE

This is the final mystery.
This is the hope that carries the Christian home.
He kept His wounds so we could keep our hope.

About the Author

Matthew Sardon is a Catholic author from Melbourne, Australia, whose work is shaped by the depth and breadth of the Church's intellectual and spiritual tradition. Formed through extensive theological study within the University of Divinity and nourished by years immersed in both the Roman and Byzantine rites, he brings to his writing a unified Catholic vision rooted in Scripture, illuminated by the Fathers, and sustained by the Church's liturgical life.

His research and writing centre on biblical theology, patristic anthropology, and the mystery of theosis—how divine grace heals, elevates, and transfigures the human person. He is committed to making the Church's ancient wisdom accessible to the contemporary world, offering clarity and strength where many experience confusion and fragmentation.

Matthew is actively engaged in Catholic ministry, contributing to teaching, catechesis, adult formation, and parish mission. His work as a speaker and presenter reflects the same passion found in his writing: to awaken faith, deepen understanding, and help others encounter the transforming love of God.

You can connect with me on:

🌐 https://matthewsardon.com

www.ingramcontent.com/pod-product-compliance
Lightning Source LLC
Chambersburg PA
CBHW060103230426
43661CB00033B/1404/J